ST. MARY'S
ST. MARY'S CITY, MARYLAND   20686

W9-AFC-565

# Middle East Perspectives

# Middle East Perspectives:

## The Next Twenty Years

edited by George S. Wise and Charles Issawi

**The Darwin Press, Inc.**
**Princeton, New Jersey**

Copyright © 1981 by the UNIVERSITY OF MIAMI, Coral Gables, Fla. All rights reserved.

No part of this publication may be reproduced, stored in a retrieval system, or transmitted, in any form, by any means, electronic, mechanical, photocopying, recording, or otherwise, without the prior permission of the publisher, except in the case of brief quotations in critical articles or reviews.

**Library of Congress Cataloging in Publication Data**

Main entry under title:

Middle East perspectives, the next twenty years.

Lectures given at a conference organized by the Center for Advanced International Studies, University of Miami, and held Feb. 1980.

Includes index.

1. Near East—Politics and government—1945-    —Congresses.  I. Wise, George Schneiweis, 1906-
II. Issawi, Charles Philip.

| | | |
|---|---|---|
| DS63.1.M543 | 956'.048 | 81-2562 |
| ISBN 0-87850-037-5 | | AACR2 |

Printed in the United States of America

# List of Contributors

Ambassador Tahseen Basheer
Fellow, School of International Studies
Harvard University
Ambassador to Egyptian Permanant Mission to the
    United Nations

Professor Gabriel Ben-Dor
Associate Professor of Middle East Politics
Haifa University

Professor Alexandre Bennigsen
Professor of History
Universities of Chicago and Paris

Professor June Dreyer
Professor of Politics and Director of East Asian Program
Center for Advanced International Studies

Dr. Nuri Eren
Ambassador of Turkey (Ret.)

Professor Charles Issawi
Bayard Dodge Professor of Near Eastern Studies
Princeton University

Professor Geoffrey Kemp
Associate Professor of International Politics
Fletcher School of Law and Diplomacy
Tufts University

Professor Bernard Lewis
Long-Term Member, Institute for Advanced Study
Cleveland E. Dodge Professor of Near Eastern Studies
Princeton University

Professor Itamar Rabinovitch
Associate Professor
Shiloah Center for Middle Eastern Studies
Tel Aviv University

Professor R. K. Ramazani
Edward R. Stettinius Jr. Professor of Middle East Comparative
    Foreign Policy and International Law
University of Virginia

Professor Haim Shaked
Director, Shiloah Center for Middle Eastern Studies
Dean of Humanities
Tel Aviv University

Professor Shimon Shamir
Head of the School of History
Tel Aviv University

Professor P. J. Vatikiotis
School of Oriental and African Studies
University of London

Professor Gabriel Warburg
Visiting Professor
Center for Advanced International Studies

# Contents

# Preface

THE YEAR 1979 began on an ominous note in the Middle East. In February, Ayatollah Ruhollah Khomeini gained control of Iran. This event brought about a radical change both in the internal structure of the country and in its relations with the outside world. Muslim fundamentalism became the dominant element of the Khomeini order. All power was concentrated in the Ayatollah's hands, and the government, which was formed and changed by him at will, had to compete for power with militant students, religious leaders, and a covert but quite strong leftist element. All three factors combined to create something approaching anarchy in Iran.

The advent of Khomeini also brought about a complete and radical reversal in relations with both Arab countries and the Western powers, including the United States. The Arab nations feared the spread of religious militancy from Iran to their own countries. Saudi Arabia, Jordan, Syria, and Iraq felt themselves threatened by the developments in Iran and sought to avoid upheavals in their own countries by restricting religious and opposition groups. Egypt found itself the subject of attack by its former ally, Iran, and was the target of the continuous hostility of other Arab countries opposed to the agreement with Israel. The Palestinian Liberation Organization (PLO) assumed the role of intermediary between Khomeini and the Arab countries, and used the Iranian revolution to fan greater hostility toward Israel.

The war continued between factions in Lebanon, placing a strain on the resources of Syria, which had occupied Lebanon in 1978 in an unsuccessful attempt to bring order to a country torn between its heavily-armed Muslim and Christian population.

The advent of Khomeini gave impetus to a catastrophic deterioration in relations between Iran and the United States. Oil, used since the 1973 war as a weapon by the Arab countries to impose both higher prices and their will on the Western world, kept rising in price and threatened the economies of Western Europe, Japan, and even the United States.

Very little was done by Western countries or by the United States to counteract the oil policies advanced by Khomeini and copied by other Arab suppliers. Although some countries, such as Saudi Arabia, have at times attempted to withstand the drive for higher prices, most gave in to Iran, Iraq, and Libya.

Disorder in Iran, the disruption of regional and international relations, militant religious fundamentalism, anti-Westernism, and the political manipulation of oil became the dominant factors in the Middle East throughout 1979.

Toward the end of this fateful year, two events took place that stunned the Western world and the United States and evidenced the unwillingness or inability of the West and the United States to meet and deal with the conflict in the Middle East. In November, 1979, Iranian militants captured the American Embassy in Iran and took as hostages fifty-two people. The militants refused to recognize any governmental authority in Iran except that of Khomeini. About six weeks later, toward the end of December, the Soviet Union invaded Afghanistan, thus threatening the Persian Gulf and the lifeline of Europe, Japan, and the United States.

In the face of these two unprecedented actions by Iran and the Soviet Union, neither Western Europe nor the United States took steps to remedy the situation. The United States attempted, through the intervention of the United Nations, the World Court, and Western opinion, to obtain the release of the hostages, but this effort produced only useless declarations and statements, which were ignored by Iran. Similar lack of action characterized the response to the Afghanistan invasion. There were protests and votes in the United Nations, but there was no action to undo the successful attempt by the Soviet Union to dominate Afghanistan and threaten the entire Persian Gulf area.

At the end of 1979, the world was faced with the following situation: American hostages were held by Iran and the United States had no way to release them. The oil-producing countries, primarily Iran and Iraq, were increasing the price of oil and threatening the economies of the United States, the West, and Japan. The Soviet Union was occupying Afghanistan and showing complete disregard for world opinion. The Arab countries were splintered by feuds; if they were united at all it was in their rejection of Egypt's peace initiative and in their hostility toward Israel.

We, at the Center for Advanced International Studies, felt that a review of the situation, as it existed in 1979 in one of the most important areas of the world, and a forecast of developments over the next two decades, would be helpful to student and scholar, statesman and soldier, governments and the general public. For that purpose, we decided to call a conference on "The Middle East and the West Toward the End of the Twentieth Century." We invited scholars from Canada, Egypt, England, France, Iran, Israel, Turkey, and the United States. We were pleased with the reponse to our invitations and we are grateful to the participants in the conference who shed light on the problems facing the world. While we, of course, did not expect any specific predictions as to what might happen over the next decade, the conference and the discussions helped acquaint us with the historical, religious, and cultural background of recent developments in the Middle East. The lectures given by some of the eminent scholars are presented in this volume. We hope that these will contribute to a better understanding of the problems and challenges of the Middle East in the last two decades of our century.

I am especially grateful to Professor Charles Issawi of Princeton University for accepting my invitation to serve as co-editor of this volume.

Dr. George S. Wise

Director

Center for Advanced International Studies

University of Miami

# 1

# Loyalties to
# Community, Nation, and State

*Bernard Lewis*

FOR SOME TIME, it has been our practice in the Western world to proceed on the assumption that the basic determinant of both identity and loyalty for political purposes is that which we variously call nation or country. In American, though not in European, usage these terms are almost synonymous. In most European languages, including English, they are somewhat different, although there are areas of overlap. Like most of mankind, we all tend to assume that our local customs are the laws of nature. They are not. The practice of classifying people into nations and countries and of making this the primary basis of corporate political identity was, until very recently, local to Western Europe and to the regions colonized and settled by West Europeans. In our time, this way of looking at people has, as a result of various circumstances, been imposed upon or adopted by most of the rest of the world. In many of these countries, among them countries in the Middle East, these notions are still fairly new; they are imperfectly acclimatized and even at the present time are by no means generally accepted, at least not in the sense in which they are understood and put into effect in the countries of their origin. Even such terms as "nationalism" and "patriotism," which we have come to regard as rather typical of Middle Eastern political life, are in themselves innovations of the nineteenth or twentieth centuries; for some time past, and more obviously at the present time, they have been and are being challenged by older and perhaps deeper loyalties.

There have, of course, always been both nations and countries in the Middle East, as elsewhere. There were countries, that is to say places; there were nations, that is to say people. Nations and sometimes also countries had names and were a familiar part of everyday life. But neither nation nor country was seen as a primary or even as a significant element in determining political identity and in directing political loyalty. In the Middle East, traditionally, these were determined on quite a different basis. Identity was expressed in and determined by religion, which in effect meant community; loyalty was owed to the state, which in practice meant the government.

There is some disagreement, perhaps more apparent than real, on what Islam means to different people. For our present purpose, a word or two may be useful. When we use the word "religion" in the Western world we are normally speaking of something rather limited. We are speaking primarily of a system of belief and worship —nowadays often a belief which we no longer hold, and worship in which we no longer participate. Religion in the Western conception is concerned with one part or aspect of life, and this part is distinct from—sometimes even separate from—the rest. This difference or distinction is expressed in such pairs of terms as spiritual and temporal, lay and ecclesiastical, religious and secular, and the like. In Islamic lands, the word religion has a much wider meaning than that. It is concerned not only with belief and worship, whether held and practised or not, but with the entire gamut of human existence, social and public as well as private and personal. In the West, the term religious law connotes canon law or ecclesiastical law, concerned with the affairs of the church and its personnel and devised, promulgated, and administered by ecclesiastical authorities. In Islam, religious law means the law of God as promulgated by revelation through prophecy, and, like religion itself, covers the entire range of human activity. In the Western world, we tend to think of the nation as the basic unit which may be subdivided into different religious communities. From a traditional Islamic point of view, it is rather religion or the religious community which is the basic unit subdivided into states. During the centuries-long confrontation between the states of Europe and the Ottoman Empire, the Europeans always saw and discussed their relations in terms of Austrians, Frenchmen, Germans, Englishmen, and other nationalities and Turks; the Turks saw it in terms of Muslims versus Christians. In Turkish documents the name Turk is rarely mentioned and the parochial subdivisions of Christendom are given scant importance. In the world-view of Muslims, which they naturally also ascribed to others, religion was the determinant of identity, the focus of loyalty, and, not less important, the source of authority.

But Islam is vast, embracing hundreds of millions of people on many continents. Ideally, and for a while even in practice, Islam was a single state bound together by the faith and law of Islam and ruled by a single sovereign, the Caliph. The desire to realize this ideal remained a recurring theme and a powerful motive through the centuries of Islamic history. With the collapse of the last great universal Islamic empire, that of the Ottomans, in 1918, the dream of unity was for a while abandoned and in a world dominated by the victorious Allied powers, Muslims sought to make a new adjustment to changed circumstances.

The problem was not entirely new. Since the days of the break-up of the original Caliphate, Muslim peoples had in fact, though not in theory, divided into separate political entities, had created political institutions, and had organized themselves to take political action. How did they do so?

The answer to these questions may be found in certain habits and institutions, deep-rooted in the past and still very active at the present time. One of them is the state—not the nation, not the country but the state itself, the integrated, coercive power in the community, and the ganglion of interrelated careers and interests that control it. In contrast to Christianity and Judaism, Islam has been a political religion since its inception. Its founder did not die, like Moses, before entering his promised land, nor, like Jesus, on the cross. On the contrary, he achieved success and victory during his own lifetime and created and governed a state. The resulting relationship of power and faith has remained characteristic of Islam from that time to this. A remarkable feature of the modern age and of the changes that modernization has brought to Islam has been the strengthening, not the weakening, of the state as a focus of activity. One reason for this is an important internal development. In the traditional Islamic society, the power of the state was in both theory and practice limited. There is a common tendency to think of Islamic political tradition as conducive to despotic, even capricious rule, and this view may appear to receive some support from recent events. It is based, however, on a misreading of Islamic history and law. The traditional Islamic state may be autocratic; it is not despotic. The power of the sovereign is limited by a number of factors, some legal, some social. It is limited in principle by the holy law, which, being of divine origin, precedes the state. The state and the sovereign are subject to the law and are in a sense created and authorized by the law and not, as in Western systems, the other way round. In addition to this theoretical restraint, there were also practical restraints. In traditional Islamic societies, there were many well-entrenched interests and intermediate powers that imposed effective limits on the ability of the state to control its subjects. With the process of modernization in the Islamic world, these intermediate powers have one by one been weakened or abolished, leaving the state with a far greater degree of autocratic control over its subjects than it ever enjoyed in traditional Islamic societies. And whereas the limiting powers have dwindled or disappeared, the state itself now has at its disposal the whole modern apparatus of surveillance and repression. The result is that modern states in the Islamic world, even those claiming to be progressive and democratic, are—in their domestic affairs at least—vastly stronger than the so-called tyrannies of the past.

This may help us to understand another somewhat surprising phenomenon of the recent and current Middle Eastern world—the extraordinary persistence of states once created. Before the First World War, there were in effect only two—or, we might say, two-and-a-half—states in the Middle East. The two were the surviving monarchies of Turkey and Iran, both conceived not as nation-states in the modern Western sense, but as universal Muslim empires. Both sovereigns, the Sultan of Turkey and the Shah of Iran, saw themselves and projected themselves as universal sovereigns of Islam to whom all Muslims owed allegiance, and it was only in comparatively recent times that they began to adopt territorial and national designations in their protocol and official usage. The half is Egypt, which, although under external suzerainty or domination, first Ottoman then British, nevertheless retained a very large measure of autonomy in its internal affairs. There was an Egyptian government, an Egyptian administration running Egypt, under fairly remote Ottoman or somewhat less remote British control. In this sense, Egypt has functioned as a political entity for a very long time, even if not as an independent state. Apart from these, some smaller groups managed to maintain a precarious independence in remote mountain or desert areas, while recognizing the nominal suzerainty of one or other of these states. The rest of the Middle East had had no experience of separate statehood or of the exercise of political sovereignty for a very long time. The nations who lived there had merged their identities in the larger communal and dynastic loyalties; the countries in which they lived were no more than imperial provinces; their very names and boundaries were subject to frequent change, and —with the exception of Egypt—they had little historical or even geographical significance.

As a result of two world wars and of the extension and withdrawal of European imperial power, a whole series of new states were set up, with frontiers and even identities largely devised by colonial administration and imperial diplomacy. Some of these rested on genuine historical entities; some were entirely artificial. Neverthless, in spite of the very strong ideological urge toward unification arising from pan-Arabism, not a single one of these Arab states has disappeared. On the contrary, they have shown—even the most improbable of them—an extraordinary capacity for survival and for self-preservation, often in very adverse circumstances. There have been many attempts to unite or even associate two or more Arab states; no such attempt has so far lasted for very long. In earlier days the failure of attempts at Arab unity could be and was attributed to outside influence. The record of more recent times illustrates that whatever the role of outside interference in the past, it is no longer a sufficient explanation. The barriers to greater Arab unity arise within the Arab world and the failure of the mergers testifies to the remarkable persistence and growing power of the state itself as a political factor.

Another element is that which, for want of a better term, we might call "local," that is, the smaller unit of identity, within the community and below the state. This may be national or rather ethnic—a tribe or comparatively small nation held together by a sense of common descent, real or imagined (whether it is in fact real or imagined is of no consequence; it is the conviction of common descent that matters). Sometimes, the bond may be sectarian, membership in a particular religious community. Sometimes, it may be regional—related to a place, district, or province. Or, it may be any combination of these.

One of the more interesting features of recent times has been the extent to which these regional, sectarian, or tribal entities have shaped and at times even dominated the political life of the region. In Iraq, for example, we see a kind of regional ascendancy, a domination of the country by people coming from one particular place, the town of Takrit. Syria offers a different pattern—an ascendancy which is both regional and sectarian, that of the Alawis from the northwest. In the Yemens, we see struggles among three rival denominations, Sunnis, Zaydis, and Isma'ilis, as well as tribal conflicts not entirely coinciding with sectarian differences.

Such situations do not arise from a sudden decision by the people of Takrit or the followers of the Alawi sect to get together and establish their domination in Iraq or Syria. But in a time of crumbling institutions and faltering loyalties, those who happen to seize power in one way or another soon begin to feel threatened and seek the support and help of those whom they trust and on whom they can rely. And what is more natural than for them to call their old friends of the same region, of the same family, of the same tribe or sect? When the established order weakens, there is a resurgence of these regional and sectional loyalties, present all the time but previously quiescent.

The persistence of the state and the recrudescence of local loyalties are two important legacies from the past, which will certainly continue to affect the political life of the region.

But a new idea came from the West, from Europe: that of the nation-state. This meant a state defined by territory, language and descent, by a common national identity as well as a common political loyalty. The concept came in various forms—first from Western, then from Central and Eastern Europe, at first linked with liberal and constitutional ideas, later often with more authoritarian doctrines. Sometimes the focus was a country, and the expression patriotic; sometimes a national or ethnic identity, and the expression nationalistic. This last could relate to a single nation, or to a larger group of nations perceived as kin. The political unification of Germany and Italy in the nineteenth century and the ideologies of pan-Germanism and pan-Slavism had considerable impact. The acceptance and adaptation of these new ideas and ideologies varied greatly in the different parts of the Middle East. For Egypt, a nation 7,000 years old, in a country sharply defined by both geography and history, the calls for national identity and patriotic loyalty evoke a ready response, and will no doubt continue to do so. The name Libya, exhumed from classical antiquity by the Italian colonial ministry and promulgated by Italian royal decree on 3 December 1934 to designate the union of the two colonies of Tripolitania and Cyrenaica, does not have the same resonance or appeal, and the Libyan sense of loyalty and identity, other than the state and Islam, is correspondingly uncertain. The remaining states of the Arab East, mostly created between the two world wars, lie somewhere between these extremes.

The question is, therefore, what happens next? How are these notions of identity and loyalty likely to develop toward the end of this century?

The further development of these matters—of identity by nation, by community, by state, by country, or by any other basis, will depend very largely on the fate of the region as a whole and this will be profoundly influenced, if not determined, by external factors, and above all by the actions and interactions of the superpowers.

One possibility is that the whole region, or a substantial part of it, will pass under Soviet domination. Given the recent successes of the Soviets in first surrounding and then penetrating the Middle Eastern region, such an outcome is by no means improbable. If the region or part of it passes under Soviet domination, then of course the pattern of organization and with it the determination of identity and loyalty will not be decided by Middle Easterners, nor will it be greatly influenced by the rhythms of Middle Eastern history or the aspirations of Middle Eastern society. The pattern will be imposed from outside, in accordance with the needs and purposes of a quite different political system.

In assessing the probable course of events in a Soviet-dominated Middle East, we are not obliged to rely on guesswork. Parts of the Middle East are already incorporated in the Soviet Union. North of the Turkish, Iranian, and Afghan borders lie a string of countries inhabited predominantly by Turkish- and Persian-speaking Muslims and forming part of the historic Middle East. These were conquered and annexed by the Russian Empire in the nineteenth century and have remained part of the Soviet Union to the present time. Given the extreme conservatism of Soviet practice, it is not too difficult to estimate what the Soviets would be likely to do if other parts of the still independent Middle East join those that preceded them into the Russian Empire.

The term "Soviet domination" can, of course, mean different things. In its mildest form it is sometimes called "Finlandization," an adjustment that has often been suggested for Western Europe and that some in the Middle East might almost seem to welcome as the least evil of the available solutions. It is possible that in the event of a Soviet triumph, some Middle Eastern countries might be able to persuade the Soviets to accept a Finnish kind of accommodation. It is possible, but very unlikely. Finland fought two bitter wars against Russia and, as Stalin once put it, gave the Russians a bloody nose. The Soviet-Finnish Treaty of 1948 was achieved only after six weeks of hard negotiation, and represents a genuine compromise. This is in marked contrast with the other East European treaties, which conform to a standard Soviet formula and were agreed and signed almost immediately. (Incidentally, the Soviet-Egyptian Treaty of May, 1971, and the Soviet-Iraqi Treaty of April, 1972, each took three days from the initiation of discussions to the signature of the completed document.)

Finland had some other advantages besides the proven effectiveness and patriotism of her forces. On the far side of Finland, there is an armed, neutral Sweden; on the far side of Sweden, NATO; on the far side of NATO, the Atlantic Ocean. The geography of the Middle East, both physical and political, is much less favorable to Finlandization.

Apart from Finland, Eastern Europe offers a number of different precedents: in Poland, Hungary, Czechoslovakia, Rumania, and Bulgaria. And beyond these, perhaps more relevant, there is the fate of the Soviet Middle East—of the Trans-Caucasian and Central Asian Republics of the Soviet Union.

On the basis of what the Soviets have already done in the Muslim and Middle Eastern territories under their rule, one may attempt a reasonable forecast of what they would be likely to do in any further Middle Eastern countries that they acquire or even in which they are able to exercise a predominant influence.

In Tsarist times, these countries were part of what was in effect a colonial empire. The Russians had invaded them and conquered them by land and not by sea, but in most other respects the process of acquisition and colonization resembled that of the expansion of the maritime empires of Western Europe, which was taking place in Asia and Africa in roughly the same period. In the earlier stages of the Bolshevik revolution in Russia, there was a temporary relaxation of central control, due in part no doubt to ideology, but rather more to weakness. Whatever its cause, this interruption of control from Moscow permitted the reappearance and expression of old loyalties, sometimes in a new form. The conquered peoples of the Russian Empire had produced their own national and religious leaders who had tried—unsuccessfully—to resist the Russian conquest of their countries. These were now rediscovered and celebrated by their peoples, and this history and culture of the Muslims of the Russian Empire, the overwhelming majority of them speaking Turkic and Iranic languages, formed the subject of intensive study and even of some popular literature and other media. The Muslim subjects of the Russian Empire began to rediscover their common identity and to realize that they were not, as they had previously been told, an ethnic dust of broken tribes inevitably attracted to Great Russia, but the remnants of what had once been a great civilization. This reawakening focused on the study of the great Turko-Iranian states and cultures that had flourished in the past and found political expression in movements and ideologies directed toward achieving a greater unity, in the form of pan-Turkism, pan-Islamism, and pan-Iranism.

This phase did not last long. As the power of Moscow was reestablished, it was soon realized that this awakening constituted a serious, perhaps a mortal, threat to the territorial unity and ideological unanimity of the Soviet Union. By the 1930s, this trend was severely limited; in the 1940s, it was decisively reversed. The various national heroes who had enjoyed a brief, popular revival and had been celebrated as leaders of national liberation movements against imperialism were suddenly reclassified and intermittently described as "feudal," "bourgeois," or "clericalist" reactionaries, resisting the "objectively progressive" advance of Great Russia. This change of line had consequences not only for the deceased national heroes but also—of more practical import—for the historians and writers who had been guilty of the crime of glorifying them. Henceforth, the dogma was laid down and officially enforced that the Russians, whether Tsarist or Soviet, had played an "objectively progressive" role and that the advance of Russian power had rescued these Asian peoples from barbarism and initiated them into a better life than they could ever have hoped to achieve for themselves. The arguments used bear a remarkable resemblance to those put forward in justification of the British presence in India and the French presence in North Africa during the nineteenth century. The important difference from these two cases is that any questioning of this doctrine, indeed any kind of national or religious ideology, was strictly —and effectively—prohibited.

A point of major importance in the enforcement of this doctrine was the denial of any principle of common identity among these peoples, whether based on religious grounds, as in the pan-Islamic school, or on national cultural grounds, as in the pan-Turkic and pan-Iranian schools. The Soviet authorities insisted that all these different peoples—the Uzbek, the Kirgiz, the Tatars, and the rest —were entirely separate and distinct nations. In the past, according to the Soviet historiographic doctrine, their national identities had been suppressed and obscured by Turkish, Iranian, and Islamic tyrannies, and only the liberating advent of the great Russian elder brother had freed them from these tyrannies and allowed them to develop their own "national" way of life. To argue otherwise was to commit the crime of pan-Turkism, pan-Iranism, or pan-Islamism, all of which were denounced as anti-Soviet, anti-progressive, and, significantly, anti-patriotic. The term "patriotism" is, of course, reserved to Soviet loyalty and allowed to no other within the Soviet Union.

In the empire of the Tsars, the various Turkic peoples spoke many different vernaculars, differing from each other sometimes considerably. They used, however, only two major literary languages, one in Central Asia, known as Turki or sometimes as Chaghatay, the other in Azerbaijan—the northern half of that province annexed from Iran at the beginning of the nineteenth century. Of somewhat lesser importance were the literary languages of the Kazan Tatars and of the Crimea. All these languages were written in the Arabic script. This, since it does not record vowels, to a large extent concealed dialectal variations and made it possible for the same literary language to be used, written and understood among speakers of many different dialects. In this respect, the position of the Turkic language speakers of the Tsarist empire rather resembled that of the Arab peoples, who also speak many widely differing vernaculars but share a common literary language that gives them a cultural, potentially also a political, unity. The literary and cultural heritage enshrined in these languages, though less in quantity than those of Arabic, Persian, or Ottoman Turkish, is nevertheless considerable and provided the basis for a lively cultural and intellectual revival in the late nineteenth and early twentieth centuries.

The Iranic peoples of the Russian Empire, fewer in number, were to be found mainly in the area now constituting the Soviet Federal Socialist Republic of Tajikistan, north of Afghanistan. Their literary language was simply Persian—the same language and the same script as are used in Iran and in much of Afghanistan. Here, too, the common literary language was used by speakers of various dialects, these, however, differing from each other far less than is the case with the speakers of Arabic or Turkish.

After the revolution, the Soviet government, ostensibly as a progressive and populist measure, took a major step to break up the cultural unity that had existed among their Muslim subject peoples. The Arabic script was abolished and replaced by the Latin script. In place of the common literary language, each area was given a local language based on the local dialect, all written in the Latin script, the orthographic conventions varying from one dialect to another, thus making it difficult for speakers of different dialects to communicate with each other in their own languages.

By this means, the Soviet authorities accomplished two significant results. One—certainly a major purpose—was to erect a barrier between the Turkic-speaking peoples of the Soviet Union and the Republic of Turkey. The Turkic literary languages of the Russian Empire, although different from the Turkish of Turkey, were close enough for educated people to be able to read and understand each other's writings. By changing the script, to some extent even the language, they were able to add a major reinforcement to the censorship that they had already erected, with the goal of isolating their own Turks from any potentially dangerous influences—religious, political, or other—emanating from Turkey. The abolition of the Arabic script for Tajik served the same purpose in relation to Iran.

But it was not only from their co-religionists and compatriots beyond the Soviet frontier that these peoples were separated by Soviet policy. The second result, hardly less important, was to cut them off from one another. By the abolition and for a while even prohibition of the old literary languages, Turkic and Persian speakers in the Soviet Union were confined to reading books in their own languages—in their new scripts—or in Russian. They had little contact with their own past; they had little contact even with what was being produced in the other Turkic republics and were thus impelled more and more to use Russian in order to communicate in writing or in speech with their fellow Turks and Muslims from the other republics.

If any doubt had existed as to the purpose of this operation, it was removed after 1928, when Turkey abolished the Arabic script and adopted a Latin alphabet in its place. This major reform had the incidental effect of removing the barrier that the Soviet government had erected, restoring the possibility of communication, which they had so carefully blocked. The Soviets in due course countered this by a second alphabetic reform for their Muslim peoples, by which they abolished the Latin scripts they themselves had devised and introduced, and imposed a new set of alphabets, this time based on the Russian Cyrillic. Similar changes were made in Tajik and other Iranic languages and dialects. Here again, in devising Russian alphabets for the Turkic languages, care was taken to produce different alphabets for different though closely related languages.

All this may give us some indication of a probable Soviet policy in a Soviet-dominated Middle East. The more closely the Middle East is integrated into the Soviet system, the greater is the danger of ideological "contamination"—of Soviet Muslims by their more recently acquired compatriots; the greater therefore the need for ideological protection. Larger movements for unity—"pan" movements—would be, at the very least, strongly discouraged. Pan-Arabism has so far received only mild chiding and disapproval from Soviet ideologists. Since no Arab country has as yet applied for admission and been accepted into the Soviet Union, pan-Arabism does not at present constitute a serious threat to Soviet unity. If, however, this situation should in any way change, pan-Arabism could become a serious offense in the same way and for the same reason as pan-Turkism, pan-Iranism, and pan-Islamism. Any movement of this kind, for a larger unity not focused on Moscow and not directed by Soviet allegiance, but with actual or potential centers outside Soviet control, is a menace and would be proscribed —and it will be recalled that proscription in the USSR has rather more serious consequences than are normally implied by this term in the Western world.

While larger loyalties would be forbidden or suppressed, local loyalties would be vigorously encouraged. Like the Turkic-speaking peoples of what was once the Russian Empire, the Arabs, too, might find that their common literary language is relegated to the domain of the historian and the philologist, the common identity expressed in that language abolished and declared illegal and, in their place, new separate languages and identities created, based on local dialects and written perhaps in the Latin and later in the Cyrillic scripts. Without great effort, one could envisage a situation in which the various regional dialects of the Arabic language are committed to writing, systematized, endowed with Russian alphabets, made into official national languages, and used to serve as the basis for a new kind of identity. This would be expressed, if it comes within the Soviet federation, in some form of "autonomy," a word much used nowadays in a variety of contexts. Autonomy can mean many things. In this situation, its significance would be largely dialectal, artistic, and academic. The new masters might choose to retain the existing division into political entities; alternatively, they might choose to change it. The fates of the component republics of the Soviet Union and the popular democracies of Eastern Europe offer various precedents. The major provinces of the Tsarist Empire in Central Asia and Trans-Caucasia were broken up and distributed into entirely new units. The states of the new Soviet domain in Europe, apart from the Baltic lands, which were wholly absorbed, kept their names and forms but underwent extensive territorial rearrangement. Not one of them retains its pre-war frontiers, and all those within reach ceded territories to the Soviets. The Middle East, with its multiplicity of national, regional, ethnic, and sectarian differences, including the presence of several major ethnic groups that have not yet achieved any form of statehood, even of a subordinate nature, offers wide scope for political engineering.

The contingency of Western domination in the Middle East may, for practical purposes, be excluded since in present circumstances there is neither the will nor the power to impose it. The most likely alternative to Soviet domination is a continuation, with variations, of something like the present situation; that is to say, Western contacts and influence in parts of the area, Soviet penetration or influence in others, and a chronic state of what is variously known as confrontation or coexistence in the remainder. If, as seems likely, this situation persists, the distribution of forces will no doubt vary from time to time.

The recent and current history of the Middle East offers several models that the states, countries, and nations of the region may choose to follow in the coming decades.

One of these is the unmistakably Western pattern of the territorial nation-state. Turkey provides the most consistent example of this, combining this new definition of identity and loyalty with a process of social, economic, and political Westernization. The Turks were the first of the Muslim Middle Eastern peoples to become engaged in this process, and it is, therefore, natural that they should have explored it much further than any of the others. Turkey has gone—more than once—through the successive phases of emulation, rejection, and reconciliation. Recently, there has been some opposition in Turkey to this process, and the desire has been expressed, in some quarters, for a return to a mythologized past; in others, for an advance toward an even more mythical "progressive" future. These protest movements derive most of their force from the economic troubles into which the country has been plunged, largely as a result of the dramatic increase in oil prices; they derive much of their several inspirations from across the frontier, the one group from competing brands of radical Islam, the other from the various ideologies, organizations, and governments that share the name of socialism. Both, as the electoral record shows, remain marginal to the main stream of Turkish life. It seems likely that, barring the imposition by force or by guile of another pattern from outside, the Turks will continue on the path that they have chosen —that of the secular modern nation-state.

In achieving this result, the Turks have an important advantage over most of their neighbors—a long experience of independent sovereignty. The independence of Turkey has at times been in danger; it has never been abolished or even suspended. The Turks have always been masters in their own house, and, consequently, have not had the political life of their country bedeviled and confused by the struggle to achieve independence against others, with the inevitable tendency to attribute responsibility for all that goes wrong to alien and hostile forces. With few exceptions, the Turks have not fallen into this trap. Their independence was neither granted nor taken; it was axiomatic, and that has always made it possible for the Turks to adopt more pragmatic and realistic attitudes toward political problems, above all that of their own nationhood. It takes time, experience, and the resulting self-assurance to achieve this kind of realism.

In Turkey, identity has been defined very precisely in national or, rather, in patriotic terms. This was made clear in a clause adopted in the Republican People's Party program of 1935: "The fatherland is the sacred country within our present political boundaries, where the Turkish nation lives with its ancient and illustrious history, and with its glories still living in the depths of its soil." This formula, with its insistence on the present boundaries of the Turkish republic, and on the intimate connection between the people and the country that they inhabit, involved a substantial act of renunciation. Not only were the Turks renouncing their imperial past and bidding farewell to the lost provinces of the Ottoman Empire; they were also renouncing the pan-Turkish and pan-Islamic ideologies that for a while had stirred many of their intellectuals and had encouraged some Turkish leaders to seek a new role for their country as the spearhead of a greater movement aiming at the union of all the Turks or, beyond that, of all Islam. Instead, the Turkish people were defined as a nationality rather than as a religious or an ethnic community, and their identity was delimited by their national frontiers. Although this choice has been challenged in recent years by leaders seeking to revive those religious and ethnic loyalties, the challenge has made little headway, and the basic character of the Kemalist revolution has been reaffirmed.

A parallel process of evolution may be seen in Egypt, which alone among the Arabic-speaking countries has a long history of separate political identity. In the transition toward modern-style nationhood, the Egyptians are in some respects better placed, in some respects worse placed, than the Turks. They did not possess the Turkish advantage of long-standing sovereignty, although it should be noted that they enjoyed a large measure of autonomy and that the Egyptian political entity is by far the oldest in the region after those of Turkey and Iran. To compensate, the Egyptians have a much stronger sense of continuity with the past. This was fostered by the striking unity of their country and by the massive and magnificent monuments of antiquity amid which they live. The Egyptian recovery of their ancient past, forgotten under Islamic influence, began more than a century ago and has now become an inherent part of Egyptian cultural consciousness. Pan-Islamic and pan-Arab ideologies and political forces have a more recent and more powerful role in Egypt than their equivalents in Turkey. It would be rash to prophesy that their role has come to an end. For the moment, however, Egypt seems to be set on the path toward a modern nation-state. Although the course of events in the two countries has been very different, there are nevertheless striking similarities between Turkey and Egypt. In both, the quest for modern nationhood has been linked with a turning toward the West—with an attempt to seek closer relations with the Western world and to adopt more and more of the Western way of life in social, economic, and political matters. Both countries have aligned themselves politically with the Western world; both countries—at the present time alone in the world of Islam—have entered into diplomatic relations with Israel. Egypt's task is complicated by many difficulties—by the heritage of Nasserism, the pull of pan-Arabism, the crippling economic burdens that the country and its people still have to bear. The resistance to modernization is stronger in Egypt than in Turkey. But the sense of nationhood is stronger too, and of Egypt also one may say that in the absence of interference or domination from outside, the most probable future form of Egyptian corporate self-awareness will be the pride of the Egyptians in their nationhood and their patriotic love of Egypt.

In the other Arab countries, the situation is very much more confused. Apart from the Lebanon, which enjoyed some form of autonomy far back in Ottoman times, the Arab states of the Middle East are all of recent creation and are perceived as states rather than as countries or nations in the Western sense. Although the drive toward statehood has been extraordinarily successful, the development of nationhood has been much less certain. There are still ambiguities about the very identity of many of these peoples. In some countries, attempts have been made to follow the Egyptian example and establish a link with remote antiquity. The Phoenicians in Lebanon, and the Aramaeans in Syria have at various times been claimed as ancestors, although in both cases these tendencies were by some proscribed and condemned as sectional, factional, regional, separatist treachery to the true cause of pan-Arabism. Even the patriotism of the Egyptians was denounced and derided in the Fertile Crescent, where it was known by the name of *tafar'un*, which one might translate approximately as trying to be or pretending to be Pharaonic. The most recent attempt at such a revival of the ancient past has been taking place in Iraq where, surprisingly, the present Baathist government has in recent months been laying increasing stress on the ancient past of the country, with frequent references to the Assyrians and Babylonians. In a country divided religiously between Sunni and Shi'i Muslims and ethnically between Arabs and Kurds, it might well have seemed that a sense of Iraqi nationality offered the best hope of preserving unity and that the best basis for such a sense of nationality could be found, as in Egypt, in the remote past of the country. Recent speeches by Saddam Hussein and others refer frequently to their glorious Iraqi ancestors, who are, of course, given retrospective Arab naturalization. Nebuchadnezzar is singled out for particular praise for his solution to the Zionist problem in his day.

No doubt, in order to counter criticism that this line of propaganda is opposed to pan-Arabism, it is defended as strengthening the Arab cause. This kind of patriotism, it is argued, will make Iraq strong and self-reliant, and only a strong, self-reliant Iraq can provide the leadership that the Arab world needs. Circumstance and opportunity will reveal whether this represents an excuse or a real pan-Arab program. For the moment, however, the earlier type of pan-Arabism, aimed at the unification of all the Arab states in some closer association, federal or even unitary, seems to have fallen out of fashion, and the present trend is toward the kind of cultural association and political kinship that exists between the English- or Spanish-speaking families of nations.

The position of Iran is very different. There are some twenty Arab states, and relations between them must inevitably be an important consideration for Arab politicans. There is only one Turkish state, but the Turks can never entirely forget that they are the last independent segment of the great Turkic family of nations extending from the Aegean to the China Sea, the more so since many Turkish refugees from these countries live among them. There is only one Iran and although there are Persian-speaking populations in Soviet Tajikistan and in Afghanistan, these are comparatively minor compared with the realms of Iran itself. And even Iran is far from unitary. Barely more than half of the population of Iran speak Persian as their primary language, the rest belonging to a variety of ethnic and linguistic and sometimes even religious minorities. Since the destruction of the old Persian Empire by the Arab Muslim conquerors in the seventh century, Iran has only exceptionally formed a single, unified realm. For almost a thousand years, it was either part of some vaster empire or subdivided into a number of small states. The modern empire of Iran dates from the sixteenth century, when rulers of the Safavid dynasty for the first time created a united Iranian realm bounded by the Ottoman Empire in the west and by Central Asia and India in the east. This has held loosely together since that time, although often the authority of the central government was very limited outside the capital and its immediate environs. The Safavids were Shi'ites and were successful in imposing this form of Islam on what had previously been a country of mixed denominations with at least as many Sunnis as Shi'ites. Under the Safavids and their successors, the Shi'i faith gave the Iranian realm its distinctive character, marking it off from the Sunni Turks, Central Asians, and Indians on all their frontiers.

While retaining this Shi'ite character, the late Shah tried to create a secular and territorial nation based on the language, culture, and homeland of Iran. Like his predecessors in Egypt and Turkey, he laid great stress on the ancient glories of his country and tried to inculcate a sense of a continuing Iranian identity, independent of the Shi'ite or indeed of the Islamic faith, and connecting the present-day people of Iran with the ancient glories of Cyrus and Darius and with the Parthian and Sasanian emperors. The core of the Shah's propaganda was the idea of the monarchy as the prime element of unity, stability, and continuity in the Iranian realm. The festivities amid the ruins of Persepolis, the ancient Iranian capital, were directed to this end.

This policy has, for the time being at least, ended. Political Islam, which has so far failed in Turkey and had only limited effect in Egypt, has overwhelmingly succeeded in Iran, where, if present trends continue, the leadership in that country will create a new kind of order based on Islamic rather than on Iranian or any other kind of national or patriotic sentiment. In the earlier stages of the Islamic revolution, the very idea of nationality was rejected as un-Islamic or even anti-Islamic. Should the Gulf be called the Persian Gulf or the Arabian Gulf—a point about which there had been long arguments? Neither, said an Ayatollah in Iran. Let it be called the Gulf of Islam. The Ayatollah Khomeini went even further—there are no frontiers in Islam, he said, or between Muslim peoples. Islam is one.

This had indeed always been the theory. It was at one time even

American South after the Civil War. For the time being—and for the foreseeable future—the world's need for Middle Eastern oil will continue, and the sellers and buyers of oil will in different ways impose their will on one another.

# 2
# Regional Politics

*P. J. Vatikiotis*

ONE MAY APPROACH the problem of regional politics by a consideration of the impact of the Egyptian-Israeli peace treaty and the Arab opposition to it. Second, one may suggest patterns and trends in developments, especially the shift of the focus of conflict further east to the Gulf and Southwest Asia. Third, one could attempt to identify potential problem areas or crisis points. An initial assumption is that, because of its political geology, or morphology if you wish, the Middle East region naturally generates both local and international conflict and will continue to do so in the forseeable future. And, because of the vital interests of foreign powers, especially the superpowers, the Middle East attracts their involvement.

The epochal shift that occurred in the political and strategic balance of the Arab-Israeli conflict is a result of Egypt's policy and the not too surprising, indeed anticipated, reaction of the Arab states to it. This shift is of great importance whatever may be the outcome of the attempt to implement, by negotiation, the provisions of the Egyptian-Israeli peace treaty. Among the factors that one ought to consider in this connection are, first, Egypt's massive presence in the Arab world in spite of the political differences between her and other Arab regimes; second, Egypt's ability to formulate policy based on her national or state interest and related to her historically important function in the region; and, third, the absence, so far, of an alternative and enforceable policy of peace or war on the part of the other Arab states. The mutual distrust, conflict of interest, and rivalry among the Arab states, especially between Iraq and Syria, the original leaders of the anti-Egyptian front, make it still possible for Egypt to continue her peace policy.

Having concluded that their experience of the last thirty years has been one of a counter-productive policy, having been bloodied by a terrible war in October, 1973, and being aware of the horrors of yet another one, the Egyptians believe they still have a role to play in the region, but one that is somewhat different from that of the past. They will play it now while trying to maintain a balance between their national interests on one hand and their wider interests as members of an Arab cultural entity and community of nations on the other. In a way, therefore, one finds, temporarily at least—I am not suggesting it cannot change—the proposition that Egypt can be really isolated from the rest of the Arab world somewhat absurd.

The strategic and political importance of the shift that has occurred at the very core of the Arab-Israeli conflict is balanced, however, by serious threats to this Egyptian peace policy. Yet, for the time being, the singular choice the Egyptians have made to relinquish war as a policy of dealing with Israel is having an impact on inter-Arab politics.

One consequence, which has already been alluded to, has been the realignment of several Arab states against the new Egyptian policy, but within a traditional historical context of the Fertile Crescent versus Egypt. There has also been a reorientation in the external policies of the region's states. Egypt, for example, has reoriented her policy since 1972 toward the West. Even without the Soviet invasion of Afghanistan at the end of 1979, there could still have been an array of regional forces between Mesopotamia and the Nile Valley, especially if one bears in mind that in 1978-79 there was renewed interest on the part of Egypt in closer cooperation with the Sudan.

It could be argued that the oil-rich states of Saudi Arabia, Kuwait, the United Arab Emirates, and Libya on the peripheries have tried to influence (and maintain in balance) the regional antagonism between Cairo and Baghdad. It could also be argued that the shift had been underway since the October 1973, war. Egypt perceived that a break in the conflict was possible only by shunting aside for the moment the Palestinian and inter-Arab factor in its relations with Israel and reorienting its external policy toward a closer relationship with the West.

Egyptian policy led to a split in the Arab League and the severance of diplomatic relations between Egypt and several Arab states. Jordanian opposition to the Camp David Accords has been basically a response to the rapprochement, temporary as it was, between Syria and Iraq, dependence on financial assistance from Saudi Arabia, and a special relationship with the Palestinians on the West Bank.

Heavily dependent on the financial assistance of the oil states and military assistance from Syria, the PLO has perforce played a prominent role in the anti-Egyptian Arab front. However, until now, this front has had no real effect on Egyptian policy, nor has it affected Egypt's massive presence in the Arab world, for she continues to export thousands of workers, teachers, professionals, and technicians to the Arab countries. At the same time, she continues to receive thousands of Arab students in her universities.

Another consequence of the treaty has been the change in the strategic position of the superpowers. Upon a careful reading of the text of the treaty and its appendices, some may argue that the United States has acquired the basis for a military presence in the region and a potential strategic capability resulting from its relationship with Egypt and Israel. This combination, however, may prove abrasive and uncomfortable, at least between Israel and the United States. Israel could become apprehensive over the massive rearming of Egypt by the United States and the likelihood of greater American pressure upon it to adopt a more accommodating policy over the West Bank.

But, in practical terms, the Sinai barrier between Egypt and Israel has been broken. The barrier between Israel on one side and the Palestinians and other Arab states on the other has yet to be breached. The possibility, slight as it may be, exists that the staged implementation of the treaty provisions may create new conditions favorable to change, regardless of how imperceptible it might be for the moment. For example, there could be a cumulative effect on the strategic and political thinking of all the parties involved in the conflict as these provisions are seen to be implemented. Under the treaty, Egypt is getting back the Sinai; recovery of this territory automatically improves Egypt's political posture and strategic position in the region. A stronger Egypt in the near future is perhaps one such development and a cause of apprehension among other Arab states. Then, the implementation of the treaty provisions may set in motion an irreversible process that may force others in the area to accommodate themselves to the newly created conditions. A formula of autonomy for the Palestinians, for example, may wean several groups and, possibly, one or two rulers away from the constellation of opposing forces, namely, the Arab Rejection Front.

Meanwhile, events in Iran and Afghanistan have shifted the regional center of conflict away from its Arab core to the eastern

peripheries of the Gulf and Southwest Asia. This shift in itself
directly affects the concerns of the Arab states within the region
and the relations among them.

## Egypt's Domestic Difficulties

There are, however, serious domestic threats and external dangers to Egypt's peace policy. At home, these are essentially economic
(with their attendant social consequences) and political. In fact,
the greatest threat to Egypt's peace policy may yet come from domestic difficulties, not from the opposition of the Arab states. The
country's major problem for the foreseeable future will be that of
feeding its rising population. It is staggering to think that the estimated population at the end of the century will be 65-70 million,
or an increase in twenty years of fifty percent. Forty percent of the
population now (estimated at the end of 1977 at forty million) is
under fifteen years of age. Only twenty-five percent of the total
at the moment (9.5 million) constitutes the working population in
the country. Despite the industrialization programs of the last
twenty-five years and the expansion of the service sector, nearly
half of this working population (44.7 percent) is still engaged on the
land, 35.9 percent in services, and only 19.4 percent in industry.
In the meantime, there has been a disproportionate exodus of the
country's trained and skilled human resources to neighboring,
prosperous Arab countries and overseas. Egypt, therefore, will
continue to depend on outside assistance.

The new economic policy, inaugurated in 1974 and commonly
referred to as the Open Door Policy (ODP), aims at tackling the
country's perilous economic conditions. The main features of this
policy are a shift to a free market economy in the hope of attracting
foreign capital investments, a greater determination to strike a more
reasonable and credible balance between industrial and agricultural
development, a decision to revitalize the existing public sectors
by promoting keener competition from an enlarged private sector,
and a conscious effort to provide structures for the management
of the economic and social problems that loom large on the horizon.

The ODP also intends to alleviate the employment problems
by absorbing the masses of Egyptian unemployed and underem-
ployed secondary-school students and university graduates into

an expanding private sector of the economy. With the greater attention to be paid to agriculture and food production, the policy will, hopefully, slow down the movement of population from the countryside to the city.

It is too early to say whether the ODP will create the required new economic structures. For the moment, it has established a parallel market for foreign exchange, reduced exchange restrictions, reformed banking laws, and, to some extent, decentralized the making of economic decisions. More important, perhaps, it has increased the participation of the private sector in the economy. But the ODP still faces great obstacles.

Although Egypt disposes of abundant cheap labor, most of it is ill-fed, uneducated, or poorly educated and trained. There is therefore, a manpower problem. Municipal and other services, so crucial to the success of the new policy, are poorly organized or have collapsed. Their restoration can only be undertaken with massive outside assistance, since technicians, craftsmen, artisans, and even managers of small-scale businesses are in desperately short supply. Even more serious is the deplorable condition of the state administration, with its overmanned and wasteful bureaucracy.

The ODP, or *infitah*, must be seen also as one going beyond economic considerations; it is the expression of a policy of openness, especially to the West. To this extent, it has been supported by the upper middle classes, elements of the small bourgeoisie as well as the new upwardly mobile segments of the population created by Nasser's old constituency, many of whom are now engaged in entrepreneurial activities.

Unfortunately, so far, this policy has turned out to be a consumer, not a producer, and has led to bureaucratic corruption and parasitic capitalism. It has also adversely affected income distribution, widening the gap between the masses of the poor and the few rich. The new tax laws of 1978, for instance, favor higher income groups, foreign and mixed investment projects, construction companies, and banks. The policy, on the whole, has led to inflation, the concentration of wealth in a few hands, flagrant consumerism, and maldistribution of income. Foreign capital, so far, has invested in quick profit projects. Western capital, petrodollars, and big businesses are reluctant to invest in long-term projects because (a) they fear political instability; (b) anticipate wider regional instability;

(c) are aware of a weak local infrastructure and bureaucratic red tape; and (d) observe the rampant inflation and the lack of technical and managerial skills in the country. The result has been that projects under the ODP (aside from tourism, hotels, and construction) are not developmental. For example, foreign banks deal mainly in import finance. In short, a laissez-faire policy has led to the loss of government control, at least over the direction of investment. In the process, a new class of *nouveaux riches* has emerged, aggravating further the problem of social and political stability.

A reformulation of the country's political priorities in the 1980s, both at home and abroad, will depend to a great extent on the resolution of some of its most pressing economic problems. In fact, the very success of the regime's peace policy and its ability to withstand Arab opposition rests on its ability to cope effectively with the changing domestic scene. At this point, the few loci of alternative power to Sadat in the country—most notably in the armed forces, which, in any case, on the whole support the peace policy—will react primarily to the regime's failure to deal with domestic problems.

Significantly, it is the social consequences of these economic problems that constitute the covert threat to Egypt's peace policy. A galloping inflation (currently estimated at forty percent) has eroded living standards of the small post-1952 "middle class," the educated elements in it, the salaried bureaucracy, and the army officer corps. Nor should the dangers of a psychologically-rooted national disaffection of the less well-off masses be minimized. Whereas the harsh economic conditions of the last thirty years were justified by the requirements of a war-time economy, the growing chasm between rich and poor, which is now of a magnitude never seen before, cannot be explained away so easily. This ever-widening gap between the very rich few and the vast majority of the poor may create conditions reminiscent of, and parallel to, the period 1950-52. That many of the new rich have acquired their wealth as a result of access to influence and power only helps to fuel the resentment of the rest of society.

Although the response of the vast majority of Egyptians to President Sadat's policy has been one of welcome relief, opposition continues to be spearheaded by the stirring populist religio-political movements that had lain dormant for a long time. These are led by the resurrected Muslim Brethren, who have resumed their activities among students especially and in the press. Their *Da'wa* magazine provides a platform of steady opposition to the regime and its policy of peace with Israel. The experience in Iran suggests also that an ambitious economic policy could founder upon the rocks of a stubbornly authoritarian state system. Vast demographic change in the last decade in Egypt, too, has produced a mass of up-rooted humanity that could provide militant, populist movements with political malcontents for whom Islam is the sole basis of political identity, solidarity, and social cohesiveness.

The concern with opposition to President Sadat's policy is reflected in the difference between the establishment of formal diplomatic relations between Egypt and Israel on one hand and the resistance to a wider normalization of relations between the two countries on the other. It is not only Sadat himself and his establishment who are reluctant to open the floodgates of normalization as long as Mr. Begin's government remains intransigent, in their view, over the issue of Palestinian autonomy on the West Bank and Gaza. Equally significant is the rejection of such normalization by groups of Egyptians, especially professionals, technicians, and others, who fear their isolation from the rest of the Arab world where they have a vital interest in terms of jobs and influence. Similarly, the slow returns of the ODP in terms of a marked improvement in the economy erode the earlier expectation of the benefits of a closer relationship with Israel. One fears that President Sadat's apparent over-emphasis on the external factor for the resolution of Egypt's economic and social difficulties may be misplaced and, in the long term, disastrous. Solutions to some of these problems must be sought at home.

Another more serious threat to the regime's policy may come from the potential diasaffection of the officer corps. Equally affected by inflation, officers observe their civilian relations enriching themselves in quick-return enterprises under the conditions of the new economic policy. They also view with great suspicion the better pay and conditions and the unnecessarily sophisticated weaponry of the police. They suspect the regime favors a strengthened police force as a makeweight to the army and as a means to control popular disturbances caused by economic hardship.

For the moment, in 1979, pressing economic problems at home and their social consequences have led to a deterioration of the domestic political situation. As a result, the so-called liberalization policies of the years between 1975 and 1978 have been discarded if not, in fact, reversed in 1979. There has been a tightening up of internal security and a move toward greater autocracy. Thus, two very recent legislative steps taken by President Sadat are, in the view of some, ominous. Passed after a referendum, one requires that legislation be based on religious law (Shari'a), the other decrees that the president can be elected for more than two terms. The first may be considered a way of countering extremist and militant religio-political oppostion; the second, a way of amending the constitution in such a way as to allow Sadat to remain in office indefinitely.

Yet, the first of these legislative acts has raised once again in Egypt the specter of communal conflict between Muslims and Copts. In April, 1980, there were serious clashes in Alexandria and parts of Upper Egypt. Milad Hanna's book, *Copts yes, but Egyptians*, appeared on the same day that President Sadat delivered his famous speech about a Coptic conspiracy to set up a Christian state in Upper Egypt. Coptic Patriarch Anba Shenouda's open letter in reply to the President's broadcast was not allowed to be published. Relations between the two communities remain strained, adding to the domestic turmoil and uncertainty. At a time when sectarian and ethnic conflicts are very much a part of the political landscape in other parts of the region, such a development in Egypt (historically the one country in the region least plagued by communal differences) contributes to the region's instability.

## The Arab Rejection Front

The Arab Rejection Front faces serious problems, too, which can affect regional politics. Iraq and Syria have led the opposition to Egypt's peace policy. Although during the last decade both countries have been governed by Baathist regimes, their relations have been marred by mutual distrust. They came together briefly when their interest in opposing a peaceful accommodation with Israel converged. Syria's opposition to Egypt rested on military, strategic, and political reasons, considering the Israeli occupation of the Golan since 1967, Syria's own military involvement in Lebanon, and its special relationship with the PLO. Iraq, on the other hand, saw its chance, with Egypt choosing to leave the wider inter-Arab political arena to engage in the politics of Arab leadership. The alliance between the two countries, however, was short-lived, because it rested on unstable foundations. An attempt at a union between them failed because of deep-seated enmities and traditional rivalries. Both countries suffered from internal weaknesses in their bodies politic, ranging from ethnic and sectarian conflict to narrow-based autocratic governing elites. Their domestic difficulties were such that no schemes of union between them could be implemented; nor could their joint leadership of the opposition against Egypt be made credible.

Ever since independence in 1946, every Syrian regime has been interested in carving out a major role for Syria in the Fertile Crescent. Equally, ever since independence, the rivalry between Syria and Iraq for the domination of the Fertile Crescent has also been a political fact of life, whether under *anciens régimes* or the military regimes that succeeded them after 1949, or under the Baath regimes in Damascus since 1963, or even after 1968, when the Baath party came to power in both Baghdad and Damascus.

President Asad has been in power in Damascus for ten years. He is the leading member of the minority Alawite sect (eleven percent of the population), which, during the last ten to fifteen years, has come to control the two main centers of power in Syria, the military and the ruling Baath party. This situation in itself would not be significant were it not for the fact that, despite a great measure of cultural uniformity, Syria's population is characterized by strong religious and ethnic diversity. The Sunni (Orthodox) Muslims who constitute nearly sixty-eight percent of the population consider religious minorities like the Alawites and the Druzes (three percent of the population) as heretical sects of Islam.

Furthermore, sectarian and ethnic diversity (exemplified by the presence of Kurds, Circassians, Armenians, and Turkomans) has produced a fragmented political system in Syria. Political interference by European powers in the past strengthened both the function of religious minorities as political units and their communal consciousness. Under the French Mandate (1920-46), sectarian loyalties were encouraged in order to counter the rise of Arab nationalism. This was particularly the case in the Latakia region, where most of the Alawites live, and the Jabal Druze region, where the Druzes are concentrated. As part of this policy, the French favored the military recruitment of special detachments from among religious and ethnic minorities (Alawites, Druzes, Kurds, Circassians) to form the *Troupes Spéciales du Levant*. They used these troops to suppress local insurrections. The Sunni establishment in Damascus, Aleppo, and elsewhere in the main towns of Syria—who constituted the "ruling class" of notables and merchants and who came to dominate after independence in 1946—resented this situation. In Syria, in addition to this basic sectarian and ethnic diversity, there are regional, local, and tribal divisions between cities, localities, and tribes that further complicate the political fragmentation of the country.

Minorities such as the Alawites had been for a long time underprivileged agrarian communities, whose only hope for upward mobility was to place their sons in military careers. Over the years, they attained a greater presence in the armed forces relative to their numerical strength in the population. When the Baath party was formed in the early 1940s, its secular ideology, including an element of socialism, attracted many members from the minorities, including the Alawites. For a long time, these minorities associated the traditional political parties of the Sunni establishment, including those with a platform of Arab nationalism, with Sunni Islam. They also resented their domination. Within a period of twenty years, however, minorities came to dominate both the Baath party (in power since 1963) and its military organization (in power since 1966), which military organization, in turn, came to dominate the civilian wing of the party.

It is against this background that one must consider the manifestations of opposition and discontent in Syria in 1979-80 and the challenge these present to the Asad regime. Sunnis resent the regime's assistance of the Christians in Lebanon during the civil war there against the Lebanese Muslims and Palestinians. They also resent the monopoly of state power held by Alawites and their allies from among the other minorities. The older political formations of the Damascene establishment are opposed to the Baath party and its domination by the Alawites, whom they consider heretics. There is also a widespread grievance against corruption in the Asad regime, compounded by inflation and inequality. Finally, there are rivalries between Alawite officers and political aspirants, as was the case in the 1960s between Asad, Umran, and Jadid.

In seeking to counter domestic instability, President Asad may seek greater assistance from the Soviet Union. While it is conceivable that such assistance could bolster his position in the Fertile Crescent and within Arab politics generally, it cannot resolve his domestic political difficulties. All the same, considering the crises in Iran and Afghanistan, a greater Syrian dependence on Soviet military support (including at some critical stage the transfer of Soviet troops to that country) would destabilize the Fertile Crescent and have serious repercussions in the region as a whole.

In addition to its rejectionist stand over peace with Israel, Iraq has recently embarked upon an aggressive Arab policy in the Gulf and South Arabia, and in view of developments in Iran and Afghanistan, it has moved toward some cooperation with Saudi Arabia. It opposes the involvement of the superpowers in the region and favors regional Arab security arrangements. Saudi Arabia's Crown Prince Fahd's most recent statement (13 August 1980) calling for a Holy War to establish a Palestinian State with Jerusalem as its capital may well be, in part, a result of the recent talks betwen Baghdad and Riyadh. Given its domestic difficulties, however, it is unlikely that Iraq in the 1980s can provide, in any combination with other Arab states, a credible regional policy, including the kind of local gendarme force that dispenses with outside guarantors of regional security. Further afield in the meantime, it has strengthened its relations with some Western states, especially France and Greece.

In the 1980s, Iraq will continue to oppose potential Egyptian primacy in the Arab area and, to this extent, will collaborate with Saudi Arabia as long as the latter country's interests also demand its opposition to Egypt. For the moment, Iraq's relations with the PLO are as strained as those with Syria. These deteriorated in part because of the PLO's unqualified support of the Khomeini revolution in Iran to which Iraq is opposed for very good reasons. It remains one of the Arab countries that could most readily be affected by developments in Iran, not simply because of its contiguous border with that country but more significantly because of the Shia majority in its population and the possible effects of a wider Kurdish separatist movement in Iran spilling over to the Iraqi Kurds.

Saudi Arabia, an erstwhile ally of Egypt, shifted its position in order to oppose Camp David and Egypt's policy. It joined the Arab Rejection Front and provided financial assistance to Syria and Jordan. Events in Iran, Afghanistan, and South Arabia, however, have prompted the Saudis to reconsider matters of domestic and external security.

Saudi Arabia in the 1980s will face the difficult problem of political stability. The major threats will come from two main sources. First, a rapid rate of economic development may have serious social consequences, ranging from demographic change to changes in life patterns; it will also at times heighten expectations that cannot be met. Second, the attending political difficulties may result from the tension between the changed patterns of life produced by a new and different economy on one hand and the desire to retain an essentially Islamic state and society on the other. These threats to the fabric of Saudi society and the nature of its polity are intertwined, not simply interconnected. Although, theoretically, these are domestic matters, they are inevitably affected by external factors of a wider Arab regional and international provenance. Of itself, the migration of Arab labor in the area, for instance, constitutes a powerful impetus for these projected changes.

There are those who argue that the Saudi Arabian ruling family will not be able to withstand for very long the pressure of demands for wider political participation and a more equitable distribution of wealth. To this extent, the prolonged intransigence of the family in the face of these pressures may create a condition of stasis in the country that may lead to sedition. Thus, there are those who have interpreted the storming of the Great Mosque in Mecca in 1979 as the first clear manifestaion of political unrest in the country by religious militants, and as a protest against the ruling family's deviation from the principles of Islam. The case could be made, however, for the future ability of the ruling family to continue to successfully balance the emerging forces by slowing down a totally imported complex of economic development, by stringent immigration policies, and by a renewal of its arrangements with the religious brotherhood of the Wahhabis, the tribal groups, and its own members. Yet, with a population of barely five million Saudis, the country must continue to depend, for its present policies, on the importation of people and technology from the Middle East, Europe, the United States, and Asia.

Saudi Arabia will remain concerned with preventing the Peninsula and the Gulf from falling under the influence of the radical Baathi regime of Iraq, the militant Iranians, or the Soviet Union through one of its satellites. At the same time, it must guard against militant, messianic religious movements at home by continually sustaining its own Wahhabi establishment. More concretely, it will seek to prevent the unification of the two Yemens (unless this takes place on its own conditions) since, in that event, Marxist South Yemen would dominate the North and allow its ally the Soviet Union greater political leverage over the Peninsula, thus threatening the sources of oil supply. Saudi Arabia will conduct its regional Arab policy in close cooperation with Kuwait, the independence of which country is in Saudi interests. It will continue to placate the PLO by running political interference on its behalf with the Western world, using oil and capital as weapons, and will support Syria and Jordan in their opposition to Egypt's peace policy. As it cannot, even in the near future, dispose of a credible military force, Saudi Arabia will continue to depend on American assistance for its security. Further afield, it will continue to compete and cooperate with Egypt in East Africa, especially around the Horn, with a view to preventing the domination of the Red Sea area by the Soviet Union or any of its client states on the African continent.

Jordan, in a way, has had to walk the tightest rope of any Arab state in the last three years. In view of its earlier position in the West Bank, its sizeable settled Palestinian population, events in Lebanon and its partial dependence on Arab financial assitance, Jordan has had to shift its policy toward a closer cooperation with the Arab Rejection Front. Until 1979, it feared the consequences of a concerted Iraqi-Syrian policy and had to embark upon a rapprochement with both of these countries. But, following the estrangement between Baghdad and Damascus and the subsequent erosion of the Arab Rejection Front, Jordan has reassessed its position. In perceiving the weakness of the Asad regime in Syria, Jordan has renewed its interest in the fate of the West Bank, hoping that an eventual arrangement in association with it might yet be a compromise solution. There has thus been, in the last two years, a renewed collaboration between Jordan and the PLO, possibly with this end in mind. This is, however, a precarious and potentially dangerous relationship in view of what happened ten years ago. Nor is it possible for Jordan to ignore the old Palestinian constituency on the West Bank that must somehow be satisfied, whatever the final arrangements. And Jordan has to contend with the 1974 Arab decision that recognized the PLO as the sole representative of the Palestinian Arabs.

The PLO has been most active in the Arab Rejection Front.

In 1979, it surfaced as a staunch supporter of the Khomeini revolution in Iran without, however, realizing appreciable political returns. Its diplomatic offensive for recognition in Western Europe and the United States had a measure of success, at least in Western Europe, but has had no perceptible impact on the conflict itself on the ground. The PLO is still caught in its own dilemma, consisting of a difficult choice between a National Covenant and the acceptance of a state on the West Bank. Constituent groups within the PLO are sharply divided over this matter. Accepting a state on the West Bank would mean abandoning the central aim of its National Covenant, namely, the recovery of all Palestine. Furthermore, it entails the risk of opposition from the local (ex-Jordanian) Palestinian leadership on the West Bank and reaching an agreement with King Hussein.

It is interesting to note that the PLO in the 1980s will probably improve its diplomatic standing and find greater favor in the chanceries of some West European states at a time when its standing and popularity in the Middle East, especially in Jordan and Lebanon, is at a low ebb. Western European concern with energy supplies from the Middle East and a parallel dissatisfaction with United States policy have been the principal factors in this development. The inconclusive negotiations between Egypt and Israel over Palestinian autonomy and the recent acts of the Begin government over East Jerusalem have contributed to it. On the other hand, the continued armed presence of the PLO in Lebanon, especially West Beirut and an enclave in south Lebanon, has alienated even the Muslim community in that country. This perhaps has been an inevitable consequence of the civil war. In Jordan, too, the events of 1968-70 have left feelings of resentment and distrust toward the PLO on the part of the long-established Palestinian community there, not to mention the East Jordanians themselves.

The role and fortunes of the PLO in the immediate future cannot be assessed separately from developments in Lebanon and, by extension, Syria and Jordan. Any future political compromise between the Muslim community of Lebanon and the recently strengthened Maronites may work to the disadvantage of the Palestinians. In order not to alienate the large Muslim community of Lebanon, the Syrians may well have to accept such a compromise or simply watch over benevolently, if not actually connive in, the PLO's eventual elimination from the Lebanese equation. For the moment, the Palestinians in Lebanon are surrounded by the Phalanges and the Syrian peace-keeping forces in the east and north and, in the south, they face Major Haddad's armed enclave and the Israeli Defence Forces on the border.

## A Composite Picture

The pattern of events in the coming decade will be marked by the continued instability of regimes. The trend of developments will be one of shifting alignments among the states of the region, with a greater involvement of the superpowers. The close of the last decade saw the virtual disintegration of Lebanon, the conclusion of the Egypt-Israel peace treaty, the overthrow of the Shah in Iran by an Islamic revolution, the Soviet invasion of Afghanistan, and the destabilization of Turkey by unprecedented economic problems and social violence.

In the Arab Middle East, the competing loci of power and rivalry of regional interests will be centered in Arabia, Egypt, the Fertile Crescent, and North Africa. Peripheral conflicts in Africa, the Red Sea area, the Eastern Mediterranean, and Southwest Asia will, naturally, affect this competition and rivalry. The pivots of conflict will be Egypt and the Arab states, Arabia and Iran over the Gulf, Iraq and Iran, Syria and Iraq in the Fertile Crescent (the Palestinians and Jordan included), Algeria and Morocco in North Africa, with Libya fomenting peripheral conflict in Tunisia, Egypt, and the Sudan.

Four trends now dominate the perception of regional politics by Arab regimes in the Middle East. One is the outcome of the Egyptian-Israeli peace treaty. Another is the long-term impact of events in Iran and the spread of militant religious-populist sedition. A third is the apprehension over the Soviet incursion into Afghanistan. Compounding this is the overall fear that the United States will not or cannot protect the region from the growing Soviet threat.

For a long time now, power in the states of the region has rested in the hands of older, traditional elites and "class" minorities. Vast demographic changes in the last decade now threaten these arrangements. With readier access to money and arms, the transformation of discontented masses into holy warriors or revolutionary forces becomes easier. They can be led not only against their own respective state political establishments but also against those who they presume have undermined their cultural autonomy, invariably some foreign power.

In my opinion, it is more useful to view the resurgence of Islamic militancy as a sociopolitical phenomenon than as a manifestation of a religious revival. It is a response to certain economic and social problems created by several decades of modernization, economic development, and social change. Its political thrust is directed against the governing classes, their elites at home, and foreign connections abroad. Having said this, it is important to realize that Islamic resurgence remains a protest movement in the main and is still negative in character. Yet, even as a negative protest movement, it will clearly influence politics in the region, at least to the extent that the conditions of stasis tend to destabilize regimes. If the experience in Iran so far is any indication, this movement will not succeed in making Islam a workable principle for political organization or the sole basis of a political order. It will nevertheless sharpen the dichotomy between things perceived as Islamic and those considered to be non- or anti-Islamic. To this extent, it will use this dichotomy—perilously, one might add—in the relations between states. Also, to this extent—as a challenge to the status quo or as the agent of sedition—Islamic militancy will be a threat to foreign powers with vital interests in the region.

Closely connected with Islamic resurgence is the problem of minorities, which will plague regional politics, particularly in Iran and in the Fertile Crescent, but also in Turkey and the Gulf States, which have sizeable Shia, Persian, and other non-Arab communities. It is felt even in Egypt. Apart from its adverse effect on the cohesion and therefore the stability of states, it can have extra-regional and international repercussions. The greater or more frequent the incidence of militant Islamic movements, the more critical the minorities problem will become. In the past, peaceful coexistence of minorities with majorities, and therefore their survival, was guaranteed by imperial orders and, more recently, by secular political arrangements. The longer the problem remains unsolved, the harsher the internal security arrangements of the states in the region will be.

A source of regional problems in the 1980s may be the extensive migration of labor in the Arab countries. Some view it as a factor of greater integration. Without going into the impact of this migration on labor-exporting and labor-importing countries, there is an assumption that its greater regularization via bilateral and multilateral Arab state agreements can promote the integration not only of a labor but also of a financial market. The constraints on such a development are not only economic but also political, as has been the case, say, between Egypt and Libya, Egypt and the Sudan, and Egypt and Iraq.

The disparity between oil rich states and poor ones, all of which must feed their populations, could conceivably inaugurate a new dimension of regional conflict. Libya and Iraq, for example, have already engaged in aggressive regional policies—regardless of their success or failure—that are made possible by their comparatively richer condition. The type of periodic clashes between Egypt and Libya in the past may become more common in the future.

Given these conditions, how credible are suggestions by some Middle Eastern states of a return to a policy of neutralism? Similarly, how credible are suggestions of regional defense arrangements that eschew ties with either of the superpowers? Is the reassertion of an Islamic identity enough? On the other hand, given the conflicting interests and rivalries between the states of the region, how effective or stable would be, say, any alliances between a superpower, especially the United States, and a Middle Eastern state?

## The Superpowers

General Sir John Hackett has argued that the experience of the Second World War has shown that the Middle East is not the key to winning a war, but that its control is absolutely essential to not losing it. For the West, it is a much needed fulcrum. The Soviet Union seems to have grasped the geopolitical importance of this fulcrum and, in the last decade, has established its military presence astride the Red Sea, southern Africa, and, now, Southwest Asia. In this way it can block the operation of this fulcrum. Otherwise, it is difficult to explain the Soviet presence in South Yemen, Libya, Syria, and Africa in the 1970s and, now, in Afghanistan. If this presence is to be extended to a politically-fragmented region like the Middle East, the possibilities of new centers of regional power emerging with Soviet support or under Soviet control are greater.

In the 1950s and 1960s, the Soviet presence in the Middle East had polarized regional politics. Now, the Egyptian-Israeli peace treaty, the Soviet invasion of Afghanistan, the Islamic resurgence in Iran and elsewhere, are all new causes for another, and perhaps different, polarization of the region's politics.

The argument is often made that if the priorities of the two superpowers in the region are different, they can be accommodated. In the current confrontation, it is clear that the United States has sought to exclude the Soviet Union from peacemaking at the western end of the region. The Soviet Union, in turn, has embarked upon a more adventurous policy at the eastern and southern ends, constituting a threat to the West's vital energy supplies from the Gulf. This new situation may well force Western leaders in the 1980s to consider more urgently alternative overland means of oil transport, which may be easier to defend and protect than the sea-lanes from the Gulf. In the meantime, the United States is seeking to consolidate its military presence in the Gulf (Oman) and the Indian Ocean, a development which in itself could provide a new rallying point for militant opposition in the region. Nevertheless, these developments have introduced a new kind of superpower rivalry over the friendship of the "Islamic world." Thus, while their respective interests demand a more direct involvement in the region in the 1980s, the consequences of their confrontation have introduced a new constraint on this involvement, namely, the sensibilities of Islam.

In the most recent of confrontations between the superpowers in the Middle East, the United States faces a serious difficulty that the Soviet Union for the moment does not, namely, disagreements with allies over Middle Eastern policy. Events in the region have strained the Western Alliance, whose roots lie in Europe. The dissatisfaction of the EEC with American leadership of the Alliance is expressed in a policy of appeasement toward the Middle East. Concerned as they are with oil supplies from the region, West Europeans believe in placating Arab oil suppliers with a more pro-Arab stand over the Arab-Israel conflict. Some of them have also actively tried to appease the Soviet Union over Afghanistan. In fact, they fear that a greater American military involvement in the Middle East will reduce the American contribution to the defense of Western Europe and, therefore, place a heavier defense burden on them.

In conclusion, regional politics will be affected by the recent major change in the Middle Eastern regional balance. The two main events responsible for the change are the Egyptian-Israeli peace treaty and the Islamic revolution in Iran. The first has had a destabilizing effect on the region to the extent that it has polarized the Arab states. There is now—no one can say for how long— an Iraqi attempt at a regional policy in collaboration with Saudi Arabia, aimed simultaneously against Egypt and at bringing her back to the Arab fold. In the meantime, Egypt's inter-Arab role has diminished. The second has eliminated a staunch ally of the West, rendering the "Nixon Doctrine" inapplicable and undermining the role of the United States in the area, fostering insecurity among its client states, chief among them Saudi Arabia.

The priority strategic interest of the United States and its allies is oil. In view of the recent change in the regional balance, the United States now intends to guarantee its military presence in the region directly. This it hopes to achieve with bases in Oman, the Indian Ocean, and related facilities in Egypt, Israel, and perhaps Somalia. Such a policy in itself, however, may prove problematic.

The Soviet Union, in contrast, has embarked upon a more dynamic and, therefore, threatening policy in the region. Whether its long-term strategic interest is to endanger Western supplies of oil or access to the oil reserves themselves is immaterial. It could be both. Equally important may be the acquisition of regional influence through an attempt to secure its communications from the Dardanelles, Suez and Bab el-Mandeb to the Malacca Straits, Indo-China and Vladivostok. The route is vital. Geopolitically, concern with security along southern borders may have prompted the Soviet Union to gain a more pervasive presence in Southwest Asia, the Middle East, and the Horn of Africa. In this way, it is in a better position to project power, influence events, and challenge the West.

If this is a fair depiction of recent changes, we may be entering a period of renewed imperial-type rivalry between superpowers in the Middle East. The rivalry will probably be conducted less by proxy and more by direct involvement, and regional politics will become proportionately more dangerous.

# 3

# The Arab World Between Pragmatism and Radicalism

*Shimon Shamir*

AT THE BEGINNING of the 1970s, one of Europe's leading journalists on Middle Eastern affairs, Arnold Hottinger, wrote an article in *Foreign Affairs* under the title "The Depth of Arab Radicalism." He predicted that the coming years would be a period dominated by radicalism, and his argument was quite persuasive. The failure of the Arab regimes, he said, to modernize effectively, to solve their most acute internal problems, to cope successfully with Israel—nourished a malaise that would lead the Arabs to take "the revolutionary way." He described this revolutionary path in the following terms: "The vicious circle . . . of high hopes, frustration, and more radical aims leading to new frustration—would probably be its beginning, and might continue for a long time. The answer to each new defeat would be more radicalism."

The projection was not groundless. The Arab world of the 1950s and 1960s had been dominated by Nasserism and "romantic" Baathism, which expounded the vision of the rise of an Arab nation "from the Arab Gulf to the Atlantic Ocean." This trend carried with it the promise of a solution to the basic problems of Arab society through social change and rapid economic development, with a consequent increase in the Arabs' prestige and power in the world. The subsequent failure to fulfill these promises caused widespread disillusionment with the nationalist regimes of the 1950s and 1960s. It was, therefore, only reasonable to expect that the *post mortem* would lead the Arabs to conclude that they had failed because they were too compromising, conciliatory, inconsistent, and pragmatic, and that they would seek a stronger remedy for the 1970s.

As we now know, this prediction did not materialize. The 1970s evolved not as a decade of revolution but rather one of de-radicalization, a period when the political regimes of the major Arab countries moved, to a greater or lesser extent, toward more pragmatism in their political programs. The ideological fervor and frequent political upheavals typical of the 1950s and 1960s all but disappeared. In fact, one of the most remarkable features of the political life in the Arab world in the 1970s was the stability of political systems. The list of political leaders who rose to power in 1969-70 and were still in office ten years later is impressive indeed. It includes Syria's President Hafiz Asad, Egypt's President Anwar Sadat, Sudan's President Ja'far Numayri, Libya's President Mu'ammar Qadhdhafi, and Iraq's President Ahmad Hasan Bakr with Saddam Husayn at his side. The dramatic Arabic broadcasts announcing a new *coup d'état* and the formation of yet another revolutionary council—announcements to which we were so accustomed in earlier decades—all but vanished from the airwaves in the 1970s.

This change can be partly explained by the experience gained in the 1950s and 1960s by the political elites. The ruling oligarchies and their state machineries have simply become better at dealing with domestic threats to their regimes. They are more skillful in employing the great variety of preventive measures needed to thwart potential conspiracies among the officer corps—the traditional hotbed of *coups d'état*. Thus, it has become increasingly difficult for others to seize power.

Perhaps the changes in the role and the size of the army may also have had an effect. In a number of Arab states, the army has successfully been de-politicized, and regimes are less dependent on the recruitment of qualified manpower from this source. As the military machineries in the Arab countries have grown, it has become increasingly difficult to organize a conspiracy comprising sufficient commanders and units to seize power that could yet remain clandestine long enough to succeed.

But of greater significance was the erosion in the credibility of the military *juntas*, which, preaching radical nationalist ideologies, had promised to accomplish historic breakthroughs for their societies. This combination of inspiring revolutionary ideology and a powerful military *junta* —expressed in the Arab political terminology of the 1950s and 1960s by the concept *thawra* —had initially been seen by Arab publics as a formidable force able to pave the road for the realization of the great Arab dream. There is a remarkable passage in Najib Mahfuz's famous novel *The Thief and the*

*Dogs* where he describes the idealist phase in the life of his protago-
nist Rauf 'Ilwan, an ardent revolutionary who had great influence
over the young people of his generation. "What does a young man
need in his homeland?" he would preach to them. "It is the gun
and the book." The combination of "gun and book," of ideology
and the means of coercion, was seen as a short-cut to salvation. It
was widely believed that there *were* attainable solutions to the problems; all that was needed to realize them was the right doctrine and
the power to impose it.

Not so in the 1970s. Having watched the violent struggle for
power between military factions and been subjected to their ruthless
methods of political control, Arab publics became increasingly skeptical of the supposedly altruistic motivations of the revolutionary
*juntas*. There was a similar disillusionment with ideology as the ultimate panacea. As a matter of fact, it may perhaps be correct to note
that the 1970s were the first decade, after almost a whole century, in
which no basically new ideology emerged. If we consider from the
turn of the nineteenth century on—say, since Jamal al-Din al-Afghani
—we find that in every decade there appeared a new system of ideas,
whether indigenous or imported: pan-Islam, Islamic reform, patriotism, liberalism, Islamic fundamentalism, pan-Arab and particularist
nationalism, Communism, Fascist-inspired activism, Nasserism,
Baathism, and guerrilla-Marxism or Maoism. All these ideologies
had relevance to people throughout the region and found political
expression in the major Arab countries.

This ideological fervor subsided in the 1970s; it seemed as if
the Arab world had run out of ideological options. One may point
perhaps to Qadhdhafi's Popular Revolution as a phenomenon of
the 1970s, but it was essentially a replay of trends from the 1950s;
the other Arab countries frequently ridiculed it as an outdated and
eclectic absurdity.

In broad terms, this development was part of a universal trend
depicted in Daniel Bell's *End of Ideology*, which reached the region
late. But it is with the particular historical factors at work in the
Arab world that we are concerned here, and most of those were
connected to the failure of the nationalist *thawra* regimes to fulfill
their promises. The limited and sometimes negative outcome of
their revolutions, dramatically and symbolically manifested in the
1967 defeat, drove the disenchanted Arabs to seek other approaches

to their problems. The more radical alternatives—Communism, fundamentalism, and fascism—had systematically been suppressed or co-opted by the nationalist regimes, and, anyway, their novelty had considerably faded. The only radical movement that managed to thrive on the disaffection with established regimes was the Palestinian Fedayeen; but with all the enthusiastic support they received in the Arab world, their message was hardly deemed relevent to the main problems of the existing states. For the most part, disillusioned Arabs did not attribute the cumulative failures to the mildness and shortcomings of the prevailing ideologies but to the doctrinaire approach itself, which had been revealed as excessively verbal, detached from reality, and ineffective. Consequently, there has been a tendency to turn away from all-embracing programs and to deal instead with the immediate internal problems of each society in an increasingly pragmatic fashion.

This has brought about the emergence of a different balance between *wataniyya* (the term now used in the Arab world to refer to local nationalism) and *qawmiyya* (or pan-Arabism). Whereas in in the 1950s and 1960s *qawmiyya* was predominant, and local nationalism was labeled "separatism" and regarded as a betrayal of the national cause, the 1970s saw a considerable growth in the relative importance of *wataniyya*. Whether in Egypt, Jordan, Iraq, or Syria, particularist nationalism was becoming more and more legitimate, more and more relevent, as a conceptual and operational framework for coping with real problems.

This gravitation toward *wataniyya* is bound to the shift toward pragmatism, despite the fact that particularist nationalism had assumed various radical forms in the 1930s. In the realities of the 1970s, *wataniyya* was associated with the tangible problems that every Arab experienced in his actual environment and native country, while *qawmiyya* reflected messianic expectations focusing on a vast entity existing only in the doctrines and visions of Arabism. *Wataniyya* called to mind the down to earth liberal-nationalists of the pre-revolutionary period whereas *qawmiyya* was upheld mostly by the doctrinaire *thawras*. *Wataniyya* has usually been rationalistic, empirical, and evolutionist; *qawmiyya*, millenarian and revolutionary.

Furthermore, it should be borne in mind that in the Arab world the anti-Western posture is associated with radicalism, whereas closeness to the West often corresponds to pragmatism. Now, *qawm-iyya* is definitely anti-Western; the very concept expresses a Promethean struggle against the West. It invokes the polarity of *'uruba,* Arabism, on the one hand, against "Western imperialism" on the other. *Qawmiyya* carries the torch of the historical struggle against Europe, the continuous *jihad* from the rise of Islam, through the Crusades and the Reconquista, up to the modern age. In contrast, *wataniyya* often focuses on the heritage of the ancient civilization of each country, stressing the contribution of that civilization to those that succeeded it in the West, and thus regarding them all as one historical organism. This is especially salient in the case of Egypt, where particular nationalism stresses connection and contribution to Mediterranean civilization and thus, directly and indirectly, to the West.

Another factor that should be mentioned in this context is the Soviet Union. Many aspects of the Soviet Union's role in the modern history of the Middle East remain controversial, but there is no question that the Soviet influence in the 1950s and 1960s worked to destabilize the region. While it is true that the Soviets gave little support to Marxist revolutionary parties, they definitely radicalized Arab politics. Their aim was often to polarize the region between their clients (the "progressives") and the pro-Western states (the "reactionaries"), thus heating up the political atmosphere. The Soviet attempt at polarization in order to facilitate penetration into the region can be seen in the background to the wars of both 1956 and 1967.

In the 1970s, the role of the Soviet Union in Middle Eastern politics was greatly diminished. The United States held the initiative in the diplomacy of the Arab-Israeli conflict, and the expulsion of the Soviet personnel from Egypt not only inflicted a heavy blow on Moscow's prestige in the region but also weakened Soviet leverage in those states where their presence continued. Thus, Muhammad Hasanayn Haykal, writing in 1978 on Arab-Soviet relations, subtitled his book, "The Rise and Fall of Soviet Influence in the Middle East." He claimed that a "new Middle East system" had emerged, dominated by the United States. Unlike the second half of the 1950s and 1960s—a period of equilibrium between the Soviets and the Western powers that allowed the local Arab states to conduct a policy of "positive neutrality" in the 1970s—the balance shifted to the American side, creating a *de facto* Pax Americana in the region. Unaware of the events that were about to reverse this process before the end of the decade, Arab political publics—just like Haykal—were under the impression that for most of the 1970s, the Americans would be gaining the upper hand. The Soviets ceased their attempts to polarize the Arab world and provoke another regional confrontation, and the anti-American radicals were thus considerably discouraged.

These developments in the Middle East were linked to two global trends that made their appearance in the mid-1960s. The first was the decline in the position of the Afro-Asian bloc, or rather the discovery of its inherent weaknesses. Following the 1955 Bandung Conference, many Arabs adopted the belief that the Afro-Asian peoples—with themselves in a central place among them—represented a rising power in the world that would eventually eclipse the decadent West. This belief nourished a conceited and defiant state of mind disposed to revolutionary ideologies. There was nothing neutral, passive, or pacificatory in the "positive neutrality" doctrine adopted by leading states in this bloc and by all revolutionary Arab regimes; in fact, it was a dynamic policy that supported any form of struggle or liberation movement against the West, the international position of which they sought to undermine. The pseudo-Marxist Third World jargon, which became so popular in the Arab *thawra* regimes, was harmless in itself, but it did legitimize the ideologies of radical leftist movements that until then had been considered outside the confines of the national consensus.

By the 1970s, it was widely recognized that the real power of this bloc was quite limited. Its lack of internal cohesion was exposed in its failure to prevent armed conflicts among its own members. Moreover, it was realized that it represented the world's "South"—the less industrialized and less advanced part of the world that would depend for many years to come on the technologies and productive capabilities of the "North." These realizations had a sobering effect on peoples throughout the Afro-Asian world.

The second global trend was the relaxation of the Cold War between the superpowers and the emergence of detente in the early 1970s. Even if some of the expectations that accompanied this development turned out to be over-optimistic—certainly since competition between the superpowers in the Middle East continued—

the overall effect was to calm political tensions and help eliminate the struggle between "progressive" and "reactionary" states.

But the crucial factor in the termination of the Arab ideological Cold War was oil. With a leading state of the formerly "progressive" camp like Egypt expecting to benefit from the wealth of a leading state in the formerly "reactionary" camp like Saudi Arabia, there was no longer any point in perpetuating the struggle between the two camps.

The rise of the oil-producing countries brought with it a new understanding of economic power. It introduced new concepts and rearranged priorities. Cool, practical, and realistic considerations now occupied a more central position in the Arab public life. Economists, financial experts, and top technocrats rapidly replaced the revolutionary officers and revolutionary ideologues who had occupied the center stage in the *thawra* regimes of the 1950s and 1960s. Oil gave the Arabs a sense of importance, of "a place in the sun"—precisely what the revolutionaries of the 1950s and 1960s had tried but failed to realize through their political campaigns. This goal was now achieved through oil and petro-dollars and by no less a factor than the arch-reactionaries and the despised targets of the revolutionaries' ideological campaigns. The consequences of this for the credibility of "the revolutionary path" were obvious.

It also led to a new relationship with the West, particularly among Arab elites. The strong anti-Western undercurrents that had nurtured the local radical movements—the outcome of the sense of hurt, of the distress of humiliation, and of the rage of impotence *vis-à-vis* the West—now diminished. They were replaced by a general feeling that not only had the Arabs established their proper place in the world but had also achieved the capability sometimes to determine the place that others would have in it. There was a new perception of the balance between the Arab world and the West, and a new image of the West itself. Some Arabs expressed it by saying that they now felt that the West was "manageable." No longer was the West seen as an omnipotent entity masterminding every move in the region. Arab elites learned to recognize the weakness of the Western systems; no longer was every Western blunder interpreted as part of a grand design meant to supress them.

Time also played a part in this process. The 1970s were a whole generation removed from the end of the colonial period, and the traumatic experiences of the historic encounter with the West were gradually receding. As Edward Shils and others have pointed out, the first generation after de-colonization usually tends to extend the "battle against imperialism." Its leaders, having achieved their positions through the struggle for independence, tend to continue doing what they did best, sometimes seeking new battlegrounds for confrontation. This theory explains the political behavior of Nasser's generation. But by the 1970s, a new generation was e-merging. The generation gap found expression in the dialogues between older and younger intellectuals that occasionally appeared in Arab publications. In such dialogues, the younger generation typically argued that domination by colonial governments was some-thing they had not experienced; hence, they could not share with the previous generation a whole range of attitudes that emanated from it. They would sometimes bluntly say that such attitudes were unrealistic; they wished to see a more practical approach in coping with society's real problems.

It was probably this nascent mood that accounted for the pop-ularity of Tayyib Salih's novel *The Season of Migration to the North*, which was perhaps the first exposition of a balanced and dispassion-ate attitude to Western domination. "If these people came, for some reason, to our land," asks the hero of the book, a young Sudanese who returns to his native village after seven years of studies in Lon-don, "does it mean that we must poison our present and our future?" And he predicts that sooner or later his people will be able to relate to their former colonizers "without guilt and without gratitude."

Arab self-confidence was also enhanced by the October war. Whatever military experts may think about the real score at the end of that war, for the Arabs it was a sign of their growing ability to cope with their adversaries. Indirectly, it also boosted the self-image of the Arabs in the context of the historic confrontation with the West, for Israel had always been considered a symbol of Western challenge. Thus, one of the main factors underlying the demand for radical solutions has considerably diminished.

So far, I have described the Arab world by way of sweeping generalizations that cannot adequately deal with any one issue and certainly not with conceptual frameworks, where the whole range of the diverse Arab political system, social structures, and cultural patterns comes into play. Yet, to differing degrees, a certain pragmatic mood was discernable in all the major Arab countries. Even under such revolutionary governments as those of the Arab Libyan People's Socialist Republic and the People's Democratic Republic of Yemen, there were indications that some segments of opinion were affected by it. In all Arab countries, the trend was manifested most clearly in the rapidly growing technocratic sector, which by the nature of its functions is often inclined toward pragmatism.

Arab political elites, which in many Arab regimes considerably overlap the upper echelons of this technocratic sector, seemed to be quite comfortable with this approach. This phenomenon also existed—as students of Islamic history know—in the classical Islamic empires dominated by the *jihad* and *shari'a* belief-systems, where the ruling elites (including the upper echelon of the ulama as well) usually let themselves be guided by worldly and practical considerations rather than by unwavering adherence to the tenets of the prevalent doctrine.

Nowhere in the Arab world was the shift from revolutionism to pragmatism more marked than in Egypt, where it was identified with the decline of Nasserism and the accession of Sadat (even though it had in fact appeared in Nasser's last years). Sadat's perception of what the political scientist K. J. Holsti has termed the "national role" was quite different from Nasser's. Despite their common revolutionary background and close association, Sadat had no difficulty in disengaging himself from Nasser's grandiose vision of a great Arab entity led by Cairo. Sadat's own vision depicted an Egypt that would perhaps desire some international prestige and regional influence but would mainly be self-centered, aspiring to economic development, social evolution, and political stability. Sadat wanted an Egypt of *infitah*, meaning not only economic open door but also conceptual openness, practical experimentation, and an open door to the external world. One of the favorite themes in his speeches was the repudiation of the previous regime's doctrinairism, which, he said, led not only to internal oppression but also to a series of major policy failures. Unlike Nasser, Sadat did not seek to change the established order inside and outside Egypt, but to find a way of living with it. Whereas Nasserism thrived on political upheavals, Sadat aimed at stability and sought the cooperation of forces that were similarly inclined. For him, international politics was not a series of heroic combats and crucial zero-sum struggle, but a process of collective bargaining in search of deals that could benefit all parties.

There can be no doubt that it was the rise of pragmatism that paved the road to Sadat's peace initiative and the Egyptian-Israeli peace process. The acceptance of the state of Israel and the readiness to establish full peace with it, proclaimed in Sadat's trip to Jerusalem in November 1977, would have been unthinkable in the 1950s and 1960s. This was a glaring violation of the Arab anti-Israeli doctrine, which totally rejected any notion of reconciliation with the Jewish State. Only as the conditions favoring pragmatism began to emerge in the 1970s, as described above, did peace with Israel enter the range of possible options before Arab decision makers.

The new constellation of pragmatic forces that crystallized in the Middle East toward the mid-1970s held in it the elements conducive to peace in the context of a regional Pax Americana. This constellation included the Middle Eastern power centers—the Shah's Iran, with its oil and extensive military build-up; Saudi Arabia with its petro-dollars; Israel with its military might and modern systems; Egypt with its large population and centrality in the Arab world—as well as lesser powers such as Jordan, Sudan, and Morocco. While these forces differed among themselves, they were united by their American orientation, a desire to check the rise of radicalism, a stress on economic development, a desire to keep the Soviet Union out of the region, and a wish to avoid another military confrontation in the Middle East. The convergence of basic interests among these countries prepared the background for the Egyptian-Israeli peace process.

In the domestic arena, the peace process was facilitated by the rising concern with local socio-economic hardships, particularly in Egypt. It can be related directly to a diminishing readiness to bear the costs of the various campaigns conducted by the previous regime throughout the region. The prevailing mood sought practical solutions to the immediate problems, and peace with Israel was seen as such a solution. Thus, the peace that was being negotiated in the late 1970s was a purely pragmatic one; it did not result from an ideological reformulation of the nature and the rights of the State of Israel but rather from the demotion of ideology itself in the hierarchy of Egyptian priorities.

An examination of the politics of the Israeli side is outside the scope of this paper, but it may be relevant to point out that in the very same decade, or rather in the second half of it, developments in Israel took exactly the opposite direction. The new government that came to power in 1976, after almost three decades of Labor control, represented a doctrinaire outlook rather than a pragmatic one. Commitment to ideology had of course been a salient feature of Labor governments as well, but the long period in which they carried responsibilities of power and had to consider the expediencies of political realities somewhat eroded this element in their politics. The Likud, on the other hand, came to power with an almost absolute attachment to ideology and without having been subjected to the moderating effects of experience in government.

Fortunately for the peace process, the negotiating teams on the two sides did not constitute political monoliths. There was a diversity of approaches on *both* sides of the fence, and it is striking to note how each team was the mirror image of the other. In the Egyptian team, openness and a bold imaginative approach were represented in the personality of the top decision maker, President Sadat, while his entourage—including such persons as Baz, Tuhami, and Ghali—shared an adherence to traditional political vocabulary and ideological rigidity. On the Israeli side, the opposite was the case: Premier Begin proudly displayed his unwavering adherence to ideology, while the aides who surrounded him—people like Weizman, Dayan, Tamir, and Barak—represented resourcefulness and readiness to reconsider basic tenets of the Israeli positions in the light of a changing situation. One may thus say that the peace agreement eventually materialized when the pragmatists on both sides converged.

If my analysis so far is correct, the prospects for the 1980s are not very bright. The "new Middle East system" of the 1970s—to use Haykal's expression—which was expected to enhance moderation and stability throughout the region, has been shattered. The fall of the Shah's regime removed the kingpin of this system; while the invasion of Afghanistan demonstrated that the Soviet Union, far from being in retreat from the Middle East, has the strategic capability to thrust deeply into the region and may use future opportunities to continue its advance.

Soviet-backed Marxist-Leninist regimes have become firmly established in the peripheral zones of the Middle East—in Ethiopia,

South Yemen, and Afghanistan. Even the anti-Communist brand of radicalism expressed by Qadhdhafi's regime has received the blessing of the Soviets, who have set up in Libya a huge arsenal, evidently not designed to serve the needs of the Libyan army alone. These regimes' neighbors, some of which are quite vulnerable domestically or strategically, feel the pressure of the radical dynamism. Key areas, like the southern opening of the Red Sea, the Persian Gulf, the major oil fields, and the sources of the Nile, which are imperative to the major non-radical states, are all within the range of these strategic threats.

The weakness that the United States has demonstrated in the course of these recent crises has decreased Arab confidence in the value of the American strategic umbrella, and key states like Saudi Arabia have sought additional insurance by working out deals with the radical forces. The Afghanistan affair has once again polarized the Arab world, bringing about a new pro-Soviet camp in the Arab world that tries to thwart the attempts of non-radical Muslim states to show solidarity in face of this invasion of a Muslim state. The Soviet Union has used the Arab Rejection Front as a basis for the new pro-Soviet alignment, with Syria playing the leading role. An important member of this radical camp is the PLO, which, far from moderating its position, as Western sympathizers expected, has actually hardened it.

These developments have seriously affected the American-sponsored peace process and hindered the attempts to extend it beyond the Egyptian-Israeli circle. The two Baghdad conferences have in fact become demonstrations of opposition to Carter's peace by all Arab states, including pro-Western states, whose support for the process was almost taken for granted. The isolation of Egypt was thus far greater than Sadat ever envisaged.

These environmental constraints on the peace process have been compounded by the difficulties emanating from the bilateral interaction itself. With the transfer of the Sinai into Egyptian hands proceeding smoothly, attention focused on the West Bank and Gaza, which constitute a much tougher problem. Whereas the issues in the Sinai were basically strategic and economic (oil) and the considerations essentially utilitarian, finding a solution for the West Bank and Gaza means coping with some of the most sensitive ideological problems inherent in these territories—those relating to Jerusalem and to historical rights in Palestine/Eretz Yisrael. In 1980, the positions of both Egypt and Israel have, to a considerable extent, been re-ideologized—as is clearly evident from the discussions of their respective parliaments, both of which passed declarative "Jerusalem Bills." It is no coincidence that the Egyptian press was allowed to revert to the pre-peace language of anti-Israeli doctrines; nor that the pragmatists in the original Israeli delegation to Camp David have one by one left the scene and lost their influence on the process.

The fall of the Shah's regime has not only shown the weakness of the pro-Western alliance facing external threats, but has above all emphasized the internal threats to the non-radical regimes. The Western-inspired development formula of these regimes, as against the quasi-Marxist formulas of their radical rivals, has usually been one of reliance on extensive employment of capital and technology to achieve economic and social progress. Iran had enjoyed abundant financial resources and was given large-scale technological assistance, which allowed her to register impressive achievements in development, yet the system collapsed. The experience of Iran has underlined that while pragmatic development policies of this kind can be quite effective in purely economic terms, their social consequences are less predictable, and rapid modernization may in fact bring about a violent backlash from the masses whose lot it is supposed to improve.

Despite all the obvious differences between Iran and the Arab countries, some of the lessons of Iran are relevant—in differing degrees—to a good many of them. One cause of the upheaval in Iran was massive migrations to the cities, where rapid development offered ample employment opportunities. This created agglomerations of dislocated masses who felt increasingly alienated from their new environment and were easily stirred to political protest. Although these workers earn more than before, they still suffer real hardships when difficulties in regulating economic activities give rise to occasional unemployment and shortages of vital commodities, or create inflationary pressures. Thus, the rising expectations are harshly frustrated, creating more and more bitterness.

Similar trends can be discerned in most cities of the Arab world, where social tensions are intensified by another type of population migration: the massive flow of workers from the poorer part of the region to the oil-producing states. The rapid growth in the numbers of such foreign workers—e.g., the Yemenites in Saudi Arabia or the Palestinians in Kuwait—adds another dimension to the existing tension and increases the dangers of social upheaval and political radicalization.

Another factor in the background to the Iranian revolution that can be detected in the Arab world as well is the flagrant increase in the riches of the upper classes. Their access to development funds and involvement in the execution of huge projects facilitate the rapid accumulation of wealth and produces among them a mentality of consumerism, unrestrained display of class privileges, and sheer corruption. Such attitudes are quite evident among the members of the ruling families in the Arabian Peninsula, and, in a different form, within Egypt's "new upper class." The behavior of these *nouveaux riches* provokes the resentment not only of the alienated lower classes but also of the middle classes and particularly the intelligentsia.

Closely associated with this problem is the extensive influx of Western experts and businessmen, which creates friction with the local society. The influence of these foreigners is often regarded as corrupting and disruptive, and there is an increasing tendency to blame them for all the ills of social transformation. Although none of the Arab countries (except perhaps Saudi Arabia) have allowed the foreign presence to reach the proportions it assumed in the Shah's Iran, the potential for the development of a similar problem exists in a number of states.

All this creates among various social groups a sense of insecurity, of grievances, and disorientation. They feel that their way of life, norms, values, and traditional institutions are under attack, and they may thus become amenable to radical solutions.

The radical movement that thrives best on this state of affairs is fundamentalist Islam. It is almost the natural choice for an aggrieved Muslim who seeks to express his reaction to Western penetration, defend indigenous authenticity, protest the stresses of modernization, and lash out against the secularized, corrupt upper classes.

Toward the end of the 1970s, fundamentalist Islamic movements mushroomed throughout the area. Khomeini's revolution had its echoes in neighboring countries with Shi'i communities—in the Persian Gulf and, more significantly, in Iraq. Muslim Brethren were engaged in a violent struggle with the Baath regime in Syria, coexisted with the Hashemite regime in Jordan in a comfortable symbiosis, and enjoyed a status of semi-legitimacy in Egypt, thus allowing them rapidly to augment their constituency. The movement manifested itself in various forms of Mahdism among the subversive groups in Saudi Arabia and in the politics of the Sudan. In Palestinian society, the upsurge of Islam found different expressions among Israeli Arabs, within Fath, and in the Palestinian diaspora. It would be wrong to regard all these diverse manifestations as identical in nature, but they do have a common denominator of which the conviction that Islamic beliefs, sentiments, and aspirations should be channeled into radical political action forms a part.

Compared to the massive dimensions of Islamic fundamentalism, the radical leftists, handicapped as they are by the stigma of alien origins, have benefited only marginally from the present malaise in the Arab world. However, the guerrilla and terror tactics employed by various radical groups among the Palestinian Fedayeen and underground movements in the Persian Gulf can turn even a small group into a threatening force if it is dedicated and well organized. The radical left can also gain considerable influence by allying itself with the other opposition groups into "national fronts." In a situation of crisis, in the Fertile Crescent states or in Egypt, such alignments may enhance the radicalization of the whole political system.

It may thus very well be that Hottinger's projection was valid after all—only made one decade too early. But then, he may well turn out to be completely wrong. There is no proof of the inevitability of radicalization. It is difficult to tell if it can attain the necessary credibility to make it sufficiently attractive for a substantive part of Arab society. It may even be argued that the limited gains radicalism has made so far have been counterproductive: that the Khomeini regime in Iran has become a liability to other fundamentalist Islamic movements as Marxist revolution in Afghanistan now has become a deterrent to leftist movements elsewhere. The challenge of the Soviet-backed regimes and of the recent thrust into Afghanistan may in retrospect turn out to have given the non-radical forces in the area and the Western alliance in general the necessary stimulus to mend their fences and prevent further encroachments.

Whether this, or other, developments will take place, is impossible to predict, and we must be aware of our limitations. It is very hard for us to break away from the confines of conceptions imposed on us by today's realities, and rise above the horizons of the present in order to draw some guidance for our actions. We are expected to discuss the present in terms of the future, but all we actually do is discuss the future in terms of the present.

# 4
# Strategic Problems in the Persian Gulf Region

*Geoffrey Kemp*

IN THIS ARTICLE, a few observations will be made about the current military balance among the superpowers in the Persian Gulf region. Thinking back over the last ten to twelve years, it appears that a crucial date was 1968. In that year, the British government, burdened with economic problems at home, announced to a not particularly receptive world that it would withdraw its forces from the Persian Gulf by 1971. At the time, the announcement was received with complete aplomb, primarily because the United States was then deeply embroiled in the Vietnam War. Furthermore, in 1968 there was no talk of an energy crisis.

The United States reviewed the British decision to pull out of the Gulf and subsequently formulated the so-called Twin Pillar policy. The argument was that Iran and Saudi Arabia were the natural pro-Western, anti-Communist countries in the region, which had some limited capability to act as policemen in the area in which the British had operated for many years. In particular, Iran had the manpower and money. But when the United States took this decision to back Iran and, to a lesser extent, Saudi Arabia in the late 1960s, Iran did not have unlimited revenue to spend on arms. Thinking about the potential buildup of the Iranian capability from an American point of view, it was quite reasonable to suppose that there would be severe limits on the amount of equipment Iran could purchase on the open market.

The policy of supplying Iran and Saudi Arabia with arms was already in effect in 1973 when the crisis broke over the Arab-Israeli war and the subsequent oil embargo, and the quadrupling of oil prices occurred. As a result, Iran, and to a lesser extent the other oil-producing countries, were able to purchase on the open market a whole array of weaponry that in the past had merely been a figment of their dreams. This led to the massive infusion of weapons into the Persian Gulf region, particularly Iran, between 1973 and 1977.

This policy fueled the "mythology" of the Persian Gulf to which the State Department contributed. This was the belief that with enough technology and infrastructure, sooner or later the modernization process in Iran and, ultimately, Saudi Arabia, would transform that area, as J. B. Kelly has put it, from the Persian Gulf into the Chesapeake Bay within twenty years. This, of course, did not happen. The 1979 crisis and the fall of the Shah ended any hope of sustaining the Iranian pillar.

Now the issue is, to what extent should the United States rely on Saudi Arabia as a military surrogate for Western interests in the region. Without a lengthy discussion of the weaknesses of the Saudi regime, one may simply suggest that if the United States erred in thinking that Iran could absorb and operate a very advanced military infrastructure in a short period of time, it would quadruple our problems to think Saudi Arabia could do so.

However, there was one element of the Twin Pillar policy that was absolutely correct and that the United States will have to live with in the future. The United States is unable to project its influence and power in this critical area without the support of regional friends and allies. Close relationships must be developed at both the political and military level. The reasons for this are the fundamental problems of geography and the basic asymmetry faced by both the United States and the Soviet Union regarding this region from a military point of view. I would argue that there are certain fundamental constraints on both superpowers irrespective of their current or future policies. A number of these asymmetries may be cited. From a strategic Soviet perspective, there is the immediate military advantage of proximity to the Persian Gulf-Middle East region. There is the long natural border with Turkey and Iran in particular. In addition, over the last ten years, Soviet airlift—the capability to lift troops quickly from their own airbases in the southern Soviet Union to the Middle East—has improved markedly. Remember that even in 1973, when the Soviets threatened intervention on behalf of Egypt, Soviet airlift capacity was constrained compared to what the far more distant United States could project into

Israel. Those Soviet figures are changing very rapidly, and the air barrier around the southern Soviet Union, which for so many years restricted their capacity to deploy far from their air bases, is gradually being eroded. This is compounded by the fact that the current regimes in the region, with the assumed exception of Turkey, are really in no position to resist Soviet overflight. Certainly, Iran would not be able to challenge Soviet violation of its airspace.

The most dramatic change of all is in Afghanistan. A simple example will illustrate why this is so important from a military point of view. Prior to the Soviet takeover in Afghanistan, United States ships that were deployed—and still are deployed—in the northwest quadrant of the Indian Ocean were relatively secure from the type of air threat the Soviet Union could bring to bear against them. The primary reason is the air superiority capabilities of United States carriers, which are very good. Also, the types of bombers operating out of southern Soviet bases were—with the exception of a few Back-fire—relatively slow, second generation, long-range aircraft. In other words, the Soviet Union was not capable of providing air cover with fighters for its long-range attack planes. As a result of the take-over in Afghanistan, Soviet fighters, particularly Mig 23s using bases in the south of that country, could sortie from those bases and provide escorts for their slower bombers. This could have a very significant impact on the balance of maritime air power in the approaches to the Persian Gulf. This may be a nickel-and-dime argument if looked at globally in political terms, but from a military point of view it is extremely significant. It suggests that the maritime balance in any part of the world can be changed by changing access to real estate; one need not necessarily add ships to a navy. This also highlights the potential danger the West faces if the Soviet Union were ever to gain access to a base on the Indian Ocean littoral. In Iran, or Pakistan, or Baluchistan, such a base would in one fell swoop overcome the greatest current disadvantage the Soviet Union has in this region, namely, its difficult access to the Indian Ocean from its home ports.

Imagine for a moment a map of the world. Where do the Soviet fleets operate from, and how do they get into the Indian Ocean? The Black Sea fleet must come through the Dardanelles, which are controlled by Turkey. If the fleet succeeds in that, it must transit the Suez Canal or the Strait of Gibraltar, both of which the West hopes would be in friendly hands. Even if the fleet reaches the Red Sea, the Bab el-Mandeb Straits at the other end are potentially vulnerable to Western mining. If the Soviet Union sends its fleet through the South Atlantic and around the Cape of Good Hope, it is a very long way. Apart from the port calls in Angola and Mozambique, the fleet can be escorted most of the way by Western forces. The projection of Soviet naval capabilities into the Indian Ocean from Pacific ports requires transit through the Japanese straits and then through the Straits of Malacca in Indonesia. In short, it is extremely difficult for the Soviet navy to operate in the Indian Ocean at the present time because it does not have assured access to secure bases and ports. The USSR does have access to facilities in Yemen, which are of growing importance, but has no major base in the region that could compare, for instance, to United States bases in the Philippines. Thus, while Soviet maritime capability is improving in the Indian Ocean, the USSR still faces problems and probably could not conduct a major campaign against Western oil tankers except in the early days of a conflict.

If the Soviet Union had access to a port on the Indian Ocean, three things could happen. First, that access would give the Soviet Union the capability to close the Straits of Hormuz, essentially by exercising control over Iran. The consequences of such an action would be very far-reaching. Second, the USSR could threaten commercial shipping throughout the Indian Ocean, not just in the Persian Gulf and Straits themselves. Third, it could deploy forces from the Soviet Union down to the Indian Ocean, which would radically alter the air, land, and sea balance.

By comparison, the United States still has advantages in access to the Indian Ocean because the straits through which we, too, must pass are currently in friendly hands. However, that is about the only advantage we do have (unless forces are permanently stationed in the Indian Ocean), aside from the fact that we have carriers and they do not. American carriers are much more sophisticated at the moment and will remain so for some time to come. The enormous disadvantage the United States has is its distance from the theatre. Sometimes, it seems, the United States is mesmerized by technology and does not pay enough attention to distance and the importance of logistics and support facilities. One of the reasons is that the United States was able to fight the war in Vietnam, thousands of miles from home, seemingly with no trouble at all. There was never any trouble in getting to Vietnam; the problems faced were those encountered in the jungles. That was because the United States was blessed at the time with an extraordinary infrastructure of support facilities and friendly bases from which naval and air forces and ground power operated. The United States had bases in Japan, the Philippines, Vietnam itself, and access to Hong Kong, Singapore, and Guam. This infrastructure of bases was extremely important; in fact, it was essential to United States military operations in Vietnam.

In the Persian Gulf region, the nearest base that the United States has in that part of the world is the British-controlled island of Diego Garcia, 2,300 miles from the Persian Gulf. That is why there has been so much recent discussion about seeking access to bases or facilities nearer to the Gulf itself. In fact, it is essential to do so if the United States is to have a timely presence in the region, let alone some capacity to fight. The areas in which we would like to have facilities are controlled by sovereign states and operations on or above their soil or in their territorial waters require their permission; hence the delicate nature of negotiations to try to secure these base rights.

Far more than access to an airstrip on Masirah Island or access to a port in Somalia is required. What the United States must be assured of, if it is to retain some semblance of capability in that region, is an infrastructure of bases extending far beyond the immediate area of the Indian Ocean and the Middle East itself. Without the Philippine bases, for instance, it is extremely difficult to support United States naval capabilities in the Indian Ocean unless we draw down very heavily the Sixth Fleet in the Mediterranean. Access to facilities in the Mediterranean, therefore, becomes as important as access to facilities in the Pacific if one wishes to project power in the Indian Ocean and the Middle East. A look at the actual countries with which the United States has friendly relationships, and upon which we could draw in times of crisis, can produce some rather optimistic scenarios, depending upon what sort of political hat one is wearing at the moment. Similarly, the nature of the United States-Soviet confrontation in the Middle East-Persian Gulf region is highly sensitive to the assumptions made about the prospective friends and allies ranged on either side. For instance, suppose the

Soviet Union were to inject airborne forces similar to those used in Afghanistan into Saudi Arabia after a coup had taken place. The excuse would be an appeal by a new regime for support. This scenario might occur with the active connivance of Iraq and the tacit or active support of Iran. This, surely a worse case from the United States point of view, would be very different from one in which the United States might be invited into Saudi Arabia in anticipation of a coup. In this case, the United States might expect the active support of Turkey, Israel, Oman, Somalia, and other pro-Western countries in the region. In other words, it is terribly easy to pick a scenario to prove any point regarding the use of force in this region. It is also impossible to predict anything happening in this region in the next year, much less the next ten years or twenty years.

The possibilities mentioned above make it extremely difficult for the policy-makers to formulate anything other than a broad-brush approach toward the practical realities of American power in this region at present. Therefore, it would be foolish of any policy-maker to elaborate a dogmatic statement of objectives and a very tightly argued and spelled-out doctrine. That does not mean, however, that there are not certain factors that the United States must take into account in pondering its strategy over the next few years. Looked at from the American strategic point of view, the first and most important thing is that the Soviet Union cannot be permitted a "free ride" in this area. We do not have to be able to challenge, if necessary with military power, every conceivable Soviet option in the region, because we cannot. What we have to be able to do is to raise the costs to the point where any rational Soviet decision-maker would think twice before putting troops over the Iranian border or placing troops in Pakistan, or flying airborne forces into Saudi Arabia.

To what extent can this be done alone, and to what extent must it be done with allies? To conclude, it seems that from an historical point of view there have always been multiple options. There was and is no clear strategy, nor is there one set doctrine as to what should be done. The British regarded the region in this manner, and the same applies to the United States and its allies today. One option, of course, would be to look at Western strategic interests in the Middle East from a disinterested, somewhat cynical, perspective, and say that the real solution to our problem in this region is securing access to the oil for a finite period of time until the development of alternative sources. If this is United States policy and if the United States accepts the fact that the Soviet Union will also need access to that oil because of its own growing energy problems, why not think quite bluntly about a spheres-of-influence approach? Thus, one would think more in terms of the 1907 Anglo-Russian model of partitioning Persia. That particular point of view is unlikely to find favor either in the United States or the region. However, it surely has been thought of by local countries and by the more far-sighted strategists in the Soviet Union because a spheres-of-influence policy does have advantages if the situation really deteriorates.

The extreme alternative to the spheres-of-influence policy would be for the United States to have, essentially, a unilateral strategy in dealing with its requirements in the Middle East. As suggested above, this is virtually impossible. It is totally impossible in the short run given the inadequacies of our current military capabilities. This leaves the third alternative: to rely on friends and allies to provide bases and access and, one hopes, some military support in the event of a serious crisis with the Soviet Union. The second strand of this approach would be to reach some agreement with friends and allies about an equitable distribution of tasks within the overall Western alliance.

The Europeans and Japanese are often mentioned as countries that have an even greater stake in Middle East oil than the United States. However, in reality, they are highly unlikely to take dramatic action to help the United States militarily in the region in the near future. There are two reasons for this. The first is that they cannot, for they lack the necessary forces. The second reason is that they are not politically inclined to do so. This leaves the option of reaching, either unilaterally or as an alliance, an agreement about re-distribution of responsibilities. If it is agreed that the United States should maintain a naval presence in the Indian Ocean permanently, or at least until the current Iran crisis ends, this cannot be done in the short run without drawing down United States assets in the western Pacific, in the Mediterranean, and probably in Europe. This is because such a presence requires marine amphibious capabilities to back it up, and a rapid deployment force that could move into the area in a time of crisis. Therefore, it must be accepted that either Japan will play a greater role in the Pacific, or United States Pacific capabilities will be diminished. Given the problems we face in that area, with Korea and the growth of Soviet maritime presence in that region, this would not be a viable policy. Yet no one expects the Japanese to move into the Indian Ocean even though they need that oil. Therefore, one is left with the conclusion that Japan will have to play a more assertive role in the Pacific. In fact, there are already signs that Japan is doing just that and is planning to expand its maritime capabilities quite substantially over the next five years.

In the case of the Europeans it has sometimes been suggested that NATO should expand its mandate beyond Turkey to include the Middle East since, clearly, the Middle East is of vital importance to NATO. This is not going to happen, for the NATO alliance does not think and work this way. It is a peacetime alliance. There is an enormous difference of opinion throughout the alliance as to how to assess threats and where to devote resources if the challenge is to be met. Therefore, NATO will not redraw its map. What is quite possible, however, is to get individual members of NATO to reassess their own interests and capabilities. There would then be a contribution on a bilateral basis to a more substantial Western effort, both in the NATO region proper and in the context of Middle East contingencies. This very dramatically highlights the importance of Turkey. Turkey is not merely an extraordinarily important member of NATO, but is, if you like, the front line of any Middle Eastern strategy that the Western world desires. I hope this leads to a rapid reassessment of the current American ambivalence toward Turkey, especially within the United States Congress. Such a re-evaluation would release arms that Turkey needs for its essential defense.

In conclusion, looking at this problem from a military point of view and also taking into account many political subtleties which have been ignored here, there is no alternative in the short run to increasing the amount of money spent on defense. The Carter doctrine does not go nearly far enough toward dealing with the overall global problem the United States faces in confronting Soviet military power. In this particular context of the Middle East and Persian Gulf, the United States will have to take the initiative. The United States does have potential allies in the region who certainly can provide us facilities and do much more as well. Taking this approach and assuming that we will spend more money and build up our capabilities, then at least we have a chance to deter the ultimate Soviet challenge. Their aim is not to fight a war with the Western world but, rather, to achieve the political coup of the century: the political control of the Persian Gulf without firing a shot. That would mean the end of the Western alliance as we know it. That would be, indeed, the most dire crisis since the Second World War.

# 5
# Intellectual and Cultural Trends

*Tahseen Basheer*

WE HAVE BEEN subjected in the Middle East to very rapid social change. It is so rapid that it is difficult to discern all the major trends that are floating on the surface, floating either in the public mind or floating by the engineering of different governments. We are finding difficulty in discerning these changes. One of the great shocks the world has seen is the inability to understand what has happened in Iran recently; despite all the scholars, intelligence reports, and knowledge about Iran under the Shah, very few people were able to understand the undercurrents that flowed, and when they emerged one day they looked as if they were something new. So this trend of the iceberg is still with us. The second trend is that all the intellectuals and analysts have been overtaken by events. But the change, in itself, has faced them with realities that are very difficult for them as yet to understand, accept, and analyze. So, we are faced with a period of change without information—change without assessing the meaning of that change and whether it is positive or negative.

Now, there is an imbalance, as a result of this phenomenon, between what is taking place in the real world and what is taking place in the minds of people, in the hearts of people, in the political ideologies of the people. I would submit that during the 1980s and 1990s we will see attempts at grappling with this imbalance. The intellectuals from the right, the middle and the left, the new ones, the old ones, will address themselves, as they indeed have started, to try and explain this change.

The second most important shift in the Middle East today is to the present tense. The Middle East has many scholars and historians, and used to be seen in terms of its past; rich, checkered ups and downs of civilization that took place there suggested many theories to many people. The Middle East was looked upon mostly as a living museum of a past that lingers on. However, the Middle East in terms of its own people is caught in the dilemma, the predicament, of the present tense. The past and the future are seen more acutely in terms of the present, and that awareness of the present is the core of public attention, and it also presents the complexity of trying to understand what is happening. With what thermometer can we gauge that attention today?

The third trend in the Middle East, which envelops all ideologies, all governments, is a pragmatic outlook. Even Khomeini tries to address the present from his own context, and he tries to answer with what to him is a pragmatic answer to an existential problem. Looked at by others, it might be completely different. But the goal is how to answer pragmatically, practically, our problems today. This pragmatic look tends to envelop all the theories of yesterday. The Arab Nationalists in all their varieties, Arab socialists, the anti-Arab Nationalists, the sectionalists are still with us, but there is a new pragmatic outlook in trying to answer these questions.

The fourth trend that I see is the maturing of the anti-colonial drive, because the basic trend in the Arab world from the nineteenth century to this part of the twentieth century has been to assert independence, to fight against colonialism coming predominantly from the West, but equally from the Soviet Union. This anti-colonial problem has matured, has almost reached its end. The only question that remains unsettled is the Palestinian problem. But aside from that, this issue is no longer the core, the dominating idea in the Arab world today.

The new idea is the search for authenticity, what it means to be Egyptian or Arab. What it means in my relation with myself, with my community, with my society, with the neighboring Arab states, and with the world. The search for authenticity, the ability to integrate within oneself and one's immediate and surrounding environment is the great burning desire that is moving the people. With that search for authenticity, all the ideologies of the 1920s and 1960s have been found to be inadequate. We have not met the challenge. So now we have a new language. The language that has spread is the language of Islam. There is, in dealing with Islam, a lot of confusion about what Islam means, because Islam to the Muslim means something different from Islam as used in the English language. But in the new trend, the use of Islam as a vantage point is a declaration of the inadequacies, the failure, of the ideologies that existed before and the hope of returning to the source to start building from there. Islam has managed to prove that it is the language of the people, not the intellectuals, not the educated classes, but the language of the mass of the people, the language in terms of words, in terms of signs, of signals, the psychological language. The real language is the language of Islam. If you want to talk to the people and not simply to import models of change that are alien to the majority, the models must be translated into terms the people understand; thus, the language of Islam has prevailed once again, in every Arab country and not simply in Iran, as the language that can evoke, on a massive scale, understanding by the people. The closer you go to that vantage point, of Islam confronting the present tense and the needs of the people, both now and tomorrow, you see what the Muslim world must confront and tackle.

I humbly submit the following: the Arabs, and Muslims in general, will take many years in which they will debate and re-debate what is a Muslim society in the twentieth and twenty-first century. One revival after another will take place till we reach one day a new *ijma'*, a new consensus, as to what modern Islam means today. This phenomenon is a recurring phenomenon. It started after Muhammad Ali, with Afghani and Abduh. It keeps coming and going. We are now at a new cycle of its revival. But the answer to this question is not simple. The answer to this question is difficult even in the West, when you reach a predominant consensus as to what Christianity or Judaism means to you. Islam will continue to be a source of reference, but what it needs is to be translated into working policies and living ideologies in all aspects of human living is another question mark, and it is another nagging question mark at this moment.

The fifth trend that I see is that the 1960s and 1970s witnessed the *strength* of the state. The state, whatever kind of regime it was, an old monarchy like that in Morocco, new budding monarchies that existed and exist in Saudi Arabia and the Gulf, which are a new phenomenon—these shaykdoms were not old monarchies, but are new monarchies in a state of "becoming." States, through elitist parties like the Baath, the charisma of leaders like Nasser and Sadat, were able in the 1960s to perfect state power. And the state became the strongest dominant shadow over the lives of the individual and society. What we witnessed in Iran is a new phenomenon: the rise of the people, mostly unarmed, against a very strong state, a whole evolution of unfolding rejection of the social order, the political order, the economic order, and the search for something new. The new order might not stay for long. But the search is there, and it is a genuine search for community, different from the simple absolute power of the state. And I would submit again that in the years to come there will be an awakening of society. The state alone, without participation, will not be able to meet the rising demands of the people. One of the mainstays of power that Sadat managed to discover, and many intellectuals in Egypt neglected, was the re-discovery and reintroduction of the countryside. In the 1950s and 1960s, the power of the city was dominant. But now there is a whole process of urbanization. If you apply the definition given by the United States census as to what is an urban center, you will find ur-banization dominant in Egypt, and with it the countryside is playing a greater role and sharing in economic goods, in participation, in the direction of the state.

Now the sixth and most important trend, though not recognized by many so far, is peace. And I shall tell you in what way the first steps, meager but crucial, in reaching peace with Israel will have a tremendous impact on our area, on Arabs and Israelis alike. Now, what we have of peace is the removing of the immovable wall of hatred, of enmity, of no contact. We breached that wall. We have proven that where there is a will, when there is imagination, we can tackle what many analysts thought to be untouchable. But what is important about peace is the following: First, peace is not simply ac-cepting reality, good as accepting reality is, which for many years the Arabs and the Israelis refused to accept. The Arabs refused to accept Israel; Israel refused to accept the Palestinians. So, facing reality is in itself laudable. But more than the simple act of accepting reality is the innovation of peace, the ability to use innovation, to allow human beings to break through the obstacles—which signifies a greater maturity than the simple acceptance of reality.

The second important element of peace consists not in simply recognizing the enemy as existing, but in recognizing him as different and legitimate. And this will have an impact on more than Arab-Israeli relations. It implies recognizing within each society that those who are not mentionable, or recognized, or looked upon as aliens, will have to be accepted. You cannot accept a greater peace and fail to achieve an inner peace. I would like to see many Arab countries and Israel recognize the factors of difference from within and how to cope with that difference in a way that will increase the integrity of the society, rather than avoid facing them lest it disintegrate society. We have to recognize the Kurds, the Shi'is, the Palestinians, and many in our midst, and learn how to incorporate them in a new relationship of equality. That in itself can mature the political system in the Middle East tremendously.

The third and most important part of peace is the ability to stop the infantile search after ideal images and to come to accept reasonable solutions. In the past, each side considered the other as an intrusion, not merely an enemy that deprives one from achieving one's own fulfillment. If one seeks ideal images, the Middle East will never be able to achieve peace. But if the Middle East is to mature, it must accept that, although each side has ideals, yet each can cope with reasonable solutions, and cannot discount the difficulties as totally non-existent or totally negative. The solution and the touchstone of Israeli maturity will be Palestinian recognition and a mutual Palestinian-Israeli recognition. The touchstone of many Arab regimes will be to accept Israel as it defines itself, just as we want Israel to accept the Arabs the way they define themselves, and not continually impose on the other side our own definition of what the other should be.

The fourth part of peace is accepting how to deal with each other in building an integrated Middle East—not a combative, competitive Middle East. How to build integration of our area, while accepting the uniqueness of all the blocks that make the Middle East, is the great and difficult challenge we shall face in the 1980s and 1990s.

The fifth element, and above all the most important, is to have an ideology of peace. So far, most Israelis and most Arabs tend to regard the present and the future as a replay of their own chosen period of the past: Biblical, Umayyad, Abbasid. Everyone has a golden age to which he attaches himself, thinking that history is a replay of the past. The Israelis of today are not the Israelis of yesterday or the Judaeans, nor are the Arabs of today the Arabs of the past. Both of them come from a different milieu and different tradition and face new realities, and though they relate to the past, ideologically and religiously, they have to reinterpret their present and future in terms of the present tense and the future tense. They will need to rebuild an integrated Middle East lest they disintegrate into quibbling, fighting, nagging small states. The Middle East cannot be aligned with other people, let alone aligned unto itself, unless it is able to face this challenge.

There is also a sixth, a different challenge, that relates to some issue that we have tried, so far, out of politeness, to dismiss. That is the religious difference. I was not surprised at the statement made by the Agudat Israel party, objecting to normalization between Israel and Egypt. We have, in the Arab countries and Egypt, many religious people who are afraid of normalization on similar grounds. We have to deal, on the issue of the spiritual reconciliation between Judaism and Islam, not in terms of the past, medieval relationship, but in terms of the future.

My seventh point is the importance in the Middle East of self-reliance. We are not building a Middle East to become an American satellite, or a Russian satellite, or an English satellite as of yesterday. We ended with pan-Ottomans; we ended with the British Empire; and now we have to build a Middle East, which, although needing external help for some years to come, aims at self-reliance.

To conclude, by way of an eighth point, on the relationship between the East and West: For a long time the Middle East was seen by the West, and maybe also by the Soviet Union, in terms of functionalism, in terms of utilitarianism. We are not seen as "people," but as oil-producing people, strategically-located people. The people here are only a very small aspect of the whole; "oil" is big and the strategic aspect is big. What you are going to see in the 1980s and the 1990s is the people. You have to deal with people, their difficult struggle to define themselves, to build a new Middle East. There is no inherent clash between the Americans or the Russians or anybody achieving his own fulfillment and coming to enjoy reasonable re-

lations with us, provided it is not imposed by the gun or the manipulation of governments, or the dictates of short-term political considerations. We must regain that element in East-West relations that
was once with us. Just to remind you, self-determination as set forth
by Woodrow Wilson has been a greater American tradition in the
Middle East than any other: the rights of man, the rights of people,
the acceptance of diversity. Maybe one day the Middle East will
learn about federalism and we could achieve, in the federal sense,
in the legal sense, what you have been lucky to achieve in your country. But in the East-West relationship, while objecting to colonialism, new or old, we want to be accepted as people; and as people
we shall commit mistakes. But we need to discover the rules of the
game, so that we can evolve our own destiny, and you can evolve
yours; and we hope we can both do so in harmony and in peace.

# 6
# A Look Into the Economic Future

*Charles Issawi*

I HAVE BEEN asked to take out my crystal ball and look to the year 2000, which makes me uncomfortable. I remember a remark made by Secretary of Labor Marshall, who said, "when it comes to predictions there are only two kinds of economists, those who don't know and those who don't know they don't know." I definitely belong to the first group. And I also remember another remark, made some twenty years ago by the London journal *The Economist*, which said that anyone who knows what is going to happen in Iran is misinformed. And how right they were. At best, as my colleague W. A. Lewis put it, "Economics is like meteorology, much better at explaining the weather than at predicting it"—and, I might add, quite incapable of preventing or controlling an economic blizzard.

So, with this cheerful beginning, let me start with an optimistic scenario and then try and give you a more pessimistic one, which comes more naturally to me, but nevertheless dwelling more on the optimistic. Let us do a bit of simple extrapolation of what per capita incomes will look like by the year 2000. We start with the 1978 level, and we divide the region into four sets of countries.[1] First, Saudi Arabia, Kuwait, Libya, and the Arab shaykhdoms—small countries that are big oil producers. Their 1978 per capita incomes ranged between $7,000 and $14,000 per year, which means that they are among the highest in the world or the very highest. If we assume that they grow at only one or two percent, real growth, per annum that will keep them among the very richest nations. I don't think we need worry too much about them.

The second set consists of one country, Israel, which had a per capita income of $4,100; that is, about the East and South European

---

* For a much more detailed discussion of recent developments, and much fuller statistical data, see Charles Issawi, "Economic Trends in the Middle East and Future Prospects," in 96th Congress of the United States, 2nd Session, Joint Economic Committee, *The Political Economy of the Middle East: 1973-78*, 21 April 1980, Washington, D. C., pp. 7-24; see also other essays in the same volume.

level, but below the West European. If we assume a three percent growth level: then by the year 2,000 we have a figure of $8,000, which means the present level of France, Germany, and Benelux. So let us leave it at that.

The third set consists of Iran, Iraq, and Algeria; large countries that are also large oil producers. Their incomes ranged from $1,300 to $2,000; Iran has declined in the last couple of years, but we do not know how much. If we assume a five percent growth per capita, which is not extravagant, then we are at the $4,000 to $6,000 level— almost at the West European level.

Lastly, we come to the bulk of the region: Turkey, Egypt, Morocco, Sudan, Syria, Tunisia, the Yemens, Jordan, and Lebanon. Their incomes ranged widely from $1,200 in Jordan to as low as $250 in the Sudan and $400 in Egypt. We can take, rather arbitrarily but not unjustifiably for our purposes, $600 as a figure, and assume a four percent growth per annum. By the year 2,000, we have a figure of $1,500, which means roughly where Brazil, Chile, and Uruguay are today. There are some countries, like Turkey, that are a bit higher, whereas some of the others are somewhat lower. Although this does not represent affluence, it means that they could give their citizens a decent life, some amenities, and more education and social services.

Having extrapolated these figures, for what that is worth, we come immediately to the question of income distribution. It is all very well to talk about per capita incomes, but how are these distributed? In the course of the last two or three decades, most of the Middle East has moved in the direction of greater equality. There have been land reforms, there has been a nationalization of industry, commerce, transport, and finance, and there has been a wholesale takeover of large amounts of property held by foreigners and members of minority groups. This happened in Egypt, Iraq, Syria, Sudan, South Yemen, Algeria, Libya, and Tunisia; and now it is happening in Iran. The major exceptions are the Arabian oil countries, where although some of the oil income has seeped down, most remains at the top and inequality has sharply increased. In the other countries, after the initial movement toward equality, a new shift toward inequalization took place, as it tends always to happen; in all of them you have a new bureaucracy and a new class attracting a lot of attention. But on the whole, there is much less inequality today than, say, thirty years ago, and I think that it is fair to say that in terms of inequality, there is nothing in the Middle East quite like

Brazil and some Latin American countries. So we can be optimistic and assume further equalization or, more precisely, that the poor get a greater share of the increment than the rich do, without suggesting anything terribly drastic.

Now we come to the next point: how will this growth show itself in the various sectors? We may start with agriculture.[2] In the Middle East, as in other less developed countries, agriculture has been the lagging sector. It has been growing at about, or somewhat below, three percent per annum, which just about keeps pace with population growth. But nowhere has the agricultural output come near keeping pace with demand. Because the income elasticity of demand for food is high, the rise in general incomes has meant that the demand for food has gone up by five or six percent per annum or more; as a result, the Middle East has become a huge importer of food—ten to fifteen million tons of wheat are imported each year alone. And because industrial production has risen quite fast, the demand for fibres and other agricultural raw materials has risen sharply.

The reasons for the lag are obvious. The methods are poor, the yields are one ton or less of wheat per hectare for the greater part of the region, whereas in Egypt they are close to three tons and in Western Europe, still higher. Output per man is a tiny fraction of what it is in the more advanced countries. There is a huge scope for improvement. One could double, or even triple, output per acre in a relatively short space of time. But this demands sustained efforts on at least four fronts: land tenure, agricultural organization, techniques, and more valuable crops.

Let us first take land tenure, where the bulk of the work has been done. Egypt, Syria, Iraq, Iran, Tunisia, and Algeria have had various land reforms; Morocco is badly in need of them, and Turkey is taking a few steps. In the other counties—Israel, Lebanon, Jordan, and Sudan—land tenure is not a major problem. However, breaking up estates and dividing them among the farmers is only one measure, a most important measure, but by no means enough. There is a lot of work to be done in consolidation and so forth, and this is very difficult. (Far more advanced countries like Switzerland, France, and Germany struggled for years with that problem.) And there is the provision of credit and technical assistance to the new owners.

Then there is the question of organization. By this is meant roads, storage installations, and other facilities required for the proper functioning of agricultural production. Here, some good work has been done, but very much more remains, and there is still an enormous amount of spoilage and waste, because one cannot get the crops to market for lack of adequate transportation or because they rot after harvest or get eaten by birds or rats in storage. There is also some provision of credits and cooperatives, but not much. The governments have tried. They founded banks, and channeled money through cooperatives. But their efforts have only scratched the surface, and by far the greater number of the many millions of farmers in the Middle East and North Africa still rely for their credit needs on non-institutional sources (i.e., relatives, merchants, money-lenders, and landlords or prosperous farmers) and pay exorbitantly high rates of interest. A closely related matter is that of agricultural research and extension. Only in Egypt and Israel has any significant research been done, and only in Israel have appropriate institutions been established for conveying the results of the research to the farmers. Here, too, much remains to be done.

We now come to the third front—techniques. Irrigation, which is vitally important to the Middle East, could be expanded considerably; an irrigated acre can yield four, five, or even eight times as much as a rain-fed acre and grow more valuable crops. In certain parts, irrigation has been extended, but not always wisely. In Iran, and even more in Iraq, a lot of land has been salinized, and spoiled, by bad irrigation. In Egypt, there is the question of the High Dam, just upstream of Aswan, which has been highly controversial. On balance, it has probably been a good thing, but we are waiting for the final results. The greatest potential in this field is in the Sudan, but there is a lot to be done there. However, with improved irrigation techniques, and adequate transport, Sudan could become the bread-basket of the Middle East. Mechanization has not made much progress except in Israel and Turkey. Then there is the question of improved seeds. Egypt has been leading the way in cotton since the nineteenth century. Israel and Lebanon have done a lot, but the other countries have entered this field only recently. Turkey, for instance, has only just begun. The Green Revolution has had less impact in the Middle East and North Africa than, say, in India, Pakistan, or Latin America, and there is as much scope in the region as in the others. The same is true of chemical fertilizers, widely used in Egypt, Israel, and Lebanon, but in few other places until recently.

It is encouraging that the use of chemical fertilizers in the Middle East and North Africa rose from 340,000 tons in 1960 to 1,100,000 in 1970 and over 2,000,000 in 1975, increasing the region's share from 0.6 to 2.3 percent of the world consumption.

The last question deals with the shift to more valuable crops. The Mediterranean part of the Middle East is uniquely situated to supply two huge markets with valuable crops. One market is Europe (and by Europe is meant both Western and Eastern Europe). The region grows both winter fruits and vegetables (such as citrus and tomatoes) and flowers, which blossom long before those of Italy, Spain, and France. Israel is the only country profiting from these opportunities for some time, but others are beginning to participate quite actively, notably Lebanon, Jordan, Egypt, and Morocco. The other market is the Persian, or Arabian, Gulf. These markets present a very great opportunity, but one that demands investment and facilities, and above all, it demands a loosening of bureaucratic formalities. You cannot export flowers under elaborate controls: they will not wait if you have to get twenty-five or thirty signatures, as is the case in so many countries. So, in summation, if one wanted to be optimistic, one could say that agriculture, instead of increasing at three percent per annum, could increase at five percent per annum, which would make a great difference to the welfare of the region.

Having discussed the first sector, agriculture, we come to the second, industry. In the last thirty years, the Middle East and North Africa have industrialized faster than any other major region in the world. Between 1950 and 1959, the annual growth rate was 13.5 percent per annum; between 1960 and 1973, it was 10.6 percent per annum. The corresponding figures for Africa were 6.9 and 7.4 percent; for Latin America, 6.6 and 7.3; for Asia (excluding Japan), 7.2 and 7.3; for all the less developed countries, 6.9 and 7.5 percent; and for the advanced countries, they were distinctly lower.[3] Many countries have shared in this upsurge: Iran, Turkey, Israel, Egypt, Lebanon, and, more recently, some of the oil countries— Algeria, Iraq, Libya, Saudi Arabia, and Kuwait. Now, this high rate can be maintained, or very nearly. There is, first, the petrochemical industry, of which the Gulf is becoming one of the main world centers, partly because it has the raw materials, partly because it has become a "dirt haven." (Countries that do not want to have air

pollution will tell the oil-producing countries to do the refining for
them.) Ethylene, fertilizers, and plastics are also produced. There
is a huge amount of gas, which is produced by the oil fields and which
is mostly flared. Huge projects are under way, and although many
have been scaled down, I think the big jump in Middle Eastern
production will soon be weighing heavily in world markets. Indeed,
the Europeans are already worried about the competition. The
gas is also being used for energy-intensive industries, such as aluminum smelting in Bahrein and Dubai and steel in Algeria.[4] Then
there are the older industries—textiles in Egypt, food processing
in Turkey, precision instruments in Israel, and cement everywhere—
less glamorous than the newer, petroleum or gas-based industries,
and with a far lower output per man, but they employ a far larger
number of people. For example, in the mid-1950s, the Egyptian
textile industry alone had a larger labor force than the whole Middle
Eastern petroleum industry. Output in all of them has been rising
rapidly, and, in view of the governmental encouragement of the
development of manufacturing, one can confidently state that there
will be a lot of movement on the industrial front.[5]

Next is services, and one should always remember that the Middle East has been in the business for a very long time. Well before
the Christian Era caravans carried incense from South Arabia to
the Mediterranean, and that was a transit service. Herodotus came
to stare at the pyramids and tell tales, and that was a tourist service.
And then there were religious services: Jewish, Christian, and Muslim pilgrims coming to the region. Consider tourism. There is a
huge potential because of climate and history, which present a combination unmatched anywhere in the world. And again only two
countries, Israel and Lebanon (until the recent civil war) took full
advantage of it. But Tunisia, Egypt, Jordan, and Morocco have
developed it, and Turkey and Syria, which have great potential,
are just beginning to. There is transit, and one need only to mention
the Suez Canal, airlines, and pipelines. Financial services can be
very lucrative: Beirut built up an impressive base, and now Bahrein
and Dubai are trying to take over the business. Shipping could be
developed, especially as regards tankers to carry the region's oil,
but there are also other possibilites. The Greeks, just next door
to the Middle East, have shown what can be done in this field, and
the region is just beginning to wake up to it.

So, over a very broad front, very much could be done. What does this development need? It needs both capital and labor, using both in the broadest sense. Capital is required for investment in agriculture, industry, services, and various forms of infrastructure. Where can that capital come from? If we are still being optimistic, there should be no problem. The Arab countries can get all their capital from the major oil producers: Saudi Arabia, Kuwait, The Emirates, Qatar, and Libya—after all, this is the biggest source of capital surplus in the world today. Iran has its own revenues, which are fully adequate to meet its needs, even at the greatly reduced level that its present government seems to favor. As to Israel, the United States has supported it, and if the political problems were solved and Israeli armaments expenditure reduced, it should not be too difficult to continue supplying it with funds. Israel's needs for development, as distinct from defense, are not that great. Turkey has been helped by the United States and the European community, and they could and should continue.

Labor presents far greater difficulties, because literacy rates are low, and skills are still scarce. But there has been progress, and the Middle East is producing technicians and managers in impressive numbers. An industrial labor force has been developed in the leading countries—Egypt, Iran, Israel, Lebanon, and Turkey—and in most places wages are low; hence, in spite of poor productivity, labor costs are usually not too high. Middle Eastern farmers, though uneducated and conservative, do not lack skills and are responsive to economic incentives. Given half a chance, in the form of ownership or security of tenure and reasonable prices for their produce, they will increase their output. Today as in the past, however, governments, whether civilian or military, continue to favor towns at the expense of the countryside and to squeeze farmers by means of artificially low prices and compulsory deliveries.

So, we have provided capital and labor and solved all the problems. But what does all this presuppose? At the very least, that seven major conditions be satisfied. I shall discuss them only briefly.

The first one is that the region is not taken over by the Soviet Union; if it is, I do not think there is much point in trying to predict the results. Given the choice, Middle Easterners would not choose to be absorbed by the Soviets any more than by the United States. By and large, the peoples of the region prefer Western products and technology, and find the Western way of life and the Western culture more appealing. This applies even more to the European than to the American variety, since, like other old peoples, Middle Easterners tend to be cultural snobs and look up to other old peoples, such as the French, British, Italians, and Germans. But as an example of successful modernization the Soviet Union does exert a strong attraction in some circles. And it also seems that certain leaders, such as the Ayatollah Khomeini, judge Western ways to be even more "Satanic" than the Soviet. And one should bear in mind that, whereas Western-type liberty means relatively little to Middle Easterners (for it is not part of their tradition), equality and justice are an integral part of the Muslim heritage. A Persian proverb states that "Equality in Injustice is Justice," and to many in the region the Soviet Union seems to provide just that.

However, if the Soviets are going to take the region, they are not going to bother to consult its peoples, any more than they have consulted the Afghans, and the question is who can stop them. Not the Middle Eastern armies, nor the Europeans, who lack both the power and the will and who are behaving like scared rabbits facing a boa constrictor. As for the United States, has it got the necessary determination, staying power, and—at a distance of 6,000 miles—the military strength?

The second condition is that the oil fields are not destroyed by sabotage or in the course of a local or international conflict and that the supply routes are not disrupted. All one can say on this subject is that the outflow of petroleum is concentrated in about a half a dozen installations, all of them highly vulnerable.

Thirdly, that some settlement is reached in the major conflicts of the region, notably the Greco-Turkish, Arab-Israeli, Algerian-Moroccan, and Lebanese Civil War. To an outsider, such quarrels over a few square miles of not very valuable territory have all the characteristics of the civil war in Lilliput, but to the peoples concerned, they are matters of life and death. And as long as they deem them as such, they will go on spending twenty percent of their Gross National Products on defense. By now, the Middle East is the major world market for the most expensive types of armaments, and this is one branch of business that is not likely to be adversely affected by world recession. One should also, for the sake of completeness, mention other smoldering conflicts: the Kurds are bound to make another bid for independence in Iran, Iraq, or Turkey, and relations between Iran and its Arab neighbors are not good.

The fourth condition is that some kind of political stability be maintained. None of the governments of the region is stable, and it is only a matter of time before most of them are overthrown. The only question is whether the ensuing revolution will be mild, or even on balance beneficial, like the Egyptian or North Yemeni, or disruptive like the Iraqi (from which the country is just recovering), or of the Iranian type.

Fifthly, that effective measures are taken to slow down population growth. At present, the Middle East and North Africa have the highest rate of increase in the world except for Latin America. A few countries, notably Tunisia, have taken steps to limit births, but even if much more is done, the regional population in the year 2,000 will be nearly twice as large as it is at present.

The sixth is that more cooperation for economic development takes place between various countries, especially between oil-rich ones and the others. Here the record is dismaying. One can illustrate it by examining economic relations between Iran and Turkey, two countries with much in common, with no outstanding conflicts and with obligations under the Regional Cooperation for Development Agreement of 1965 to coordinate their economic policies. The fact is they have done next to nothing. Or take Iraq and Syria, whose economies are crying for coordination and both of which are governed by branches of the Baath party subscribing to the same political and economic ideology. Not only have they not implemented joint schemes and failed to agree on the utilization of the waters of the Euphrates, but their quarrels over the allocation of revenues from the pipeline carrying Iraqi oil through Syria reached a point where Iraq shut down the pipeline and, at the cost of billions of dollars, built one pipeline to the Mediterranean through Turkey and another to the Persian Gulf through its own territory. And schemes to integrate the Maghreb states, which would benefit all the countries concerned, have so far led to no results. Again pipelines provide an illustration: Algeria and Tunisia managed to agree on a pipeline to carry Algerian gas through Tunisia to Sicily, but the project for a similar line through Morocco and under the Straits of Gibraltar to Spain has been stalled, and an alternative project is being studied for one from Algeria directly to Spain, involving a much larger and far more expensive submarine stretch.

Ever since 1945, the Arab governments have been talking of economic cooperation, and in 1964 they actually formed an Arab Common Market. But so far, the main oil-producing countries have failed to join it, and intra-Arab trade continues to account for less than five percent of total Arab foreign trade.[6] However, certain joint Arab projects have been implemented, and billions of dollars have been advanced in the form of loans or grants by the oil-rich governments to other countries in the region and outside it. Perhaps even more important have been the movements of labor and capital. At present, there are over 2,500,000 foreign workers in the oil-producing countries of the Gulf and Libya, of whom the bulk have come from other parts of the Middle East and North Africa, and the remittances they send home are running at $3,000 million, or more, a year.

Lastly, that economic and social management improves. Most countries have islands of excellence; for example, the Suez Canal in Egypt and Alia Airlines in Jordan, but they are surrounded by seas of inefficiency. The takeover of the bulk of urban activities by the governments—banking, insurance, foreign trade, transport, industry, etc.—has made things far worse since the cumbrous bureaucracies set up to deal with such matters are proving patently incompetent.

Perhaps the best way to gauge the economic and social performances of the Middle East and North Africa is to compare them with the so-called Gang of Four: South Korea, Hong Kong, Taiwan, and Singapore.[7] This is done in the table on page 103, which gives some economic and social indicators for these countries and for two groups in the Middle East and North Africa, one representing the more affluent countries and the other the poorer ones. Malaysia has also been shown separately, since it shares certain characteristics with the Far East as well as the Middle East. What might be called the "pure oil economies" have been omitted, since both their income levels and their rates of growth are determined almost wholly by the volume of oil produced and the price at which it is sold and do not in any way reflect the performance of their economy.

Before analyzing the table, some general remarks are in order. First, the Gang of Four are very poor in natural resources—they have nothing to compare with either the oil of the Middle East or the rich agricultural land of Egypt, Iraq, and Sudan. Secondly, Singapore and Hong Kong were reduced to rubble during the Second World War, as was Korea in 1950-51, and Taiwan was also badly hit. Thirdly, although Korea and Taiwan benefited from abundant American aid, the amounts were nowhere near the vast sums received by the Middle East in the form of foreign aid or oil income. Fourthly, these countries have a more equal income distribution than the Middle East and North Africa; in particular, the disparity in incomes between town and country is far smaller. Thus, in South Korea the rural per capita income is slightly above the national average, and, in Taiwan, it is equal to it; however, in Middle Eastern non-oil countries, it is only fifty percent of the national average, and, in the oil countries, a tiny fraction of it. Lastly, in the Far East, women play a prominent part in the economic and social life, whereas the Middle East and North Africa have hardly begun to tap this immensely important reservoir of talent and labor.

Many reasons can be adduced to explain the superior performance of the Far East. One can mention that the Gang of Four are Chinese or Chinese-influenced (even in Malaysia practically all the motive power is supplied by the Chinese minority, which constitutes thirty-five percent of the population) and that, except in the relatively brief period between 1800 and 1950, China has been equal or superior to any other civilization in economic matters. Or one can point to Japan's great influence—it modernized the agriculture, infrastructure, and educational systems of Korea and Taiwan, and, more recently, has drawn all four into its economic orbit and encouraged them to develop numerous industries which it was giving up in order to devote itself to more technologically-advanced ones. Or one can speculate, more grandly or vaguely, on the successive shifts of the world's historical centers from the river valleys of the Near East to the Mediterranean, the Atlantic, and now to the Pacific. Others have discerned a peculiar aptitude in post-Confucian Society for modern technology and development[8]—the Yellow Peril is now replaced by the Yellow Wizard. In this connection, I should like to mention one of my pet theories. Namely, that whereas the Greeks were interested in Ideas and not their application, the Chinese in Things and their application, and the Europeans in both Ideas and Things, the Middle Easterners have been primarily interested in Words. One may suggest, finally, that the huge war-time shocks to which these countries were exposed acted like a stimulus to economic development, as they did in Germany, Italy, and France, whereas the Middle Easterners were insulated from such shocks by the Allied Armies.

All these considerations are valid, but the humble economist has also something to say. He can point to the great success achieved by the Gang in educating their peoples and contrast this with the feeble, sporadic, and uncoordinated efforts in the Middle East and North Africa (the figures on adult literacy rates bring this out very clearly, but they fail to indicate the huge investment in skills made in the Far East). He can dwell approvingly on the intense effort to develop agriculture, the very high yields obtained, and the rapid rate of growth of total farm output and output per farm worker in Korea and Taiwan; again, the Middle East and North Africa present a sorry contrast. It is worth mentioning that the Koreans claim one-third of their territory is now covered with trees planted in the last ten years. He can observe, with deep satisfaction, that their industries are not capital intensive, which means that they employ more workers per unit of capital investment and take advantage of the Gang's only basic resource: an abundant, skilled, hard working population. These industries are so efficiently run that their products compete in the markets of Europe and America, provoking manufacturers successfully to demand protection against such imports. Their investment rates are among the highest in the world, and rising fast. In contrast with the non-oil producers of our region, however, this has been achieved by raising the domestic savings rate and not, in recent years, by drawing on outside funds. Their economies are export-oriented, and the volume of their exports is truly staggering. In 1977, exports ranged from $8,200 million for Singapore to $10,000 million for Korea; these figures may be compared with $6,200 million for India and $12,000 million for Brazil. In the Middle East and North Africa, on the other hand, the largest non-oil exporters were Israel ($3,000 million), Turkey ($1,800 million), and Egypt ($1,700 million).[9] More generally, they have ensured optimum conditions for dynamic economic growth; this has earned them very high marks from Milton Friedman, a fact that should not necessarily be held against them. Economic performance has been matched by social progress.

The wide gap between life expectancy in the Far East and the Middle East and North Africa reflects the far better health conditions prevailing there. Still more significant are the figures on crude birth rates: the Gang of Four's birth rates were just about halved between 1960 and 1977 and now stand at a relatively low level. By contrast, only three countries in our region show significant declines: Turkey, Tunisia, and Egypt. And even their birth rates are fifty percent or more higher than those of the Gang of Four, while in the rest of the region they are 100 to 150 percent higher. Nothing illustrates more clearly the deep difference between the modernization processes in the Middle East and the Far East. Birth rates reflect a people's fundamental attitude toward social relations, and such wide differences are indicative of the deep gulf separating the two regions. In this, as in so many other matters, Malaysia lies between the two culture areas.

The gap also illustrates another point, which I made long ago.[10] Compared to other regions in Asia, the Middle East's standing in economic indicators (per capita income, energy consumption, food consumption, use of cement, etc.) is far higher than in social indicators (health, literacy, birth rates, etc.). Recent attempts to construct a Physical Quality of Life Index (PQLI) show that many relatively prosperous countries, such as Iran, Iraq, as well as others like Egypt and Morocco, not to mention Saudi Arabia, Libya, and the Shaykhdoms, rank far lower than much poorer countries like Sri Lanka, Thailand, China, and the Indian state of Kerala.

We can now return to our main subject and examine the alternative scenario, the pessimistic one. What do we see? The oil-rich countries failing to channel more than a tiny fraction of their huge revenues to the have-nots. This means, among other things, that the oil-rich countries will literally choke on their own riches. The corrupting effect of riches, so strongly emphasized by ancient moralists and so blithely ignored by modern social scientists, will continue to operate with increased strength. It seems that the inhabitants of these countries believe that work is not for them: they can always hire foreigners to do anything for them, from the installation of antiballistic systems to garbage collection. What happened in Iran is likely to occur elsewhere.

As for the have-nots we may assume that the availability of capital will be limited and the growth will be slower. Let us again very quickly look at our sectors. Agriculture will just keep pace with population or more likely will fail to do so, as it has, for example, in North Africa and Iraq in the last twenty years. Industry? It will develop, with a number of white elephants kept alive by government subsidies and protection and experiencing that nightmare of the economist, a negative value added. That is, the real value produced by them will be less than the value of the resources they consume. Many industries in the Middle East fit that description today: motor car, aircraft, and most of the steel mills. In infrastructure, a lot is being built that will not be kept up; it will be left to rust and deteriorate—for instance, the excess roads, docks, and airports in the Arabian countries. More ruins will be added to the Middle East, but they will not be as picturesque as the ancient Egyptian or Roman ones. Services will not thrive because tourists will be scared off by political tensions or by ideologies, and liquid capital will flow out of the region. As for defense, expenditures will remain high and continue to absorb a large proportion of Gross National Product.

Now, even if all of this happens, the Middle East will survive. It has survived the Assyrians, the Macedonians, the Mongols, the Tatars, and many others. But, needless to say, that would mean that the greatest opportunity for development in modern times would have been wasted.

I do not know which of the scenarios is more likely to take place. Both are possible, but the outcome will be determined by many decisions that are now being taken or will be taken over the next few years, in Washington and Moscow, but also in Cairo and Jerusalem, Damascus and Baghdad, Ankara and Athens, Riyadh and Teheran. With so many variables at work, even the boldest of social science forecasters should refrain from prediction.

## NOTES

1. These figures have been obtained from the World Bank (International Bank for Reconstruction and Development), *World Tables, 1979*.

2. The most convenient source for statistics on agricultural production and trade is the Food and Agricultural Organization's publications, notably the *Yearbook of Agricultural Statistics, The State of Food and Agriculture*, and *The Monthly Bulletin of Statistics*.

3. Nathaniel Leff, "Entrepreneurship and Development," *Journal of Economic Literature*, March, 1979.

4. For a detailed study, see Louis Turner and James Bedore, *Middle East Industrialization* (New York, 1979).

5. For recent figures, see Issawi, *op. cit.*, p. 24.

6. On this subject, see, Alfred Musrey, *An Arab Common Market* (New York, 1969).

7. The following remarks are largely based on *The Economist*, issues of 22 December 1979 and 9 Feburary 1980.

8. See *The Economist*, 9 February 1980.

9. World Bank, *World Development Report*, 1979, Table 8.

10. Charles Issawi, "Asymmetrical Development and Transport in Egypt," in William R. Polk and Richard L. Chambers, *Beginnings of Modernization in the Middle East* (Chicago, 1968). For further comparison of indicators, see *idem.*, "The Economy of the Middle East and North Africa: An Overview," in A. L. Udovitch, *The Middle East: Oil, Conflict and Hope* (Lexington, Mass., 1976).

TABLE

| | (1) GNP per capita 1977 $ | (2) Percent Growth per Capita 1960-1977 | (3) Adult Literacy Rate | (4) Life Expectancy at Birth | (5) Birth Rate per 1,000 1960,1977 |
|---|---|---|---|---|---|
| Korea | 820 | 7.4 | 91 | 63 | 41-21 |
| Taiwan | 1,170 | 6.2 | 82 | 72 | 40-21 |
| Singapore | 2,880 | 7.5 | 75 | 70 | 38-19 |
| Hong Kong | 2,590 | 6.5 | 90 | 72 | 35-19 |
| Malaysia | 930 | 3.9 | 60 | 67 | 39-29 |
| Tunisia | 860 | 4.3 | 38 | 57 | 47-32 |
| Syria | 910 | 2.3 | 53 | 57 | 47-46 |
| Algeria | 1,110 | 2.1 | 35 | 56 | 51-48 |
| Turkey | 1,110 | 4.1 | 60 | 61 | 43-30 |
| Iraq | 1,550 | 3.8 | (40?) | 55 | 49-48 |
| Iran | 2,160 | 7.9 | 50 | 52 | 47-40 |
| Sudan | 290 | 0.1 | 20 | 46 | 45-45 |
| Egypt | 320 | 2.1 | 44 | 54 | 44-36 |
| North Yemen | 430 | — | 13 | 47 | 50-49 |
| Morocco | 550 | 2.2 | 28 | 55 | 50-45 |
| Jordan | 710 | 1.8 | 59 | 56 | 47-47 |

Source: World Bank, *World Development Report, 1979*. Tables 1 and 18.

# 7

# The Challenge of Populist Islam in Egypt and the Sudan in the 1970s

*Gabriel Warburg*

I would like to tell the Arab people that if Arabism were the number one objective, the prophet would not have brought about Islam. The Arab people did not unite before and will not unite on the basis of Western-imported patriotic and nationalistic principles. . . . The Arab people's identity is cultural. . . .the base of this culture is Islam. Through Islam the Arab people will not only find their unity and do away with Israel but will also be able to unite with other Islamic peoples. This will be the approach of a new humanity. . . .

(Quoted from an interview with Iranian President Abolhasan Bani Sadr in *al-Nahar al-Arabi wal-Duwali*, Paris, 24-30 March 1980.)

THE USE AND misuse of the Muslim idiom in the contemporary politics of Egypt, the Sudan, and other predominantly Muslim states has been widespread. Even if we limit ourselves to the post-Second World War period, the voluntary and involuntary role played by the Islamic establishment in legitimizing policies that in many cases were contrary to the very essence of Islam was all embracing. Al-Azhar, in particular, was exploited by President Nasser when he sought to promote policies that ranged from family planning to Arab Socialism and to *jihad* against Israel. In the Sudan, where the Islamic establishment had never enjoyed the prestige of the Azharite ulama, the political role of the shaykhs was less significant. However, popular Islamic movements, such as the *Ansar,* the *Khatmiyya*, and to a lesser degree the Muslim Brethren, emerged as prime contenders for power in the independent Sudan. Indeed, the very failure of democratic government in that country was to a large extent the result of Islamic sectarianism. However, neither the Egyptian nor the Sudanese ulama were capable of creating a meaningful opposition to the military elites once the latter had gained power. The Azharite establishment in Egypt has so far backed Sadat's peace initiative with Israel just as it had supported Nasser's militant external relations in the previous years. Indeed, in order to counter the reversals he had suffered in his relations with the Arab rulers, especially since 1977, Sadat has emphasized al-Azhar's role as the leading institution in the Muslim world. He has repeatedly claimed that al-Azhar's contribution to the preservation of Islam was so predominant that neither the Arab nor the Islamic mission could have proceeded without Egypt and without Egypt's al-Azhar. But while Sadat denounced the Arabs and their leaders—in the wake of the Arab League's meeting in Tunisia in November 1979, stating that "the latest comedy in Arab solidarity has ended. . . ."—he reiterated his belief in Arab solidarity. He prophesied the emergence of a greater Islamic League, which, according to the editor of *October,* Anis Mansur, would help the region "rise from the abyss of Arab policy to the glory of Islam."[1] On 28 January 1980, Sadat accused the Arabs of having foresaken the Prophet Muhammad's righteous path. They were being misled by their leaders, "the leaders of polytheism and ignorance," and hence it was up to Egypt to lead the Islamic and Arab peoples back to the ways of true Islam. The new league of Muslims and Arabs would, therefore, according to Sadat, not be a league of states but, rather, "a league of Arab and Muslim peoples so that Egypt may exercise through the people the leadership role of the Arab world and the Islamic world."[2]

This emphasis on Islam, as a major source for solidarity, was, according to one observer of the contemporary Middle Eastern scene, a by-product of "the end of pan-Arabism." While the quest for Arab unity, as propagated by Nasser, the Baath party, and others, presented a real threat to the particularist interests of the Arab nation-states, pan-Islam did not. As seen by Fouad Ajami "forty-eight Muslim countries and seven hundred million Muslims are a safe and distant symbol giving a semblance of 'super legitimacy' without posing a threat to reason of state."[3]

But, while the Islamic establishment has on the whole been supportive of Sadat's internal policies and foreign relations, populist Islam, especially since 1977, has attacked these policies with ever-

increasing vehemence, so much so that in a recent Islamic conference, held at al-Azhar in January 1980, to denounce the Soviet invasion
of Afghanistan, Sadat's policy was inadvertently criticized. The
conference participants, who included not only the Azharite establishment but also representatives of all Muslim associations, such
as student organizations and sufi leaders, demanded a return to
al-Azhar of its full independence and advocated the election of the
rector of al-Azhar by ulama from all over the Muslim world. Thereby, the participants stated, al-Azhar would regain its leadership role
of the Islamic *umma*. Furthermore, the conference denounced not
only the invasion of Afghanistan, which was ostensibly the reason
why it had been convened, but demanded the liberation of all Islamic
lands, starting with the occupied Islamic republics in the Soviet Union, and the Muslim lands of Spain, Palestine, and finally Afghanistan. This clearly presented a challenge to Sadat's attempts at moderation and especially to his peace initiative with Israel. For, if Spain
was still regarded a Muslim land, surely the entire territory comprising Israel had to be liberated too. It would, therefore, seem that the
impact of the more militant brand of Islam, as represented by the
Muslim Brethren and some extremist neo-Mahdist movements, is
beginning to make inroads into the hitherto docile Islamic establishment. Nonetheless, it is with populist Islam and its possible challenge to the regime with which the following remarks will be primarily concerned, not because of the latter's militancy in the recent past
but also because the Muslim Brethren have survived all previous
attempts to crush them and have surfaced again and again as the
only movement in Egypt enjoying grass-root support.

It is in their mass support and in their ability to exploit the "language of Islam" in preaching to the people that the *Ansar* in the Sudan have to a certain extent resembled the Muslim Brethren. Just
as the Muslim Brethren presented the first important challenge
to Nasser in 1953-54, so the *Ansar* were rightly regarded by Numayri
as the most serious potential threat to his regime when he came to
power in May 1969. Nasser tried to eliminate the Brethren through
persecution, imprisonment, and executions, first in 1954 and again
1965-66, but to no avail. Numayri attempted to crush the *Ansar*
in March 1970, when between five and twelve thousand supporters
of this movement were brutally killed by bombs and rockets on Aba
Island, their spiritual headquarters. A few years later, the *Ansar*

had recovered to such an extent that they could openly challenge the legitimacy of Numayri's regime and try to overthrow it in the second half of the 1970s. But unlike in Egypt, the Islamic establishment in the Sudan never enjoyed the prestige of the Azharite religious leadership. Hence, Numayri, in his quest for Muslim support, had to rely on popular Islamic movements such as sufi orders, especially the *Khatmiyya,* and on the Islamic Charter Front founded by the Brethren. He even tried to create a cleavage between the offspring of the Mahdi, in order to gain the support of at least part of the *Ansar.* Indeed, he went so far as to praise the role of Mahdism in bringing about the victory of Islam in the Sudan—and has attempted since 1977 to reach an accommodation with the leaders of the opposition headed by Sadiq Mahdi, the leader of the *Ansar.*

Populist Islam therefore may at present be regarded as a challenge binding the two sister countries of the Nile Valley. But there are other reasons why it would be useful to look at Egypt and the Sudan within a common framework. The Sudan is Egypt's hinterland, and even if one were to disregard historical ties binding these two countries, their fate is connected through the Nile, the Red Sea, the affinity of their peoples and cultures as well as their fear of common foes. Among these foes, the Soviet Union would definitely be selected by both Sadat and Numayri as the most dangerous. Ever since Sadat was forced to sign the infamous treaty of friendship with the Soviets in May 1971, he has regarded them as a threat to Egypt and to the region's independence. Hence, he was delighted to intervene militarily on Numayri's behalf when the Sudanese Communist party staged an abortive anti-Numayri coup in July 1971. One year later, Sadat expelled the Soviet advisors from Egypt. Since 1974, both Sadat and Numayri have viewed the growing Soviet presence in Ethiopia, the Horn of Africa, and South Yemen as the major threat to the region, and they have continuously offered their help in order to overcome it. In a typical editorial on 11 January 1980, the Cairo daily *al-Ahram* dealt with "Egypt's Arab and Islamic Commitments." The most important commitment, according to *al-Ahram,* was Egypt's role in confronting "the danger of the Red advance on all the Islamic and Arab fronts as well as on the Red Sea and the Horn of Africa." As long as Numayri is in power in the Sudan, the special fraternal relationship between that country and Egypt will probably be preserved, creating a united front against Soviet incursions.

But there are additional spheres in which the Sudan under Numayri's rule has demonstrated its loyalty to Sadat. Numayri has supported Sadat's peace initiative with Israel ever since it started. Sudan did not attend the 1977 and 1978 Baghdad Arab Summit meetings in which Sadat was condemned as a traitor. Even after Numayri attended the November 1979 Tunisian Summit conference, he did not join the anti-Sadat chorus. The only visible sign of change in Sudanese-Egyptian relations was the recalling of their respective ambassadors. On the Sudanese-Arab front, Numayri's "closing of the ranks" was greeted by the PLO and the Iraqi government as a major achievement, and it brought about the renewal of diplomatic relations between Iraq and the Sudan. But Sadat has not denounced the Sudan nor expressed his contempt for Numayri, as he had done to other Arab leaders. On the contrary, a little over a month after Numayri signed the anti-Egyptian declaration in Tunisia, he received from Sadat the customary congratulations on the occasion of the anniversary of the Sudan's independence. Sadat emphasized the fraternity of the two states and their everlasting friendship, a sentiment affirmed by Numayri in his interview with *al-Sharq al-Awsat* on 30 January 1980. It would, therefore, be premature to regard Numayri's attendance at the Arab Summit in Tunis and his subsequent move toward solidarity with the Arab line as an indication of an impending rupture in Sudanese-Egyptian relations. The Sudanese authorities continue to distinguish between their military and political alliance with Egypt, which they regard essentially for the Sudan's security and probably for their own survival, and their solidarity with other Arab states, especially in criticizing the Camp David Accords. The latter may in part be a sincere indication of displeasure with Egypt's role in undermining Arab solidarity in the face of growing pressures, but it is at least as much the result of economic realities, which make continued Arab (mainly Saudi) support imperative for the Sudan's survival. Thus, while Numayri recently came back from a visit to Riyadh with some $450 million in economic and military aid, and with promises of two million tons of Saudi oil, plans for coordinated Sudanese-Egyptian development in the spheres of agriculture, irrigation, and construction continue unimpeded. Even in the religious and cultural spheres, the establishment of a branch of al-Azhar in Khartoum is being planned, and the "Islamic Integration Center" has been charged with the planning of religious and ideological coordination. In other words, Numayri has succeeded, at least for the time being, in enjoying the support of both Egypt and Saudi Arabia. He presents them with an essential bond in their anti-Soviet front, one gaining in importance and perhaps essential throughout the 1980s. But even Sudan's economic dependence on Saudi Arabia is not one-sided. The Sudan's economic potential, especially in agriculture, may begin to bear fruit in the 1980s and is of significant importance to Saudi investors. Moreover, if the Sudan will also manage to start exploiting its newly discovered oil, its economic viability, and hence its political independence, will be enhanced considerably.

## Populist Islam Under Sadat

When Sadat came to power in October 1970, many of the Brethren arrested in 1965 were still in detention camps; Sadat released them in May 1971, after purging Nasser's major power blocs. Indeed, with his bitter fight against the leftists and the Nasserist elite, which was part of what he later called the "corrective revolution," Sadat was in need of allies. He had the army behind him, as proven in May 1971, but the Brethren, with their bitter memories of Nasser and his clique, were ideal partners in Sadat's search for mass support in universities, industries, and the rural areas. Sadat, though aware of the political ambitions of the Muslim Brethren since his early meetings with their founder, Shaykh Hasan Banna, in the 1940s, was willing to accept their collaboration as long as it did not challenge his authority and policies. This period of voluntary cooperation lasted until 1976-77, deteriorating after the Camp David Accords of September 1978. However, even while cooperation lasted, the Brethren challenged several of Sadat's policies, and it would be misleading to describe the post-1978 period as one of open or total opposition to Sadat. But, while in the pre-1976 period the Muslim Brethren could be counted on as a useful partner against both the leftist and the militant neo-Mahdist movements, this has no longer been true in the last two years, during which the Brethren have often been a threat to established order and hence had to be neutralized.

In a recent study, Israel Altman distinguished three major ideologies within the Muslim Brethren. The moderately progressive Brethren are those grouped around the Kuwaiti journal *al-Muslim al-Mu'asir* ("The Contemporary Muslim"), while on the most extreme and militant wing are those who preach Mahdism, and are allegedly supported by Qadhdhafi. The strongest and central group of the Muslim Brethren is that whose views are expressed in two Egyptian journals *al-Da'wa* and *al-I'tisam*. *Al-Da'wa*, which has been permitted to renew publication since June 1976, following twenty-two years of forced silence, may indeed be regarded as the most outspoken and most representative organ of the Brethren in Egypt today. The radicalization of the Brethren's policies and their more open criticism of Sadat started after the January 1977 "food riots," when the Brethren were called upon to support the government against the "Communist conspiracy." Since then, both leftist and Nasserist opposition groups have been largely suppressed, leaving the Brethren unopposed, especially among the mass of students.[4]

In the study, "The Students Under Sadat: 1970-77,"[5] Hagai Erlich ascribed the victory of the Muslim Brethren in the December 1977 students elections in most Egyptian universities to the following reasons. The first is the students' alienation, brought about by the enormous growth in their numbers (from some 100,000 in 1962-63 to about 400,000 in 1976); inadequate increase in the numbers of faculty (in 1977 the ratio of faculty per students was one to 666); and poor teaching facilities. The second reason is the students' realization that their prospects for a promising future are rather gloomy. Hence their alienation and their willingness to march against the regime whenever a cause may appear, as they did in January 1972 and in January 1977. Another reason, as mentioned above, is the suppression of Communists, Marxists, and Nasserists on the campuses after the January 1977 riots. Hence, when elections were held, the students had only two alternatives, to vote for the government-sponsored Misr party or for the Muslim Brethren, with the latter having the upper hand. Two years later, in December 1979, the Brethren complained bitterly against the government's rigging of the student elections, and in some universities they even boycotted the elections, seeing that they had no chance to win. The reason for this change was the growing extremism of the Brethren, which went through the gradual transformation from mere criticism to an outright attack on the establishment.

Since 1972, the Muslim Brethren have pressured the government for inclusion of Islamic principles in the constitution and in the legislative process, and, in line with Saudi Arabian practices, they have demanded the implementation of penalties (*hudud*) prescribed by Islamic law (shari'a) for offenses such as assault, theft, consumption of alcoholic beverages, adultery, slander, and apostasy. They believe that a prompt and strict implementation of these penalties—on all Egyptians, regardless of religion (a clear departure from Orthodox Islam)—would have an immediate, positive impact and would reverse the social and moral degradation from which Egypt allegedly suffers. Already in June 1977, *al-Da'wa* called upon Sadat to adopt an Islamic policy, coordinated with Saudi Arabia, in order to combat Communist-leftist atheism, which was being broadcast, so the Brethren claimed, over the mass media and was undermining Islam.[6] Indeed, since their reappearance in 1976, *al-Da'wa* and *al-I'tisam* have openly criticized the government's shortcomings. They attacked Arab pop-music and criticized the authorities for encouraging indecent and vulgar programs on television and radio instead of others devoted to Islamic topics. The few religious programs broadcasted were, according to the Brethren, of little moral value since they only included ritualistic Muslim practices, such as prayers, fasting, or the pilgrimage. The whole educational system in Egypt came under bitter attack, as Islam had again been relegated to the margins. But even more far-reaching was the claim that Egyptian school and university graduates, including those of al-Azhar itself, were not properly taught classical Arabic and hence were in effect cut off from their Islamic heritage. The Brethren also criticized Sadat's so-called economic open-door policy. While maintaining their denunciation of Nasser's Arab Socialism, they denounced the new policy for raising false expectations among the masses and creating consumerist attitudes that could not be satisfied. An open-door policy would benefit the foreigners and the upper-classes only, while the bulk of the population would become even poorer. The solution, according to the Brethren, was to adopt an economic system based on Islam as the only way to increase productivity, and they claimed that only Islam would turn labor from a chore into religious activity.[7] But one of the Brethren's most bitter grievances against Sadat was the fact that despite his so-called liberalization, the Muslim Brethren had not been allowed to form their own political party or platform. Sadat has continuously warned against introducing religion into Egyptian politics, as this, he claims, would antagonize religious minorities such as the Copts, and, hence, might harm national unity. The Brethren argued that in Islam state and religion formed a single system and hence Sadat's argument was without foundation. Moreover, they pointed to the record of their cordial relations with the Copts as proof that Sadat's fears were unwarranted. Finally, they actually threatened Sadat that if their demands were not met they would be forced to found a clandestine organization.

Whatever past records of intercommunal relations may prove, Coptic opposition to the Brethren's demands regarding the application of the shari'a, and especially the *hudud*, to all Egyptian citizens is a matter of record. In April 1979, there were reports about anti-Christian activities in the University of Asyut. Muslim student groups were accused of violent attacks on the Copts and of distributing pamphlets against the Coptic church's spiritual leader, Patriarch Shenuda III, while an anti-Sadat paper accused the regime of "stirring up sectarian dissension in order to suppress political movement and to fragment national opposition."[8] The fact is that tension has indeed increased as a result of militant Islamic propaganda.

Until January 1979, Sadat and his government were willing to tolerate the Muslim Brethrens' criticisms, even when they were aimed against Sadat's peace initiative. But in January 1979, *al-Da'wa* came out with an open attack on Sadat himself, accusing him of collaborating with the United States secret services and Israel against all Muslim movements, including first and foremost the Brethren themselves. *Al-Da'wa* claimed that Sadat had decided to implement a secret report, written ostensibly for the CIA by Dr. Richard Mitchell, in which the leadership of the popular Muslim movements were to be lured into the religious establishment by offers of money, while those leaders who could not be bought would be exterminated.[9] The government promptly ordered the closure of the magazine and vehemently denied its allegations. In an interview with the London-based paper *al-Arab*, on 30 April 1979, the Egyptian deputy prime minister, Hasan Tuhami, stated that the CIA report for quelling the Islamic movement in Egypt was a mere fabrication. He claimed that "anti-Muslim evil scheming hands are behind this and have fabricated this report . . . . Its aim is to foment sedition, which we hope that God Almighty will spare the Islamic nation."[10] But Sadat went even further when, in a speech to the faculty of Tanta

University, he accused the Russians of fabricating this report and then using Qadhdhafi to smuggle it into Egypt.

The Muslim Brethren were on the whole more outspoken in their criticism of the regime's internal politics than they were of external relations. Their rejection of Nasser's Arabism, depicted by them as a distortion of Muslim history, was probably one of the reasons that attracted them to Sadat. The Brethren claimed that history textbooks, used in Egyptian, Syrian, and other Arab schools were in fact a declaration of war against Islam. Arabism had replaced Islam in these textbooks, while the pre-Islamic *jahiliyya* was being extolled because of its Arabism, despite its barbaric and anti-Muslim nature.[11] But, while the Brethren thus supplied Sadat's new regional policies with Islamic-ideological backing, they also denounced the new creed of "Egypt first," labelling it a "pagan pharaonic approach."

But, by far the most important challenge to Sadat's foreign policy was waged by the Brethren against his peace initiative with Israel. Their *jihad* against the Jews in Palestine, even before Israel became an independent state, had put the Brethren in the forefront of those fighting against the so-called Zionist threat. Their secret army—the *Jawwala* (Rovers)—continuously fought against the Jews, especially in south Palestine, both before the Arab countries invaded Palestine on 15 May 1948, and after. Martyr's Day became an annual commemoration of the Brethren's martyrs, many of whom had indeed fallen in the "holy war" against the Jews. It was, therefore, no wonder that *al-Da'wa*, since its reappearance in 1976, bitterly and continually denounced Israel. It viewed World Jewry as an agent whose services were used by the United States and the Soviet Union alike against the Muslim world. Peace with Israel was therefore tantamount to treason, while every Muslim was obliged to take part in the *jihad* against the Israeli threat. While these anti-Israeli attacks were going on in 1976-77, Sadat had not yet undertaken his peace initiative; hence, they reflected to a large degree official Egyptian thinking. But Sadat's trip to Jerusalem in November 1977, and his signing of the Camp David Accords were both unacceptable. Israel's true aim was the destruction of Islam and hence peace with it was a betrayal. In a special editorial dealing with the Camp David Accords, the editor of *al-Da'wa*, Umar Talmasani, denounced the agreement because it did not compel Israel to withdraw from Muslim Jerusalem. Moreover, Talmasani stressed that the Brethren, unlike the Nasserists and the Communists, opposed the peace treaty on religious grounds because, according to Islamic law, it is a sin to leave any Muslim land in the hands of usurpers.[12]

One month later, *al-Da'wa* came out with the announcement that, according to the *Qur'an*, reconciliation (*sulh*) with Israel was forbidden. In a direct challenge to Sadat, the Brethren declared that Islamic history would pass judgment on those who were willing to sell their dignity and beliefs for questionable material benefits. Thus, in the first half of 1979, Sadat felt compelled to openly denounce his Muslim antagonists, and accused the Muslim Brethren of attempting to create a state within a state. The attempt to mix politics and religion would, according to Sadat, not be tolerated.

The phenomenon of neo-Mahdist movements in Egypt, though interesting in itself, does not seem to be at present strong enough to present a real challenge to Sadat's regime. Since Sadat came to power, several such neo-Mahdist groups have appeared, especially on university campuses, where they openly defied the regime. Their appearance, made possible by Sadat's more liberal policy, enabled such groups to be established; once they had become strong enough, they committed sabotage or assassination under the banner of their Islamic puritan principles. It was then that the government stepped in, arrested as many of the movement's leaders and members as it could lay its hands on, and had those directly responsible imprisoned for long terms or even executed. Altman lists four of the most notorious Mahdist groups, which were all accused of enjoying the support of some external enemies of Egypt, in most cases Qadhdhafi's Libya.[13] Of those, one of the better known was the *Shabab Muhammad*, who in an attempted coup in April 1974, stormed the military college in Cairo. But the best known and most extensive was *Jama'at al-takfir wal-hijra*, whose leaders were executed following their July 1977 kidnapping and assassination of Shaykh Husayn Dhahabi, a former minister of *waqfs*. Indeed the reappearance of another *jihad* movement in Egyptian universities, with views similar to those of *Jama'at al-takfir wal-hijra*, was reported in December 1979, by the Kuwaiti *al-Anba'*. Most of the members of this movement were apparently rounded up and imprisoned in October 1979. However, one of its leaders, Ali Mustafa Mughrabi, was only caught a couple of months later in his hideout in Alexandria. He confessed before he died of his wounds that he and his followers had planned to disrupt public order by throwing bombs in places of worship. In an article titled "Blind Cairo Sheikh Rallies Poor with Fiery Islamic Creed," the *New York Times* (11.28.79), reported on another such populist fringe movement, that of Abd Hamid Kishk, a blind imam of the *'Ayn al-hayat* mosque, whose weekly sermons attracted thousands of followers. Shaykh Kishk attacked the inequities of contemporary Egypt, and denounced the government for subsidizing such luxuries as the *hajj* (pilgrimage to Mecca) while thousands of Egyptians were hungry and naked. Most of these fringe movements believe in a *mahdi* or a caliph who was sent by God to bring the world under Islamic rule. They believe, not unlike the executed Muslim Brethrens' ideologue, Sayyid Qutb, that society in general is in a state of decay, or *jahiliyya*; hence, *jihad* is the only way to restore true Islam, even to the so-called Muslim countries. Most of these groups declare themselves as the only true custodians of the shari'a and vehemently oppose any innovations introduced in the name of modernization or progress.

Despite the recent upsurge in populist Islamic militancy, it would seem that at present the Egyptian regime is not confronted with an insurmountable challenge. The Muslim Brethren continue to criticize Sadat's policies, and the student clashes between Muslim militants and Christians in the universities of Asyut and Alexandria in March 1980, tend to suggest that violence is increasing. Moreover, the "language of Islam," having emerged from near-obscurity under Nasser, is finding growing support, not only among the lower and middle classes, but also professionals and the intellectual elite. However, Sadat seems to enjoy continued support and popularity within large sections of the population. Even more important is the confidence of the army, which, having rid itself of Soviet patronage, seems to back Sadat's policies without meaningful dissent. Under these circumstances, the Muslim Brethren, despite their popularity and militancy, would probably stop short of an outright challenge to the regime. The bitter lessons of their persecution under Nasser in 1954 and 1965 still seem to linger, and a realistic appraisal of their real power will probably convince the Brethren's leadership that co-existence with Sadat is preferable to an outright confrontation, which might lead to their renewed suppression and even martyrdom.

## Populist Islam Under Numayri

Mahdism, which in Egypt had never achieved any prominence, has dominated the political scene in the Sudan ever since the 1880s. The *Ansar*, who renewed the Madhist mission between the two world wars, have, since 1945, formed their own political party—the *Umma*. Here lies one of the main differences between the *Ansar* and the Muslim Brethren. The latter have, on the whole, shied away from active politics, whereas the *Ansar*-dominated *Umma* party has not only competed for power but actually been at the helm of government for long periods before the Numayri coup. It seems that on the eve of Numayri's coup, the Mahdist leaders were on the verge of seizing power. In fact, Muhammad Ahmad Mahjub, leader of the *Umma* and a close associate of the *Ansar*, relates in his memoirs how Hadi Mahdi and Sadiq Mahdi, respectively the spiritual and political leaders of the *Ansar*, had agreed on 23 May 1969, to unite forces with the *Khatmiyya*-oriented Democratic Unionist party and realize their ambition of turning the Sudan into a presidential republic with an Islamic constitution. The two Mahdist leaders also declared their intention to compete in the forthcoming elections, the first for the presidency, the second for the post of prime minister. As Mahjub related with some bitterness, "They thus seemed to consider the rule of the state a booty to be inherited and divided between them, to the exclusion of the other members of the (*Umma*) party who did not belong to the Mahdi family."[14] A few days later, the Numayri coup brought this dream to an end. Therefore, it would seem that, unlike in Egypt, the populist Islamic leadership supported the status-quo as long as it enjoyed power.

Their fight for an Islamic constitution was probably one of the *Ansar's* major concerns in the pre-Numayri period. Why was it so difficult to declare in a Sudanese constitution that Islam was the religion of the state and that the shari'a was a major source of legislation? The main reason was the precarious political unity of the Sudan, which depended not only on a Muslim majority but also on the non-Muslim southern Sudan, which accounted for nearly one-third of the population. The southern uprising, which started in August 1955 and was only brought to its end in February 1972, after seventeen years of civil war and enormous bloodshed, centered around southern fears of northern Muslim domination. This domination had already, in 1953-55, expressed itself in concentrated efforts to enforce Arabic and Islam on the tribal population of the south. It was southern fear of Arab-Muslim domination that led to proposals for a federal type of government or, as the more extremist southerners demanded, southern independence. In fact, the southern leadership only supported the northern plan for an independent Sudan in December 1955, with the clear understanding that federalism, and equality of Christianity and English with Islam and Arabic, would be seriously considered by the Constituent Assembly. However, in December 1957, southern demands for regional autonomy were rejected out of hand by the northern Muslim majority as an "expensive façade." It was on these principles that the southerners fought the February 1958 elections. But, while the south overwhelmingly supported these demands, the *Umma*-dominated government forced a new constitution on the Constituent Assembly. Fears of Islamization and Arabization were thus the main reason for the southerners' boycott of the Assembly as of June 1958. Under General 'Abbud's military dictatorship, in 1958-65, Islam and Arabic were forced on the south, despite courageous and, at times, desperate resistance. English was barred from the schools, and Arabic-teaching Muslim schools were opened instead. Lastly, on 27 February 1964, Islamization was further boosted when all Christian missionaries were expelled from the country. However, the basic demands of southern autonomy and of equal status for Christianity and Islam, and English and Arabic, continued to stir up strife in the south and were to a large extent instrumental in overthrowing the Abbud regime in October of that year. And so, in 1965, the new parliamentary government once again faced the same dilemma. A draft constitution was finally worked out, but it was never ratified. Muhammad Ahmad Mahjub, who as prime minister was directly involved in the constitutional debate, wrote in the retrospective:

> There should have been no quarrel on whether the constitution should be Islamic or secular. The Sudanese could have had a constitution without calling it Islamic, thereby practicing their Islamic faith and using the tolerance embodied in its tenets. This would have allowed us to have a permanent constitution without much trouble.[15]

This statesmanlike approach might have helped the Sudan overcome the conflict had Mahjub fought for it in his own *Ansar*-dominated *Umma* party while he was prime minister before Numayri's coup. However, all the major Sudanese parties, with the sole exception of the Communists, supported an Islamic constitution. Even the National Unionists, led by Ismail Azhari, who prided themselves on their secularism, did not oppose an Islamic constitution, probably for fear of losing support. Oddly enough, in May 1965, while the only serious negotiations to work out a logical compromise with the south were in full swing, Azhari publicly declared the centrality of the Muslim-Arab heritage for the united Sudan. It is no wonder, therefore, that the Muslim Brethren, organized in the Islamic Charter Front, openly advocated an Islamic constitution, stating that they could not have a God who cared only for religion, since in Islam God cared for all aspects of life. Thus, the question of whether or not Islam was to be declared the religion of the state was much more detrimental in the case of the Sudan than it was in Egypt. For the Sudan, voluntary unity between north and south depended on religious and cultural tolerance. True, Abbud's dictatorship and even the sectarian Muslim-dominated parliamentary governments succeeded in forcing Arabization and Islamization on the reluctant south. But the price was enormous: continuous bloodshed and destruction as well as a growing alienation and hostility of the southern population, of which some three million escaped across the borders to Ethiopia, Kenya, Uganda, Zaire, and the Central African Republic.

This was the situation when Numayri came to power in May 1969, and a month later announced his plan for granting regional autonomy to the south. Indeed, only a strong military dictatorship could have adopted a plan so bitterly opposed by all major political parties and unpopular even among the conservative Muslims in the rural districts. However, Numayri and his colleagues did not face elections, nor did they fear uncensored opposition in the press. The solution they adopted, which ultimately led to the Addis Ababa peace settlement between north and south in February 1972, was largely based on the program advocated by the Sudanese Communist Party ever since 1954. However, stable peace in a united Sudan required a new and tolerant approach to the divisive issue of the constitution. In September-October 1972, a Peoples' Assembly was elected for the sole purpose of drafting a permanent constitution, which was approved and promulgated on 8 May 1973. In part one of the constitution, the Sudan was declared a "unitary, democratic, socialist, and sovereign republic . . . part of both the Arab and African entities," while non-Muslims were granted the right to be governed by their own personal laws. But even more significant was the wording of article sixteen, where both Islam and Christianity were stated to be: "the religion," the first "of the majority," the second "of a large number of citizens," thus overcoming southern fears of Islamic domination.[16]

This policy of limiting Islam to fulfill the purely religious role of personal beliefs was part of a general drive to end sectarianism and especially to crush the *Ansar*, a task that, as mentioned above, was undertaken with great brutality and efficiency in March 1970. Numayri and his colleagues must have lived under the misapprehension that once they were free of *Ansari* political pressure they could move toward a secular society. An example of this illusion was the so-called cultural revolution initiated by the Revolutionary Command Council in the summer of 1972 with the aim of "reshaping society in its trends, values, practice, and skills," hardly a modest endeavor. In the long debates concerning this "revolution," modernization, science, and technology were definitely regarded as more important than Islam. The late Ja'far Ali Bakhit, who had been a central figure in drafting the constitution, expressed critical views of the traditional Muslim value-system of the Sudanese masses. He demanded "a shakeup in the traditional society that now exists, in such a way that it leads to the creation of vacuums that, in turn, lead to struggles leading themselves to predominance of values." There can be little doubt that the values Bakhit sought to implant were not the traditional Islamic ones. His colleague, Professor Abd al-Rahman Aqib, expressed his contempt for the old values even more bluntly when he defined the cultural revolution as an expression of "indignation at all the obsolete legacies" and an invitation to society to change its prevailing views.[17]

However, these expectations were as premature in the Sudan as they had been in Nasser's Egypt. Already in 1972, the three major traditionalist parties had formed the National Front, whose declared aim was to overthrow Numayri and then to initiate the "revival of Islam" in a modern democratic state. The three founding parties were the *Umma*, the Democratic Unionists, and the Islamic Charter Front, representing the major sectarian divisions in Sudanese Muslim society. It was, therefore, quite clear that the *Ansar*, despite the March 1970 massacre, were again on the march, united, at least temporarily, with their erstwhile rivals, the *Khatmiyya* and the Muslim Brethren. The two most prominent leaders of the National Front, Sadiq Mahdi and Husayn Sharif Yusuf Hindi, representing the *Umma* and the Democratic Unionists respectively, were the grandsons of two of the most venerated sectarian leaders of the Anglo-Egyptian Sudan. Following the massacre of the *Ansar* in 1970, Mahdi had been exiled to Egypt, where he was for some time under house-arrest. Once he was allowed to leave Egypt, he started to organize the anti-Numayri Front. Hindi, who on the eve of the Numayri coup had served as Minister of Finance in the last civilian coalition government under Muhammad Ahmad Mahjub, had escaped to Aba Island, the *Ansars'* stronghold, when Numayri assumed power. Once in exile, Hindi had joined forces with Mahdi and the *Ansar* as well as with the Islamic Charter Front. The newly formed National Front soon enlisted the aid of several of the Sudan's unfriendly neighbors, headed by Qadhdhafi's Libya, but including at times such curious bedfellows as Saudi Arabia and Marxist Ethiopia. The Front, with its new allies, tried unsuccessfully to topple Numayri's regime at least on two occasions, in November 1975 and July 1976.

In order to overcome the mass following enjoyed by the sectarian popular Islamic movements, Numayri tried to institutionalize popular support for his regime. Following in Nasser's footsteps, he set up the Sudanese Socialist Union (SSU) as the only legitimate political organization in the country. However, like the Arab Socialist Union in Egypt, the SSU was supposed to demonstrate its loyalty to the regime without gaining any real stake in the political system. Thus, a large part of the activity of its branches revolved around demonstrations of support for government policy. Genuine and open debate on government policy were few and unimpressive. The SSU became a mass organization, lacking grassroot support or independent leadership, with a top-heavy bureaucracy made up largely of presidential appointments. In order to overcome the SSU's inherent weaknesses, Numayri, following now in Sadat's footsteps, announced his intention to liberalize the political system, relax censorship, and encourage greater popular involvement in Sudanese politics. However, as long as the leaders of the National Front remained in exile and were doing their utmost to overthrow Numayri, there could be no real liberalization of the political system. Following the abortive, *Ansar*-led coup in July 1976, both the opposition leaders of the National Front and President Numayri decided to reconsider their previous strategy. The July 1976 coup attempt had been the most dangerous challenge to Numayri's regime since the abortive Communist-inspired coup of July 1971. It was led and executed by well-trained and equipped *Ansar*; and, by the time the fighting had ended, some seven hundred lives had been lost and ninety-eight additional *Ansar* were later executed. The failure of this coup, despite the fanaticism of *Ansar*, who fought to the bitter end, was due primarily to the loyalty of the Sudanese army and to the immediate support of Egyptian army units stationed in the Sudan. The coup's failure convinced the leaders of the National Front that Numayri was too strong to be easily toppled. It convinced Numayri, who at first claimed that the coup had been executed by foreign mercenaries emanating from Libya and Ethiopia, that the National Front and especially the *Ansar* were too strong to be ignored. He then sought a "national reconciliation."

For Numayri's regime, the return of the National Front leaders to the Sudan as partners within the SSU presented benefits and potential dangers alike. It was clear that neither Mahdi nor Hindi would become docile "collaborators" of the regime and that their presence could create an active opposition within the SSU. However, Numayri probably believed that as long as they were willing to denounce sectarianism, join the SSU, and work within the regime, their presence in the Sudan would outweigh the dangers of their continued exile. On 8 July 1977, Sadiq Mahdi was therefore invited to Port Sudan in order to discuss the details of reconciliation with President Numayri. The eight-point agreement reached between the two leaders was revealed by Mahdi in a number of interviews. According to Mahdi, Numayri agreed to important changes in the political system, the release of political prisoners, a revision of the constitution, and neutralism in the Sudan's international relations. In return, the National Front agreed to end its armed opposition, dissolve its foreign-based training camps, and return to the Sudan to take part in the national reconciliation. Indeed, Mahdi openly declared his belief both in the role of the army in the politics of developing countries and in socialism as an essential model for economic development. The one-party system, exemplified by the SSU, was, according to Mahdi, essential for the present stage of Sudanese politics; all he asked for in return was the restoration of political and civil liberties and a general amnesty for himself and his colleagues. Curiously, Islam did not seem to loom large in Mahdi's interviews. The agreement was ratified by the executive of the National Front on 14 July 1977, and at the end of that month some nine hundred political prisoners belonging to the National Front were released on Numayri's orders. Indeed, a law granting general amnesty for "illegal acts" committed against the regime was passed on 7 August. This enabled Mahdi, accompanied by twelve leading *Ansar*, to return to the Sudan on 27 September 1977, after more than seven years in exile. Reconciliation was prepared in the Sudan not only through amnesty but through major changes in the electoral law to the People's Assembly, which were announced on 26 September 1977. Furthermore, a special committee was appointed by Numayri in the same month, whose task it was to facilitate the integration of the returning political exiles into the political, economic, and social fabric of the Sudan.

The elections held in February 1978, may be regarded as one of the major fruits of reconciliation. Out of the 304 seats in the People's Assembly, candidates supported by the two main groups within the National Front, the *Ansar* and the Democratic Unionist Party, won thirty seats each, while the Islamic Charter Front won twenty seats. If one takes into account that about sixty additional seats were won by so-called independent candidates, especially in rural areas, the fruits of reconciliation seem impressive. On 21 March 1978, Numayri appointed six new members to the SSU political bureau, a substantial figure in this prestigious twenty-nine member body. The new members included Sadiq Mahdi, Ahmad Ali Mirghani, and Dr. Hasan Turabi, the respective leaders of the *Ansar,* the *Khatmiyya,* and the Islamic Charter Front. Even more far-reaching were the appointments of fifty-one new members to the Central Committee of the SSU, which included the above three leaders as well as many other former anti-Numayri activists. At the time, Ahmad Ali Mirghani, in line with *Khatmiyya* tradition, refused to be drawn into active politics and declined the honor conferred upon him by Numayri. Mahdi also declared that he regarded his appointment as premature. Yet, a few months later, on 3 August 1978, he reached an agreement with Numayri to join the central bodies of the SSU.

However, even at this stage, when reconciliation seemed to progress smoothly, two questions remained unanswered: first, Mahdi's political-executive role in the Sudan and, second, his ability to stand by the agreement to bring the anti-Numayri opposition from

Libya and Ethiopia back to the Sudan. Right from the first agreement of July 1977, there were consistent rumors that Mahdi would be offered the Sudan's premiership. Indeed, when, in one of his periodic government reshuffles, Numayri assumed the office of prime minister, it was generally assumed that he had done so in order to eventually hand the post to Mahdi. These rumors persisted despite constant denials both by Mahdi himself and by Numayri, who declared that Mahdi was not yet ready to assume executive responsibilities. The second, and from Numayri's point of view, the more crucial problem, was Mahdi's ability to persuade the National Front exiles, and especially the Front's armed forces, which were concentrated primarily in Libya, to return to the Sudan and be absorbed peacefully into society. Mahdi undertook several trips in 1977-78 to Libya in order to convince his followers to return to the Sudan. But despite constant reports regarding the success of this operation, many exiles remained in Libyan and Ethiopian camps as late as December 1978, when it was already clear that reconciliation was not progressing as smoothly as Numayri and Mahdi had once thought it would. Indeed, by October 1978, Mahdi had already submitted his resignation from the political bureau of the SSU, and left the Sudan for the United States, ostensibly for private reasons. However, while Mahdi did not at that stage declare that reconciliation had failed, he clearly indicated his dissatisfaction with two aspects of Numayri's policy: first, his subservience to Sadat's foreign policy, and especially his backing of the Camp David Accords; and, second, the lack of progress with regard to the promised amendment of the Sudan's constitution along Islamic lines. Two months later, in January 1979, Hindi stated that reconciliation had come to an end and that armed struggle, both in Sudan and from across the borders, would be resumed. Mahdi, though more cautious, gave his tacit support to the renewed struggle, giving Numayri's Middle Eastern policy as the main reason.

Toward the end of 1979, the rupture between the National Front leaders and Numayri seemed to be complete. In one of his most outspoken attacks on Numayri's regime, Hindi accused the president of blatant opportunism and of selling-out Arab and Palestinian rights for his opportunist alliance with the "traitor Sadat." Hindi further claimed that demonstrations and strikes, which were spreading in the Sudan, had the support not only of the stu-

dents, workers, and the Jazira cotton farmers but also of the Sudanese army. Therefore, in Hindi's view, Numayri was doomed and
reconciliation was no longer possible. Indeed, even if Numayri
would now change face and sell out his partner Sadat to the highest
bidder, the forces of the National Front would never again negotiate
with him. But, while the government continued to insist that the
disturbances in the Sudan were limited to high-school students in-
stigated by Iraqi foreign agents and that reconciliation was progressing steadily, there was evidence that pressure on Numayri was
mounting. In the first half of October 1979, the Iraqi news agency
reported an attempted military coup against Numayri, mass demonstrations of students, and workers' strikes against the government's support of Sadat's policy. And while one had to be skeptical
about the news, for Iraq was a self-proclaimed enemy of Numayri,
it became quite clear in subsequent developments that all was not
well with Numayri and his regime.

On 25 October, Numayri held a meeting with army and police
personnel to call for national action in order to prevent sabotage
by the enemy of the revolution. On the same occasion, Numayri
emphasized the Sudan's Arab identity and reiterated its loyalty to
the Arab cause. Even more telling was Numayri's attendance at the
Tunis Summit Conference organized by the Arab League in November 1979. Having refrained from participation in the Baghdad
Summit in November 1978, his attendance indicated a definite
change in policy. The change became clear when, on 25 November,
Abd al-Hamid Salih, chairman of the Sudan's People's Assembly,
made a statement on the Middle East peace process. In it he asserted
that the Sudan had never fully supported the Camp David Accords;
furthermore, since Sadat's peace efforts had failed due to Israel's intransigence, the Sudan fully supported Arab solidarity regarding the
Arabism of Jerusalem and the creation of a Palestinian state ruled
by the PLO. This point of view was reiterated a few days later by
the foreign relations committee of the SSU.[18]

So it seemed that the combined economic and political pressures were at last bearing fruit. Numayri was constantly accusing
Iraq of plotting in the Sudan, but it became quite clear that the "power blocs" who were accused of being involved in these intrigues within the Sudan were not limited to the Communists, the usual scape-
goats. In a recent purge of the SSU political bureau and the re-

organization of its secretariat under Numayri himself, the two sectarian leaders Sadiq Mahdi and Ahmad Ali Mirghani were ousted.
It would therefore seem that national reconciliation, which had
once been declared as the most important aspect of Numayri's policy
since July 1977, has, at least temporarily, been shelved. Of the three
sectarian leaders of the National Front, only Dr. Hasan Turabi is
still active in Sudanese politics. Sharif Hindi, who lives in London,
continues to attack and to denounce Numayri, promising his audiences that Numayri's days are numbered and that a popular revolution is not far off. Sadiq Mahdi seems to have chosen a more am-
bivalent attitude. In the wake of the Tunisian Arab Summit, Mahdi
has once again returned to the Sudan and has apparently acted on
Numayri's behalf in helping to resume diplomatic relations with
Iraq and cordial relations with Libya. In an interview with the Kuwaiti *al-Watan*, conducted in Khartoum on 23 March 1980, Mahdi
explained his views regarding the Soviet invasion of Afghanistan.
He rejected all Soviet explanations regarding this invasion as unacceptable and stated that he had accepted a Soviet invitation to
hold more discussions on this topic.[19] So it would seem that Mahdi,
having resigned from the central bureau of the SSU, is nonetheless
maintaining a rather low-profile role in Sudanese politics.

In the meantime, Numayri has proceeded with his plans to de-
centralize his government and to divide the Sudan into six regions,
which would be governed by their own regional assemblies and governments, similar to those of the south. Should this plan be realized,
it could change the fortunes of the Sudan and satisfy the diverse
ethnic groups that make up the checkered map of the Sudanese
population. However, decentralization might also be exploited by
sectarian leaders. Populist Islam of the *Ansari* brand could, for
instance, attempt to exploit its power among the Baqqara tribes
in Kordofan and Dar-Fur, or among the Fallata in the Jazira and
the Blue Nile region. Thus, regionalism could be a mixed blessing,
which, as happened before, might be shelved before full implementation. However, the historical heritage of the *Ansar*, their
grass-root support, and their concentration in certain regions of
this vast country, tend to suggest that their challenge to central government is still acute. If we take into account that the Sudan is torn
by immense problems in practically every sphere and that Numayri
after more than ten years in power has not succeeded in bringing

about any real solutions, with the possible exception of the southern problem, the dangers of a populist Islamic uprising in the Sudan seem greater than in Egypt.

## NOTES

1. Interview with Sadat, quoted by FBIS-MEA, V. 252 (31 December 1979), from *October* (30 December 1979); Mansur's editorial quoted from *October* (6 January 1980), by FBIS-MEA, V. 5 (8 January 1980).

2, FBIS-MEA, V. 20 (29 February 1980), quoting Radio Cairo (28 January 1980).

3. Fouad Ajami, "The End of Pan-Arabism," *Foreign Affairs* (Winter 1979), p. 364.

4. Israel Altman, "Recent Radical Trends in the Positions of the Moslem Brothers," Shiloah Center Occasional Papers (Tel Aviv 1979) [in Hebrew], p. 2 [hereafter Altman 1979].

5. Shiloah Center, Occasional Papers (Tel Aviv, May 1978).

6. Israel Altman, "Islamic Movements in Egypt," *The Jerusalem Quarterly*, 10 (Winter 1979), pp. 87-94 [hereafter Altman, *JQ*].

7. E. Sivan, "How Fares Islam," *The Jerusalem Quarterly*, 13 (Fall 1979), pp. 4-5.

8. Joint Publication Research Service, *Near East Report*, 1966 (18 July 1979), quoting *al-Hawadith*, London, 27 April 1979; while denouncing Egyptian authorities for stirring up dissent, the paper itself "hinted" that it was odd that only the Coptic grandson and namesake of Butrus Ghali Pasha, the Prime Minister assassinated for signing the 1899 Condominion agreement with Britain for the joint administration of the Sudan, could be found to sign the new treaty of "subjugation" with Israel.

9. Altman (1979), p. 10.

10. *FBIS-MEA*, V. 85 (1 May 1979).

11. Sivan, pp. 39-40.

12. *FBIS-MEA*, V. 194 (5 October 1978) quoting from *al-Da'wa*, October 1978; *FBIS-MEA*, V. 199 (13 October 1978) quoting from *al-Siyassa*, 10 October 1978.

13. Altman, *JQ*, 97-99.

14. M. A. Mahgoub, *Democracy on Trial* (London 1974), pp. 224-25; for details, see G. Warburg, "Islam in Sudanese Politics," *The Jerusalem Quarterly*, 13 (Fall 1979), pp. 47-61.

15. Mahgoub, p. 181.

16. The Democratic Republic of the Sudan, *The Permanent Constitution of the Sudan* (Khartoum, 8 May 1973).

17. Joint Publication Research Service, *Translation on Near East*, No. 843 (18 October 1972).

18. *FBIS-MEA*, V. 231 (29 November 1979), quoting SUNA, 29 November 1979; *FBIS-MEA*, V. 229 (27 November 1979), quoting SUNA, 25 November, 1979.

19. *FBIS-MEA*, V. 62 (28 March 1980).

# 8
# Full Circle—
# Syrian Politics in the 1970s

*Itamar Rabinovitch*

A DECADE MORE often than not proves to be an artificial framework for the analysis of a political process. But the political history of the Asad regime in Syria during the 1970s represents an exception to this rule. In the course of one decade, a full circle was completed. Asad staged his coup on 14 November 1970, not merely as a contender for power but also as the advocate of a specific approach to the problem of power in Syria. In the early 1970s he tried, accordingly, to alter the relationship between regime and populace by making his government less coercive and more popular. This domestic orientation was matched by a pragmatic and diversified foreign policy. Both met with impressive success in the early and middle parts of the decade, but encountered increasing difficulties and finally failed as the 1970s drew to a close. Asad has overcome successive attempts to overthrow him, but in the process of doing so he was forced to undo much of what he had previously advocated and carried out. By November 1980, Syria and the Baath regime had by and large returned to their position of a decade earlier.

There is an intrinsic value to the study of Asad's attempt and his failure. Such a study also serves as a necessary basis for understanding Syria's domestic politics and foreign policies in the 1980s. Furthermore, the course of Syria's political history sheds light on several issues that are of import for the whole region.

## The Formation of Asad's Regime

Asad's "corrective movement" of November 1970 inaugurated the third phase in the history of the Baath regime in Syria. During the first two phases (1963-66, 1966-70), the Baath came to be characterized by a peculiar working arrangement combining a military

oligarchy with a subservient party organization. This formula enabled the Baath to hold power for a longer period than any of its
predecessors in independent Syria, but not to overcome two fundamental difficulties.

One was the refusal of Syria's urban Sunni (Orthodox Muslim)
population to accept the legitimacy of a regime whose leaders mostly
originated in rural and minority communities. Through a series of
clashes between the regime and its urban Sunni rivals in the 1960s, an
unsatisfactory balance was established: the opposition could not topple a narrowly-based regime that controlled the army, and the regime
could not make itself acceptable to the urban political classes.[1]

The other difficulty was posed by the endemic factionalism
and the recurring conflicts within the Baathi ruling group. Indeed,
in the late 1960s Syria's domestic politics centered on the conflict
between Salah Jadid and Hafez Asad and their respective factions.
At stake was more than a contest for power. Jadid and his faction
advocated a radical approach to the solution of the regime's underlying problem. They argued that the hostility of the urban middle
classes to the regime was incurable. The only way to broaden the
basis of the regime's support lay in a transformation of Syria's socio-
economic structure. This had to be achieved through conflict and
antagonism with the urban population, which should be held at bay
by force and intimidation. Their foreign policy was congruent with
this outlook on Syria's domestic politics. In the late 1960s, Syria
was closely aligned with the Soviet Union, pursued a radical line in
the Arab-Israeli conflict, and was at odds with most Arab states.[2]

Asad's views, reinforced and accentuated by the conflict with
the rival faction, were different. He believed that an accommodation could be reached with the urban middle classes so that the Baath
regime could be based more on consensus and less on coercion.
In foreign affairs he was for a diversification of Syria's international
orientation and for mending fences with other Arab states. The disagreements were brought to a head by Syria's abortive intervention
in the Jordanian civil war of September 1970. Syria's foreign policy
reached a dead end, and the ensuing altercations prodded Asad to
stage the "corrective movement" of November 16 and seize full
power in Syria.

Asad now turned to the implementation of the program he
had advocated. He was quite successful in forming a remarkably
cohesive ruling group. Unlike previous coup authors, he did not

seize power as the leader of a heterogeneous coalition but rather as the undisputed leader of his own coterie. Furthermore, his coming to power was not an abrupt event but the culmination of a long, gradual, and well-prepared process.[3]

It was far more difficult to contend with the hostility of the Sunni urban middle classes. Asad himself, and several of his close associates, were members of the Alawi minority community, and Asad was reluctant to risk the coherence and stability of his regime by diversifying the sources of power. The risks entailed in such a policy were certain, but the prospects of really mollifying the Baath's foes and critics appeared negligible. Asad tried to overcome this dilemma by organizing his regime on a dualistic basis. The core of the new regime consisted of Asad and his circle, army officers, and party functionaries. But this inner core was to operate through a series of institutions and organizations that would endow the regime with a constitutional and non-partisan appearance. Asad himself was the central figure in both systems, and by exercising personal leadership in a style previously unknown in Baathi politics, he sought to establish a direct link between regime and populace.

During his first years in power, Asad implemented this domestic strategy with impressive success. Syria, a closed and grim country in the late 1960s, came to be characterized by a more benign public atmosphere. A series of political and constitutional reforms was completed within two and a half years. Asad himself was elected president, a "national progressive front" (a nominal coalition comprising the Baath and its "progressive" allies) was formed, a permanent constitution was adopted by plebiscite, and a legislative assembly was elected. These measures completed the development of the formal structure within which Syrian politics have been conducted since 1973. In reality, though, actual power in Syria has continued to be exercised by the inner core of the regime; the President's informal circle and the network attached to it. This group performs three major functions: it controls the army and the party and guarantees the survival of the regime; it participates with the president in decision making; and it controls the functioning of the formal structure of the Baath regime.[4]

As a rule, this dualistic system has functioned very well, but it met with less than full success in coping with the two underlying problems in the Baath regime:

1. The Syrian urban population is well aware of the locus of

real power in the regime, and remains unreconciled to the fact that it is ruled by what it regards as a minority group. The more liberal atmosphere inaugurated by the Asad regime and the gestures it made toward these groups had been well accepted and had made their political impact in 1971-72. But in the absence of real reconciliation, it was later exploited by the regime's critics to express their opposition. The most significant early manifestation of the lingering opposition to the Baathi rule occurred in February 1973 when large-scale demonstrations were held to protest the text of the proposed draft of the new permanent constitution. The regime could break the demonstrations by force, but its leaders preferred a political solution and altered the text of the proposed constitution. The uneasy truce between the regime and the opposition was thus maintained, although the softer terms in which it was couched did not eliminate its explosive potential.[5]

2. Despite the unprecedented cohesiveness of the ruling group around Hafez Asad, it was not entirely free from rivalries and disagreements. Thus, in 1972 General Muhammad Umran, an exiled Alawi former Minister of Defense, was assassinated in Lebanon; he was said to have been plotting with Alawi army officers. In 1975 Asad was embarrassed by the strong opposition of radical and pro-Iraqi elements, which manifested itself in the Syrian Baath party organization.

## Asad's Foreign Policy

The early success of Asad's domestic policies was complemented and reinforced by his foreign policy exploits. Its initial aims were rather modest: to end Syria's isolation and to diversify her regional and international relations. Accordingly, Syria joined the (rather nominal) Egyptian-Libyan federation and began to develop her relations with West European countries. The Syrian-Egyptian rapprochement laid the political and military foundations for Syria's participation in the October 1973 war.

Syria's participation in the war was far from being fully successful, but the experience of the war and the subsequent political developments were the turning points in the process, which led the Asad regime to embark on a new regional policy. The new policy sought to build a power position from which Syria could play a more autonomous role. It was to rest on Syria's influence in Jordan and

Lebanon and over the PLO, on her increased military power, and on her ability to conduct diversified Arab and international policies.

Asad was prompted to adopt this new policy by the lessons of the years 1973-74, which underlined the importance of the American and Saudi positions in the region and the unreliability of the Egyptian and Soviet alliances. The vacuum created by the decline of Egypt's regional position and the opportunities available in Lebanon and Jordan facilitated the implementation of the new strategy. By early 1977, Syria had acquired a position of hegemony in Lebanon was closely allied with Jordan, had considerable influence over the PLO, dealt with both Moscow and Washington, developed her armed forces, and played a crucial role in formulating the Arab world's policy toward Israel.

But, in fact, processes were then at work which a few months later confronted the Asad regime with a grave and lengthy crisis. Like his earlier success, Asad's difficulties were caused by a combination of domestic and external elements. These were expedited and aggravated by Syria's involvement in the Lebanese crisis.

## The Crisis of the Asad Regime

In moments of smugness in the years 1975-77, various spokesmen for the Asad regime suggested that Syria was about to take away from Egypt the role of leadership in the Arab world.[6] The truth of the matter was that even the more limited vision of regional hegemony envisioned by Asad was beyond the capabilities of his regime. This was painfully demonstrated by the domestic and external impact of Syria's intervention in the Lebanese civil war, which revealed that one fragmented polity could not afford to try and regulate the affairs of another such polity.[7]

In Syria the regime's military intervention in Lebanon and the direction it took were widely construed as an essentially sectarian policy, a Christian-Alawi alliance against the Palestine and Lebanese Sunni Muslims. This exacerbated communal tensions in Syria and the urban population's hostility to the Asad regime. Furthermore, the army's lengthy stay in Lebanon resulted also in internecine squabbling in the regime's upper echelons and in inflationary pressures. The latter fomented public criticism of the government and induced Asad to launch an abortive and counter-productive "anti-corruption" campaign.

But the most important domestic consequence of these developments was the radicalization of the opposition to the Asad regime. The intensified objection to the regime and its policies was now reinforced by greater aid from the outside (primarily by Iraq and the PLO), and by the emergence of new, activist militant Islamic groups that viewed the traditional Muslim Brotherhood opposition to the regime as too tame.[8] They launched a new offensive against the Baath, which unfolded in three stages:

1. A campaign of terror and assassination aimed at public figures, army officers, Soviet advisors, and party and public buildings. The campaign was very effective in creating insecurity, fomenting inter-communal tensions, and generating discord in the regime's upper echelons.

2. An attempt to bring the country to the verge of civil war by pitting Alawis against the Sunnis. The most salient act in this regard was the massacre in June 1979 of some sixty Alawi cadets at the artillery school in Aleppo.

3. A campaign seeking to organize civil disobedience against the regime in northern Syria, which in the winter of 1979-80 forced the regime to dispatch large army units to Aleppo and northern Syria in order to break the backbone of the opposition.

The domestic difficulties were matched and exacerbated by a foreign policy stalemate. Many of the difficulties were inherent in the policy itself—it had been too ambitious for Syria's resources and collapsed when the opposition proved to be too powerful. But there was also a clear linkage between domestic and foreign policy: the domestic crisis crippled Asad's foreign policies, and the latter's failure reflected adversely on the regime's legitimacy and standing at home.

By 1978 several of the Asad regime's foreign policy difficulties and failures had become apparent:

1. The Syrian-Iraqi conflict is essentially a political dispute between two rival wings of the same party and two hostile leaders. Superimposed on this core are several additional layers: a dispute on the two countries' respective shares in the waters of the Euphrates, the transit of Iraqi oil and foreign trade through Syrian territory, the Kurdish problem, and divergent Israeli and Arab policies. Until 1975 Syria appeared to be the stronger party to the conflict, and she did not hesitate to use military threats against Iraq. But later on,

the balance changed. Iraq settled her dipute with Iran, quashed the Kurdish rebellion, and laid alternate pipelines that eliminated her dependence on Syria. Iraq now used her large army and economic resources and her own Baath party organization to exert a very effective and destabilizing effect on Syria.

2. In the course of 1977, Syria and Asad played a cardinal role in shaping the Arab world's policy toward Israel and effectively curtailed the policies of Egypt's President Sadat. But when the latter (largely as a result of this Syrian conduct) took his journey to Jerusalem, Asad found himself incapable of responding to the new challenges. The opening of a direct Egyptian-Israeli settlement destroyed the policy developed by Syria after 1973. Nor could Asad organize an effective Arab front that would isolate Sadat and foil his policies. Such a front was meaningless without Iraqi participation, and Iraq's terms for reconciliation with Syria were unacceptable to the Asad regime.

Consequently, Syria's policy in the Arab-Israeli conflict reached a dead end. Syria was not moving toward a political settlement that would return the Golan to Syria so as to match Egypt's gains in the Sinai, nor was it building a credible military option. This paralysis was exploited by the regime's foes in and outside Syria, and its leaders' explicit and implicit responses to such criticism are a clear indication of its effectiveness.[9]

## Syria's Position in Lebanon

The Riyadh and Cairo agreements of October 1977 provided Arab endorsement of Syria's hegemony in Lebanon, and the long-term prospects of consolidating that position looked good. But in 1978 and 1979 the political price for retaining and developing that position seemed prohibitive. In 1978 Syria fought with the Christian militias and suffered heavy casualties. In 1979, when large forces were required in order to reimpose the state's authority in northern Syria, the presence of some 30,000 troops in Lebanon was taxing the resources of the Syrian army. And throughout the period the Syrian authorities were embarrassed by the problem of South Lebanon, which became the main theatre for military conflict between Israel and the Palestinians. Syria did not want to intervene on the PLO's behalf, so as not to be drawn into a military confrontation under disadvantageous circumstances. But her failure to support the PLO during the Litani Operation (March 1978) and during Israeli air raids exposed the Asad regime to domestic and external criticism.[10]

## Syria's International Orientation

In the years 1975-77, the Asad regime was very successful in maneuvering between the two superpowers in a fashion reminiscent of the hey-day of non-alignment. This was based on Syria's position as an object of American wooing, on her regional influence, and on the regime's ability to control all domestic opposition to the government's pragmatic foreign policy. Thus, Asad could in 1976 coordinate his intervention in Lebanon with the United States and engage in an open controversy with the Soviet Union. In the spring of 1977 Asad met with both Carter and Brezhnev on his own terms.

But the domestic political crisis and the decline of Syria's regional position also eliminated the regime's capability to manipulate the superpowers. The Syrian-American dialogue came to an end and Syria lapsed into a position of dependence on the Soviet Union. Syria's support of the Soviet invasion of Afghanistan was one clear symptom of the new state of Soviet-Syrian relations.

## New Domestic and Foreign Policies

There have been two aspects to the Asad regime's response to the Islamic opposition's challenge. First came the effort to break the backbone of the opposition by sending large and loyal units to Aleppo and other parts of northern Syria. All centers of opposition were sealed off, house-to-house searches were conducted with great brutality, and violent pressure was exerted on the population. This probably aggravated Sunni-Alawi relations beyond repair, but in the short run it quelled northern Syria and broke the active opposition to the regime by the end of the summer of 1980. There remained the need to respond to the opposition's more fundamental challenge. With this end in mind the Baathi leaders formulated a new domestic stategy in the spring and summer of 1980 which amounted to a dismantling of the Asad regime's original domestic platform. The change was apparently based on the conclusion that the attempt to regain at least the passive support of the urban classes was indeed bound to fail. Therefore, the regime had to base its domestic policies on the support of the army, party, and those social groups that had a stake in the regime.

While they continued to argue that their challengers were a tiny and isolated minority, the regime's spokesmen began early in 1980 to depict a historic and profound antagonism between the social groups supporting and those opposing the "revolution." The original Asad strategy, which sought to obliterate social and political divisions and conflicts, was thus discarded. In the same vein a National Guard was formed, in a fashion reminiscent of the 1960s, to "protect the revolution." The National Guard is not actually needed for the regime's protection—this function is performed efficiently by the army and the security services. But it has proven its usefulness in the past as an effective instrument for popular mobilization and for radicalizing the public atmosphere.[11]

The same trend has been evident in the Asad regime's foreign policy during the same period. Throughout the 1970s, Asad had rejected all Soviet offers and pressures to conclude a treaty of friendship and cooperation like the ones signed by the Soviet Union with Egypt and Iraq in 1971 and 1972. Such a treaty would have gone against the grain of Asad's policy at the time. But by the end of the 1970s the roles had been reversed. A treaty with the Soviet Union seemed to Asad a measure bound to guarantee a greater measure of Soviet aid and commitment and as a signal to friend and foe alike that at least in Soviet eyes Asad was still an asset worthy of further investment. The Soviets, in turn, had to be persuaded that this indeed was the case.

The result was lengthy negotiations and finally a treaty. The treaty is couched in very general terms but the text itself and several press reports and commentaries suggest the possibility of secret annexes.

The signing of the treaty was preceded by a Syrian-Libyan aggreement on (a nominal) union between the two countries. Asad's chief motivation was apparently the support of a regime, which, while controversial, has a distinctive Islamic and Arab nationalist identity. One certain result of this rapprochement has been to place Syria much more clearly and firmly in the radical end of the Arab political spectrum.

The similarity to the circumstances of the late 1960s is readily apparent. The Baath regime, itself affected by factional strife, and enjoying a limited measure of public support, is confronting a hostile opposition in Syria's major cities. The population in the rural areas and the provincial small towns, the Baath's natural constituency, is still not politicized and does not serve as an effective basis of support. Measures have been taken by the regime in order to radicalize Syrian politics, although a desire to avoid a total confrontation is still evident. Syria is again close to and dependent on the Soviet Union and, aside from its alliance with Libya, isolated in the Arab world. A radicalized Baathi Syria in the late 1960s radiated a destabilizing influence across her borders; this pattern may well repeat itself in the 1980s.

## A Regional Perspective

The changes that occurred in Syria in the late 1970s or, to put it differently, the failure of Hafez Asad's political strategy, have so far been presented in the context of Syrian politics. They can, indeed, to a great extent be explained in terms that are inherent in the political circumstances of Syria and the Baath regime: Syria's ethnic and political diversity, the earlier political history of the Syrian republic, the entrenched antagonism between the Baath regime and a sizeable sector of the urban political classes, and the regime's own errors and miscalculations.

Yet, several of the developments that took place in Syria during the past decade were not unique to it but part of broader processes that affected the whole region. They were, according to the circumstances, the particular manifestations or reflections of general trends or contributors to their emergence and evolution. Thus, the conflict betwen Sunnis and Alawis in Syria should be seen in the context of the exacerbation of communal relations in the Arab world of which the Lebanese civil war and the Sunni-Shi'i conflict in Iraq have been two other important manifestations. Nor should the surge of Sunni fundamentalist militancy against the Baath regime in the late 1970s be divorced from the resurgence of political Islam—a cardinal fact of international politics during the same years.

The rise and evolution of the Asad regime in the early and mid-1970s were construed at the time as an important aspect of the trend toward moderation in the central countries of the Arab world. Together with the development of Sadat's regime in Egypt, and, to a much lesser extent, the Baath regime in Iraq, Asad's politics and policies represented—or seemed to represent—stability, pragmatism, readiness to settle with Israel, a movement away from the Soviet Union, and willingness to deal with the West, if not directly with the United States. The trend has been evidently checked in Syria. It had never been very strong in Iraq. Together with other potential developments in the region—exacerbation of the Soviet-American rivalry, confrontation between rich and poor Arab states, recrudescence of the Arab-Israeli conflict, domestic upheavals—a new radical phase in Syria could be the harbinger of a similar phase in the region as a whole.

## NOTES

1. For general works dealing with the early years of the Asad regime, see Malcolm Kerr, "Hafiz Asad and the Changing Patterns of Syrian Politics," *International Journal*, Vol. 28, pp. 689-706; Talitha Petran, *Syria* (London 1972), pp. 239-257; and Moshe Ma'oz, *Syria under Hafiz al-Asad, New Domestic and Foreign Policies*, The Jerusalem Papers on Peace Problems, No. 15, 1975.

2. For the Asad-Jadid controversy and conflict, see O. Tabor, "Syria," in D. Dishon (ed.), *Middle East Record, 1969-1970* (Jerusalem 1977), pp. 1127-1164, and N. Van Dam, *The Struggle for Power in Syria* (London 1979), pp. 83-88.

3. See I. Rabinovitch, "Continuity and Change in the Ba'th Regime in Syria," in I. Rabinovitch and H. Shaked (eds.), *From June to October* (New Brunswick, N. J. 1977), pp. 219-228.

4. See I. Rabinovitch, "Syria," in Colin Legum (ed.), *The Middle East Contemporary Survey, 1976-77* (New York 1978), pp. 604-618.

5. For the 1973 crisis in Syria, see Abbas Kelidar, "Religion and State in Syria," *Asian Affairs*, Vol. 61, pp. 16-22.

6. One revealing instance of this mood was the statement made in November 1975 by the Syrian Minister of Information to an A.P. correspondent. The Minister enumerated the factors that enabled his country to claim from Egypt the leadership of the Arab world. In addition to the historical role of Damascus in Arab civilization and Hafez Asad's leadership, he explained that "Syria has increasing support and confidence of other Arab states, excellent international relations with East and West, a population united behind the regime, and a professional army of 150,000 with the latest Soviet weapons." Associated Press from Damascus, 21 November 1975.

7. See A. Dawisha, "Syria in Lebanon—Asad's Vietnam?" *Foreign Policy*, No. 33, pp. 135-150, and P. B. Heller, "The Syrian Factor in the Lebanese Civil War," *Journal of South Asian and Middle Eastern Studies*, Vol. IV, No. l, pp. 56-76.

8. Reliable information on the structure and activity of the radical opposition to Asad is difficult to come by. But some insight can be gained from the testimonies of the captured anti-Baathi terrorist broadcast by Syria's

radio and television. See, for instance, the interview with one Ahmad Salim, Damascus Home Service, 18 July 1980. For another perspective, see the interview with Issam Attar, leader of Syria's Muslim Brotherhood, who lives in West Germany, in *An-Nahar Arab Report,* 18 February 1980.

9. See, for instance, the speech delivered by Asad on 8 March 1980, the seventeenth aniversary of the original Baathi revolution. Radio Damascus, 8 March 1980.

10. One such example is the attack by the Iraqi News Agency on Syria's conduct during the Litani Operation, quoted by the BBC's monitoring service, 16 March 1978.

11. This is clearly illustrated in several references by Baathi spokesmen in the spring and summer of 1980. On March 9, in the wake of Asad's above-mentioned speech, Radio Damascus stated as follows: "the battalions of the National Guard, the battalions of workers and peasants who laid the pillars of the March Revolution are standing today, with high revolutionary alertness ready to hit anyone who might be tempted to hurt the homeland's revolution and stand."

# 9
# The Islamic Revolution—
# Is Saudi Arabia Next?

*Haim Shaked*

AS A FAMOUS proverb goes, it is extremely difficult to make predictions, particularly about the future. Nevertheless, in an attempt to be true to the main theme of this conference, I shall try and concentrate on the future and briefly discuss prospects for the stability and instability of the Saudi Arabian regime. I shall follow a dual course of analysis and shall present an outline of two alternative developments of Saudi Arabian politics.

Let us first assume that the year is 1990 and that we are participating at an academic conference that convened after a very serious crisis had occurred in Saudi Arabia, a crisis that may have toppled the regime. What would specialists of Saudi Arabian history and politics say then about the situation? How would they analyze, *a posteriori*, the causes of the Saudi Arabian crisis?

They would probably make a distinction between its immediate causes, the major trends and processes of change that led to the crisis, and permanent, basic features of Saudi Arabian society and polity that laid the foundations for the momentous events. Looked at more closely, albeit briefly, what is the picture that would emerge? There are a number of noteworthy fundamental features that might contribute toward a possible crisis. Saudi Arabia is a vast country geographically, with a very small population—both in relative and absolute terms—estimated at five to six million indigenous inhabitants and about two million foreign workers of different occupations and origins. Geographically, and socially, Saudi Arabia is a country of very sharp differences, and such differences tend to breed regional tensions. The distinctions between the heartland or uplands and great deserts of Saudi Arabia, the West (the Hijaz), and the Eastern coastland along the Persian Gulf are not confined to topographic features. They have far-reaching social and political implications. Each of these geographical units is inhabited by a number of tribal confederations bound by shifting alliances that rouse animosities among them. Indeed, Saudi Arabian history could not be fully understood without an allusion to these tribal coalitions and rivalries and the ways in which they have affected Saudi Arabian policies in the past. Another notable division is between rich and poor—the haves, those who do not have enough, and the have-nots. Of late, a new distinction has become very important. It cuts through the educated group: those who are educated in Western institutions and ways of thinking, as opposed to the powerful ulama, or the learned men of Islam, taught in traditional schools in Saudi Arabia. One might add the divisions between tribal society, which is still an important element in Saudi Arabian life and politics, and the rising, ever-growing urban society; between those who rule and those who are ruled; and the deep-seated rivalries, which run across the ruling family itself (such as the famous competition between the "Sudayri Seven," the Jilwi, and other sons of the late king 'Abd 'Aziz). Furthermore, the geo-strategic location of Saudi Arabia, and the fact that Saudi Arabia is so rich in oil and proven oil reserves, have turned her into a coveted prize for a variety of international interests, each of which creates and exerts its own pressures, and, oftentimes, even engineers subversion. Last but not least, Saudi Arabia is a traditionally-oriented fundamentalist society and state, governed by a dynastic monarchy that has ruled the country autocratically for 200 years (with two significant interruptions). In this regard, the Saudi political system is quite archaic and anachronistic.

As an additional dimension, one might add a number of basic trends and processes that have taken place in and around Saudi Arabia in recent years. Among these, one should note the lengthening cracks which have appeared in the structure of Saudi ruling institutions. Since the assassination of King Faysal in 1975, there has been no major dominant figure able simultaneously to maintain complete discipline and mobilize the elite in an attempt to satisfy the needs and fulfill the expectations of Saudi Arabians. No one outside the inner circle of the ruling family fully knows the details of their differences concerning choices of regional and international orientation, but it is common knowledge that they do not see eye to eye on issues that are of major importance. For example, there are questions of policy toward the Iranian revolution; the response to Russian encroachment on the region, particularly Afghanistan; the American role in countering that encroachment; and the peace agreement between Egypt and Israel. It is clear, however, that these issues, and possibly also a number of domestic ones, do provide fuel for personal rivalries at the very top of the ruling family—a situation that does not add to the stability of the regime. To these one might add the slow but regular development of a highly sophisticated military establishment, which has been accumulating organizational skills, as well as the technical and educational means that are prerequisites for an attempt at seizing the reigns of power; the cumulative effects of corruption in Saudi Arabian society; the uneven distribution of the enormous oil income; and the indirect influence on Saudi Arabian society of the swollen colonies of foreigners—some of whom represent ways of life that are markedly different than those preferred by the Saudi Arabian establishment.

Abroad, the upheavals in the Horn of Africa, Iran, and Afghanistan, the radicalization of South Yemen, and the uneasy relations with North Yemen have all created tensions for the Saudi Arabian political system, and they represent serious threats to vital Saudi Arabian interests. The same is true of the dangers posed by Russian-Communist influence in the region. Paradoxically, another type of political activity—that between Israel and Egypt—has also had an unsettling effect on Saudi Arabia. For Saudi Arabia, in the short run, it meant not more stability or reduced danger of a major Middle Eastern war but a need to take sides within the delicate system of inter-Arab relations; the country has been steering a careful diplomatic course between other Arab countries ever since.

That imaginary gathering of specialists in 1990 would probably point, retrospectively, to certain historical turning points or milestones of the process that culminated in the overthrow of the Saudi regime. Beginning in 1969, when there was a very serious, albeit abortive, conspiracy against the regime, they would then dwell on the surprise assassination of King Faysal in 1975. The November 1979 occupation of the *Ka'ba* would come next on the list of events that undermined the Saudi Arabian regime. There might be some other events between now and 1990 that would figure on this list. All these episodes, combined with the above mentioned processes—

so these specialists would argue—had accumulated, and then culminated in a crisis that engulfed the regime.

But it can also be imagined that in 1990 an identical conference
of specialists would have to deal with a situation in which the present
Saudi Arabian regime was not toppled. In attempting to explain
how it is that the fragile situation in Saudi Arabia never exploded,
that gathering would certainly point to the fact that, while in 1979
there was a serious threat to the Saudi Arabian regime, it was sufficiently resilient to absorb the external as well as the internal shocks.
They would add that in the final analysis, the regime did survive
the takeover of the *Ka'ba* without unsettling after-effects; that
in 1975, when the King himself was assassinated, the regime did
show a remarkable ability for a swift and smooth transition of power;
and that the 1969 conspiracy was detected and crushed before it
gained the momentum required to topple the regime. The same
analysis would indicate that the Saudi Arabian ruling institution
is not a small clique but constitutes a very large number of princes
(about three thousand) who have a vested interest in the continued
existence of the monarchy. It would also emphasize that the Saudi
Arabian government conceptualized a very interesting formula for
the gradual and careful implementation of modernization, without
forsaking the traditional features of society. Its careful blend of
conservatism and modernity might thus be presented as a cleverly
designed political and cultural shock absorber. Furthermore, the
existence of two armies, not just one, and their mutual neutraliza-
tion would be cited as another obstacle to a successful military *coup
d'état*. And the fact that income from oil has percolated and spread
over a large part of Saudi Arabian urban and tribal society would
be cited as a force for stability. As for foreigners—both laborers
and advisors—it would be said of them that they are strictly controlled by the security forces and are thus prevented from spreading
ideas detrimental to the integrity of the political system. The same
is true of the effects of change in the immediate environment of
Saudi Arabia and their significance for Saudi Arabia's stability. It
could be argued that the Saudi Arabian government learned the
lesson of Iran and was wise enough not to alienate the ulama while
it was strong enough to sustain any subversion levelled against it
from its smaller neighbors. The Russian danger, the argument
could maintain, and was more perceived than real, for any serious

Russian or Russian-inspired threat to Saudi Arabia would have passed the brink of toleration by the United States. It could be suggested that the basic feature of Saudi Arabia—namely, that it is a very large country with several centers—meant that it was therefore extremely difficult for a conspiratorial group to seize the country at one stroke. The geographical differences and their social implications could be dismissed as mainly theoretical and relevant more to scholarly literature than to real life.

The juxtaposition of these two imaginary future conferences brings out some of the complexities of assessing the direction of Saudi Arabian politics. The combination of little authoritative knowledge of how decisions are really arrived at behind the palace walls and a lack of sufficient information about the actualities of Saudi Arabian political life reduce prediction to guesswork. Nevertheless, one cannot escape the urge, and need, to look from the present into the future, and, in retrospect, it would appear that toward the end of the 1970s, there were some major changes in the area, which raise questions concerning the stability of a regime such as this one. The aggregate picture is presently such that more weight should be put on the possibility that the Saudi Arabian regime may crumble than on contrary assurances that it will survive.

In the beginning of 1979, a short while after the success of the Iranian revolution, many specialists believed that Saudi Arabia was next in line and that revolution there was imminent. At about that time, a conference on Saudi Arabian affairs took place under respected auspices in New York; the members of the panel, all specialists in Saudi Arabian affairs, had a very difficult time in arguing for the likelihood of the Saudi Arabian regime lasting for more than a year. Well, the end did indeed come, and the Saudi Arabian government demonstrated a remarkable ability to withstand the first shock-wave created by the Iranian revolution and the growing pressure exerted by the Soviets and their allies, in spite of the United States' failure to act decisively in the crisis. This, however, does not mean that the proper forecast for the foreseeable future is "more of the same." The Saudi Arabian situation seems to be changing, and there are indications of a serious and constant erosion. A number of international, regional, and local factors seem to have crystallized into an actual threat to the Saudi regime. Therefore, while in the beginning of 1979 the present author was convinced that Saudi Arabia could survive the immediate effects of the Iranian revolution and other developments in the area, he can no longer be sure that Saudi Arabia can do so for long. One major cause of this change of assessment has been the successful takeover of the *Ka'ba* in November 1979. Short-lived as it was, it exposed the relative strengths and weaknesses of the Saudi Arabian regime and its inability to detect and control the seeds of serious domestic conflict. Saudi Arabia's posture toward the Iraqi-Iranian war further accentuated some of the country's inherent weaknesses.

In the conclusion of an article on Saudi Arabia written together with Dr. Steven Rosen and published in *Commentary* in June 1978, we stated that "Saudi Arabia has become not part of the solution but part of the problem (of American policy in the Middle East)." In the beginning of the 1980s, Saudi Arabian stability begins to look not merely like a problem, but a highly explosive one. It is impossible to foretell exactly how and when it will explode, but the situation seems to have reached a critical point warranting an assessment of Saudi Arabian vulnerability and instability more thorough than at any time in the past.

# 10

# The Palestinians and
# the Future of Middle East Politics:

## A TENTATIVE EXPLORATION OF SOME
## ALTERNATIVE SCENARIOS

### *Gabriel Ben-Dor*

Palestine is a historical memory, an ideological figment, which may, like others of the same kind, become a political reality or may slip back into the oblivion from which it was recovered; the issue is not yet clear. The Palestinians, however, are real people, with a real problem, the solution of which is long overdue.

Bernard Lewis (1975)

The Palestinian people believe in Arab Unity. In order to contribute their share toward the attainment of that objective, however, they must, at the present stage of their struggle, safeguard their Palestinian identity and develop their consciousness of that identity, and oppose any plan that may dissolve or impair it.

Palestinian National Covenant (1968), Article 12.

Egypt, Israel, Jordan, and the representatives of the Palestinian People should participate in negotiations on the resolution of the Palestinian problem in all its aspects . . . The solution from the negotiations must also recognize the legitimate rights of the Palestinian people and their just requirements. In this way, the Palestinians will participate in the determination of their own fate . . .

Camp David Accords (1978)<br>"The Framework for Peace in the Middle<br>East," Section A.

THIS ESSAY IS not an attempt at a prediction. Rather, it is an attempt to forecast some probable trends in the future of Middle East politics as they relate to the role of the Palestinians. The difference

*147*

between a prediction and a forecast should always be borne in mind.

"A prediction usually dispenses probabilistic interpretation, a forecast is always conceived within a certain probability range. A prediction is generally made in terms of a point or event; a forecast is made in terms of alternatives. A prediction focuses upon one outcome; a forecast involves contingencies. The composite distinction between predicting and forecasting—in terms of probability, contingent outcomes, and specification of alternatives—lies at the core of the existing approaches to the future."[1]

The reluctance to engage in prediction is enhanced by the dismal record of predictions in the 1970s. If we look back upon the dramatic events of the 1970s in Middle East politics it seems that very few of us could have predicted them at a conference of this kind held in 1970. Consider such events as the Yom Kippur War; the twists and turns of Lebanon's Civil War in 1975-76; the ascent of the Begin government in Israel in 1977; Sadat's initiative and trip to Jerusalem that year; the Iranian revolution of 1978-79; these are the most important events that shaped the political evolution of the Middle East in the 1970s. It seems that these could have been predicted only in the most general way as possible trends. No one could have predicted exactly when the 1973 war was to break out, how it would be conducted, how it would end. No one could have seen all the particular twists and turns of the Lebanese Civil War, although a variety of experts could have predicted that the Lebanese political system was up against strains and stresses which might e-rupt in something of the sort. Electoral trends in Israel, particularly those relating to the changing voting habits of younger people and Jews of Oriental origin, could have prepared us for a possible change of government in Israel. Changes in Egyptian policy toward Israel and the Arab-Israeli conflict ever since the 1967 war in general and the 1970 war of attrition in particular could have prepared us for further dramatic change in Egyptian policy toward Israel, but not Sadat's initiative to Jerusalem. And again, a great many experts on Iran had been predicting for many years the eventual downfall of the Shah's regime, the glaring weaknesses of which were obvious and were there for every analyst to see. However, the particular chain of events that brought about the Shah's eventual downfall, the rapid disintegration of his army, the particular strength of the Islamic wave, and the charismatic leadership of one single man in opposition to the Shah, could not have been predicted, and it is highly likely that the analyst ought not to attempt specific predictions of this kind in the first place. Rather, what he ought to try and do is identify a political system, and its boundaries; the key variables interacting in the system that give it its peculiar character and then attempt to forecast the way these variables will evolve in the future; the way they will interact in the future; the way new major variables may intrude into the system; and some future trends in the environment of the political system. Then the task is to identify some main alternatives related to probabilities; it is preferable that not much more be attempted. If this is done well, at least assumptions about the future that we all hold and in the lack of which we are simply unable to conduct policy will become explicit rather than remain implicit. As explicit assumptions, they are at least exposed to serious discussion, debate, and criticism, as implicit assumptions are not. To that extent, bringing these assumptions out into the open and bringing them before the policy-making community itself may be an important service toward developing a policy-oriented political science as it relates to the study of Middle East politics. No more than that is claimed in the context of this particular paper.

Beyond these reservations, it is important to point out the philosophical but rather important fact that the future is not an "objective reality" that will come into being, which we can simply guess at, but it is rather a chain of events of our own making. Thus, really, every forecast or prediction we make has elements of a self-fulfilling prophecy. If we assume that a certain chain of events is likely to take place in the future and we adapt our behavior and our policy to that particular assumption, we are helping to bring it about. However, this is not a relevant question. It is the assumption behind the argument of this paper that guessing in a pseudo-scientific way at some objective future event is pointless; rather, we should examine possible outcomes of existing policies to the making of which we are all privy in some way.

Obviously, if we work with a very large number of debatable assumptions and if we work with a very large number of variables, the analysis will become simply unmanageable in terms of the large number of factors to be analyzed. Therefore, it is better to work with a small number of explicit *major* assumptions, to identify a small number of most likely scenarios with assigned probabilities, and analyze these in the light of what we know about Middle East politics today. Going beyond that would make the analysis too cumbersome to handle. We also have a number of other minor implicit assumptions that should become clear as the analysis goes on. However, there are four major explicit assumptions as to the future of Middle East politics in relation to the role of the Palestinians.

The first major explicit assumption is that the Middle East is a turbulent region containing many different kinds of conflicts; it is likely to remain so for a long time to come. The superpowers will not be able to divide the area into spheres of influence; thus, there will be no outside imposed solutions on the parties to the Arab-Israeli conflict. The second assumption is that peace efforts will be a central component of Middle East politics in the last two decades of the twentieth century. The Egyptian-Israeli treaty will neither disintegrate completely nor will it grow into a reality detaching Egypt altogether from the Arab world. Egypt will make further tempts to enhance and nourish the Egyptian-Israeli treaty to maturity and at the same time will attempt to recapture the leadership of the Arab world; failing that, it will attempt at least to become again a central actor in the regional political system and will not accept a pariah role in the Arab world. The third major explicit assumption is that a dramatic substantial change on the Palestinian issue is unlikely in the national consensus either in Israel or in the Arab states interested in pursuing a political solution. In that sense, the basic parameters of the so-called Palestinian problem are not likely to change, except to the extent that the Egyptian-Israeli treaty creates a partial new reality in which the context of the Palestinian problem will change slightly. The fourth is that Middle East politics will continue to be dominated to a large extent by the quest for the establishment and the institutionalization of status-quo oriented states not superseded by pan-Arab or pan-Islamic loyalties on the behavioral level, even though homage to these ideologies will be paid all around the region. Such ideologies will influence the politics of the various states to a large extent; however, they will be contained, which has been so far the case with "Khomeinism," and thus the basic identity of the states as fundamental units in regional politics will remain unchanged. An attempt will be made to institutionalize and further advance this state of affairs.

The present stage of the Arab-Israeli conflict is really somewhat deceptive. We are at the moment in a situation of momentary lull, a "time-out," due to the tension in the Persian Gulf. There is a Presidential election in the United States; the Egyptian-Israeli treaty is just now being implemented and certain judgments as to its future stability can be made; and there is a feeling that political instability in Israel is reaching the point where for the next stage of the political process to resume there is a need for possible changes in Israel as well. As a result, the Arab-Israeli conflict is at a low intensity in its cyclical fortunes—and this has been the case several times before in the 1970s. However, when this period of "time-out" is over, perhaps sometime in 1981, the question of stabilizing what is still essentially a fragile bilateral agreement will become more pressing than ever.

Notwithstanding Egypt's visible disillusionment with the vagaries of pan-Arabism, it is nót likely (as we have argued above) to accept for long its status of outcast; this state of affairs is equally unnatural and uncomfortable to the Saudis, Kuwaitis, Moroccans, Sudanese, and many other Arabs who find themselves in a badly polarized Arab world and time and again on the wrong side of the fence, so to speak, allied with radically pro-Soviet forces confronting their natural allies, Egypt and the United States. The way out is a comprehensive settlement led by a coalition of centralist Arab forces and with active American participation, when the United States recovers (either in the wake of the Presidential elections or in the wake of a new national consensus in the United States) the initiative and the ability to again act creatively in the Middle East. As things stand, the key Arab forces needed for a comprehensive peace process are reluctant to initiate or join such a process for a variety of reasons—always citing the inadequate handling of the Palestinian issue as the main reason.

The sincerity of this argument may be questioned on historical grounds, but political prudence does give some credence to the assumption that a broad and comprehensive settlement cannot be engineered without progress on the Palestinian front. The obstacles to such progress are familiar: a strong national consensus in Israel (backed by some eighty-five to ninety percent of the Jewish population) against a third state between Israel and Jordan; the current unacceptability of negotiations with the PLO and the remilitarization of the West Bank of the Jordan by Arab armies; the Arab insistence that Israel must withdraw from the West Bank and Gaza where a Palestinian state must be created; and the Arab affirmation that the legitimate rights of the Palestinians can only be represented and defined by the PLO. Can we envisage sufficient room to maneuver between these polarized claims and can we come up with any ideas that might help satisfy the demands of the parties without forcing them to make very substantial changes in their basic stance?

This is not impossible. However, in order to check probabilities, we should now take a look at the general list of major possible scenarios as they are likely to evolve in regard to the Palestinians in the Arab-Israeli conflict in particular and in Middle East politics in general.

In considering the list of alternatives, one point is very clear. Notwithstanding the high visibility of the Palestinians in Middle East politics, it is obvious that even in the 1980s the prospects of the Palestinians depend on wider Middle East politics and are determined by them much more than the other way around. The fundamental transition of the issue in the 1930s into one which was to be determined by the collective strength and collective consensus of the Arab countries is still very evident, and from this the Palestinians have found no exit. Our analysis leads us to conclude that this will not change. The context of our discussion, therefore, has to be political and has to relate to the real world of Middle East politics. It follows, then, that much of the historical argument as to the "centrality" of the Palestinian issue to the Arab-Israeli conflict is really superfluous and is no longer relevant to what is happening in the Middle East today. What is relevant is that the Palestinian issue has a very specific role to play in Middle East politics at the present time and in the foreseeable future as well. The logic of Middle East politics requires a country like Egypt to have both peace with Israel and a leading role in the region. If indeed this is the case, and this does seem to be the case, then Egypt must seek a way to rebuild its bridges with the Arab world and re-enter the mainstream of politics in the region. In order to do that, of course, a price will have to be paid by Israel, too, and this process might help make Israel a more legitimate partner in the politics of the region. This price will undoubtably involve the Palestinian question.

THE PALESTINIANS AND THE FUTURE OF MIDDLE EAST POLITICS:
(A List of Scenarios)

A. *Decline and Eventual Disappearance of Palestinian Organizations.*
Highly unlikely, given known and probable foreseeable parameters of Middle East politics, either in variation A-1 (Disappearance of the Palestinian issue) or A-2 (a multi-laterally or bi-laterally satisfactory resolution of the Palestinian problem).

B. *Establishment of Palestinian Entity.*
    B-1 Autonomy under Israeli domination as enduring solution. Probability very low.

    B-2 Palestinian state "sandwiched" between Israel and Jordan. Probability low: problems of demilitarization; irredentism, instability; refugee problem with no feasible solution; problem of the role of the PLO.

    B-3 Jordanian-Palestinian federation, under Jordanian domination. Probability a bit higher as a short-run project. In the long run problems of minority rule, demographic and sociological developments and trends running counter to this tendency; Jordanian weakness and inter-Arab factors. Number of possible variations. Problem of PLO in this scheme.

    B-4 Palestinian-Jordanian federation, under Palestinian domination, in conjunction with Palestinianization of East Bank, reflecting demographic and sociological trends. West Bank and Gaza possibly in arrangement of "shared rule" (a variation of federation condominium) with Israel, demilitarized. Palestinian organizations eventually dominate from political center on East Bank. Probability in the long run high only if comprehensive peace and virtual new regional order negotiated and implemented. Problems of winning acquiescence of several key forces to reduction of Hashemites to virtual role.

C. *Perpetuation of Status Quo; Radical, Visible Palestinian Organizations Operating in the Arab World, Partially Controlled and Manipulated by outside Forces; Palestine Issue Alive.*
    C-1 No Palestinian entity. High probability.

    C-2 Palestinian autonomy as in B-1. High probability.

    C-3 In case of B-2 with PLO excluded. High probability.

    C-4 In case of B-3 with PLO excluded. Possibly activity concentrated in the short run against Jordan. High probability.

    C-5 In case of B-4, PLO likely to split, with majority vying for political control of East Bank center; minority factions, supported by certain rejectionist forces continuing struggle from outside. Probability uncertain as to particulars.

It is highly unlikely that in the foreseeable future any major Arab power necessary to the stabilization of Egyptian-Israeli peace would join negotiations unless an arrangement involving the Palestinians was included. Indeed, a thorough analysis shows that even the Egyptian case is not altogether different. Although the Egyptian-Israeli treaty is legally supposed to stand on its own feet, if no major movement is made on the Palestinian issue and if the question is left unresolved after the initial five years, the future for a stable bilateral peace between an isolated Egypt and Israel will look rather gloomy regardless of the *legal* linkage between the two Camp David treaties. For the *political* linkage is easy to see, and it is politics that we are talking about in this context. Conflicts—and international conflicts in particular—evolve dynamically; nevertheless, it is highly likely that in the dynamics of this particular conflict, the character of the Palestinian issue, an issue linking Egypt with the Arab world, and constituting a possible bridge for Egypt to the Arab world in the event of some major concessions from Israel on the Palestinian question, will remain central. Therefore, getting away from a historical line of argument, the following salient "political facts" clearly stand out:

1. The autonomy plan agreed upon by Egypt and Israel is not much more than an elegant way of agreeing to disagree, postponing solution of the fundamental components of the Palestinian question for a few years until the Egyptian-Israeli peace treaty might change the situation in the entire region for the better, leaving the resolution of the question easier in the long run.

2. Peace is and will remain unstable between Egypt and Israel until other major Arab powers join in the process.

3. The Arab powers essential to the process will simply not join unless more concessions are made by Israel in the direction of some independent Palestinian entity. On this point, it is not unlikely that Sadat has made a major miscalculation.

4. The Arab countries insist on the resolution of the Palestinian question not just because of the alleged power of the Palestinians but because of the commitment to this cause in the Arab world, which seems to be rather well entrenched on both the elite and the popular levels, notwithstanding abuse of the Palestinian issue by various Arab countries on numerous occasions. The fact is that the Arab commitment to a Palestinian state seems to be well institutionalized in Arab

politics, just as is Israel's refusal to agree to such a state under the conditions most often mentioned. The question is whether one of these will "give in," so to speak, and if so which, or whether in such a polarized situation, some sort of acceptable middle ground can be found at all.

Numerous observers have pointed out that the Arab states have given the Palestinians, more or less voluntarily, a virtual semi-veto power over the possibility of a comprehensive Arab-Israeli peace, since the Arab states have clearly delegated to the PLO the right to determine when the minimal rights of the Palestinian people have been satisfied. In practice, there is nothing that the Palestinians could do to force the hands of the Arab states, should these choose to abrogate this obligation. However, the Arab states seem to be absolutely unwilling or unable to do so, particularly since the Palestinian case has been given a rather good hearing by world public opinion. From the Israeli point of view, there seems to be very little that Israel can do to persuade the Arabs to change their minds radically on this particular issue, and the same goes for Egypt. For Israel, and not just for Israel, there are very few good choices. Israel and certain of those Arab countries, which consistently pay lip service to the idea of a Palestinian state, are really rather apprehensive about a radical Palestinian-Arab state becoming an island of turbulence and instability in the region, and a possible Soviet base. The choice, then, for both Israel and several of the so-called moderate Arab countries, may be between undesirable alternatives.

Yet, political reality is a powerful constraint. A settlement with the Palestinians as such, or even with Jordan, may not be worth serious concessions from Israel and others. Peace with Egypt may be worth *some* concessions; if what is involved is the possibility of a stable and comprehensive peace, then *major* changes on the Palestinian front may be justified. It is possible that against this background the admission of the Palestinians as a legitimate actor should be seen as pre-empting one of the major sources of so-called revisionism in Middle East politics, which makes the region such an island of turbulence. In such a case, some major policy changes will be in order.

It is unlikely, then, that the Palestinian issue will disappear; it is even less likely that the various Palestinian organizations funded, encouraged, and controlled by different Arab factions will disappear inasmuch as they are fairly useful for a variety of reasons to a great many political forces. It is possible that, for a while, a given Palestinian organization or the PLO as a whole may be abandoned, opposed, or even defeated militarily by an Arab country (as we saw in the 1970s), but there will always be others, given the nature of inter-Arab relations, who will be interested in encouraging, using, and, therefore, funding the various Palestinian organizations. Thus, scenario A is altogether unlikely.

As to scenario B, the assumption is that as long as peace holds, the establishment of some Palestinian entity will become a very serious possibility. On the rubric B-1, some progress has already been made, at least as far as an agreement on autonomy between Egypt and Israel is concerned. The autonomy plan does have the advantage of being the first mutually agreed scheme between Israel and a leading Arab country on the Palestinian issue. It contains a number of challenging ideas and it obviously improves to a certain extent the lot of the inhabitants; however, it does not do much more than that. It speaks of administrative self-rule without resolving the question of political rule, which is what the entire problem is really about. It assumes a Jordanian and local Palestinian participation that is simply not forthcoming. It speaks of a transitional period during which, to quote from the Camp David agreements, "a withdrawal of Israeli armed forces will take place and there will be a redeployment of the remaining Israeli forces into specified security locations." How many Israeli armed forces; when, from where, where and how will they be redeployed; who will specify the security locations; and a great many other questions have been left unresolved to the point where we must conclude that such an agreement simply cannot work in the long run, at least in this vague form, until the Egyptian-Israeli treaty, once stabilized, enables the polities to look for the kind of permanent resolution of the Palestinian issue that the autonomy plan does not allow us to imagine. The autonomy plan cannot be a basis of comprehensive peace inasmuch as it does not constitute the bridge that Egypt needs so badly in order to build an inter-Arab coalition that will back a possible comprehensive peace.

As to scenario B-2, that of the Palestinian state "sandwiched" between Israel and Jordan, this is not likely to be accepted by Israel, nor is the PLO majority happy with it. It would be difficult to expect this new state voluntarily to accept total demilitarization, which would be necessary from the Israeli point of view. It would create a great many problems of irredentism; it would be inherently unstable; and the refugee problem could not be resolved within the geographic, economic, and political constraints of such a state. It is not likely that the PLO would be able to govern a territory landlocked between its two most mortal enemies. As a rule, the Israeli arguments that such a state would be a threat to regional stability seem well taken and it is fair to argue that the so-called conservative Arab forces see it as such as well. Thus, it would be fair to conclude that very few relevant countries are really interested in making scenario B-2 a reality.

To a certain extent, the most popular solution has been that based on scenario B-3, namely, the Jordanian-Palestinian federation under Jordanian domination. Many Israelis believe that if Israel is to give up territories in the West Bank, they should be returned to Jordan under some Jordanian-Palestinian arrangement; this is the explicit official policy of the Israeli Labor Party, which is quite likely to win the next Israeli election. This scheme has a great many attractions in the short run; however, we are talking here about the long run. We must recognize that such a federation under Jordanian domination would really mean minority rule: the Palestinians have already attained a majority in the East Bank and the Palestinian population in the West Bank and Gaza is about seventy percent of the total population. The Palestinian element is becoming increasingly politicized, and it is more highly educated and technologically sophisticated than the ruling Bedouin element in Jordan. In addition to that, Jordan seems reluctant at this particular point to join in the peace process even under relatively generous terms for itself. Jordan has achieved legitimacy, respectability, prosperity, and a rather popular role in inter-Arab relations, certainly far more so than ever before, partially for having accepted the Rabat resolutions (which amounted to renouncing something that the kingdom never really had a chance to recover), and for having condemned the Egyptian-Israeli treaty. The role of the PLO, or generally speaking, the large half-million or so strong Palestinian community in Lebanon that is the backbone of the Palestinian movement in such an arrangement, is also very unclear. How would they get along with the Jordanian regime, what kind of presence would they have in the East Bank or in the West Bank? If such a role would not be satisfactory, are we not back to a variety of scenarios subsumed under C in our classification? Is peace likely to be stable and survive for a long period of time in a scheme which really runs counter to the trends of demography and sociology?

Nevertheless, this may be an acceptable starting point for a historical process that seems to be highly probable in the long-run: the largest single Palestinian community, the one in the East Bank, is becoming the majority there. Thus, any solution to the Palestinian problem that involves establishing a Palestinian entity must include in some way eighty percent of "historical" Palestine, the area having the largest single Palestinian community in the world. It is possible that under such a scheme, the beginnings of a process of Palestinization of Jordan will start, which brings us right away to scenario B-4.

This scenario could and would (obviously) become possible only in the framework of a comprehensive peace and a new regional order. This is the idea of the Palestinian-Jordanian federation, this time under Palestinian domination. The elements supporting the Hashemite regime would be reduced to the role of a minority, reflecting accurately ongoing demographic and sociological trends. To this Palestinized East Bank center, we can see the annexation of the West Bank and Gaza strip in a way which would allow the kind of latitude that cannot be created in a West Bank and Gaza state.

Such latitude will permit, for instance, the introduction of the principle of shared-rule, which is really a variation of federalism, bringing about, to give one key example, an Israeli-Palestinian condominium on the West Bank and the Gaza strip. This must be demilitarized. If the new Palestinian entity will be centered on the East Bank then the demilitarization of the West Bank is workable inasmuch as it involves less than ten percent of the total area involved and not the entire territory of the Palestinian entity. Of course, the shared-rule principle will allow Israel to have free access to the Holy Places, and the right to purchase and settle land offered voluntarily, with the consent of the local population. It will also allow Israel to protect its security interests by having a joint presence, with the Palestinians overseeing and enforcing the necessary demilitarization. However, the shared-rule principle will always have to take into account the realities of the situation, namely, that the majority of the population is Palestinian Arab, and its affairs will have to be run by Palestinian Arabs in cooperation with the Palestinian community on the East Bank where sovereignty will not be restricted. This will also enable the larger entity not only to play a central role as a respected actor in the regional politics, but also to resolve the refugee problem by providing territories for resettlement.

The Palestinization of Jordan is a long-run historical process likely to take place in any case; thus, the question to a large extent is simply this—are we going to be passive onlookers at the unfolding of a major historical process that, if not inevitable (nothing is *really* inevitable in politics), is highly likely to risk its attendant threat to peace, or are we going to harness the forces of history in a creative way in order to create a peaceful and stable solution to the problem? This requires abandoning a variety of old clichés such as the importance of the Hashemite regime for the stability of the region, the peace-loving nature of the Hashemite regime, the moderate pro-Western orientation and historical alliance between the Hashemite regime on the one hand and the United States and Britain (and tacitly Israel), and so on and so forth. However, none of this seems convincing at the moment and in the long-run none of this is bound to alter the "natural course of history." The problem of upheavals in the short-run that this historical process might create is very serious and several important political factors may be reluctant to pursue such a course of action in the short run, but it seems to me that in the long run, granted the national consensus prevailing both in Israel and the Arab countries, only a principle of shared-rule can resolve the problem of the Palestinians on the West Bank and Gaza. Such a principle of shared-rule will not be applicable unless the Palestinian entity is a large one that includes the East Bank of the Jordan. To the extent that we are able to point to long-term developments in the Palestinian question at all, this leads us to expect that the Palestinization of the Jordan River will be accomplished one way or another. If this is the case, then a solution or a scenario along the lines of scenario B-4 would not be at all improbable; it is a scenario with many attractive features. The mechanics of the shared-rule arrangement have already been addressed and some scholars and numerous publications of the Jerusalem Institute for Federal Studies refer to this quite explicitly and help us on this point.[2]

However, the question is not one of mechanics or governmental technology[3] but rather one of creating a new political order congruent with the basic trends in Middle Eastern politics, sociology, and demography. It is relatively easy to argue about the long run; at this particular moment, there is no answer to this. However, the object of this particular exercise in thinking is not to propose short-term techniques, to reconcile forces now unwilling to acquiesce in such historical processes, or to put together a coalition likely to advance a given scenario, but rather to bring before us images of possible futures. If this image looks probable as well as attractive e-nough, then the politically-oriented technical questions will be discussed in their own right.

Whatever basic scenario we adopt, it is highly likely that some component of scenario C will survive for a very long time to come. It is nearly certain that radical Palestinian organizations will continue to operate within the Arab world, partially controlled and manipulated by outside forces, thus keeping the Palestinian issue alive. The question is, to what extent will this happen and which Arab countries will support it? It is important to realize that in a conflict of such magnitude, resolving the issue to the total satisfaction of all Palestinians is well nigh impossible. Therefore, there will always be a reservoir of refugees, of the discontented, and of radicals, supported by those interested in destabilizing the status quo, whatever it may be in terms of the Palestinians. The question is how to minimize the number and the influence of such disruptive forces within Palestinian organizations and, more to the point, within the various Arab countries. Thus, whether we conceive of some eventual solution as B-1, B-2, or B-3 (with the exclusion of the PLO), it is highly likely that there will be a rather visible coalition of Arab forces manipulating the Palestinians, who will have every cause to cooperate. Only with the implementation of B-4, in which there will be a very real offer of power to Palestinians in a fairly large state, are the Palestinian organizations highly likely to split, in a contest for the capture of political primacy on the East Bank. Even if such is the case, the minority sections are likely to split and challenge that status quo. Possibly, some of them will continue to fight in the East Bank, whereas others will continue to struggle from outside, supported by Arab factions. This is an inescapable conclusion, which, however, ought not to discourage us. It merely means that the basic nature of the system will not change, and it is not likely that in the near future the Palestinian issue is going to disappear from the Middle Eastern political scene.

Of course, this whole discussion of scenarios holds a number of important variables constant. No major change is expected in the pattern of relations between the superpowers. Incremental gains by one superpower or another will appear to take place from time to time, but the basic relationship based on a balance of power will endure for the time period here specified. It is assumed that while in some respects there will be important changes in the relations between Arabs and Israel, it is not expected that the Arab-Israeli conflict will somehow just go away.[4] However, as Janice Stein persuasively argues, "peace is not the absence of conflict, it is rather a change in the rules for managing conflict."[5] Peace, therefore, is but an advanced state in the process of reducing and transforming conflict. It does not, however, have to be a utopian resolution at all. It is expected that the idea of *"antagonistic collaboration"*—cooperation within conflict—will become very important in regional politics. A basic conflict of ideologies and national movements will not disappear. Cooperation with the antagonists will become possible as the rules of the game change and as considerations of *raison d'état* in the Arab world become ever more important (as was argued by numerous scholars in the late 1970s).[6] It is also assumed that no basic pattern of change will be discernable in terms of armaments technology, such as the introduction of nuclear weaponry, that might change the balance of power in the region.

A further assumption is that there will be changes in the leadership of the various Middle Eastern political actors. However, these will be incremental changes, refining and further developing present policies without bringing about a decisive break with the policies advocated by the present main protagonists.

In the final analysis the problem is one of controlled imagination That is, we must remain within the constraints of reality and of viability, but at the same time we must exercise our imagination and creativity if our thinking about the future is to be useful at all. What is and what is not going to be viable during the last two decades of the twentieth century is not at all clear; the Sadat initiative and various other events of such magnitude have proven this fact. Our sense of the viable must therefore remain elastic and flexible. Such controlled imagination may help us to foresee probable trends without violating unduly the idea of practicality and without losing sight of political reality. Within this framework, it is obvious that we cannot expect a change in the basic Palestinian pattern. Palestinians will continue to be an important element, as they symbolically represent an issue that demands resolution. But their passivity is best manifest in the idea that what is important in the Middle East politics is not so much the *Palestinians* but the *Palestinian issue*, that is, it is not the Palestinians who must be satisfied but the Palestinian issue that must be resolved to the satisfaction of the other Arab countries. Within this context, it is important to note that those of us who expect a so-called internal solution based on local Palestinian leadership of the West Bank and Gaza may be missing the point. Rather, the whole idea of a solution to the Palestinian problem must be a broad one, involving Jordan and a broad coalition of Arab forces.

The final point to be made, a bit on the artistic side, is the main paradox in analyzing Palestinian affairs: namely, that the importance of the Palestinians increases in proportion to the chances of the peace process dominating Middle East politics. When the guns fall silent and diplomacy resumes, the Palestinian question is important for the resolution of the Arab-Israeli conflict and therefore the Palestinians become also, at least to some extent, important. When diplomacy falls silent and the guns speak out loud, the Palestinians (as we have seen in 1973) become relatively unimportant. This is an important paradox of Middle East politics that the Palestinians have never understood correctly. Only if peace efforts fail and the Arab-Israeli rivalry culminates in the outburst of massive armed conflict can the Palestinian issue be expected to recede almost totally into the background. Such a deterioration contradicts one of the main assumptions entertained in this essay. Still, the discernible paradoxes of the past and present should sensitize us to the possible paradoxes of the future. The past paradoxes had to do mostly with the Palestinians and the fortunes of war. The future we hope will reveal to them the fortunes of peace.

## NOTES

1. Nazli Choucri, "Forecasting International Relations: Problems and Prospects," *International Interactions*, 1:2 (1974), quoted in Raymond Cohen and Saul Friedlander, "A Taxonomy of Short-Term Forecasting Problems in International Relations," The Hebrew University of Jerusalem, mimeo (1975), p. 3. For an application of this approach in our context, see Gabriel Ben-Dor, "Conflict-Reduction Through Negative Peace: Exploring the Future of the Arab-Israeli Conflict," in N. Oren (ed.), *The Termination of*

*Wars* (forthcoming, The Leonard Davis Institute for International Relations, The Hebrew University of Jerusalem).

2. See also, the collection of articles and essays based on a conference explaining the shared-role principle in Daniel J. Elazar (ed.), *Self-Rule/Shared Rule: Federal Solutions to the Middle East Conflict* (Turtledove Press, 1979).

3. This question is explained to a certain extent in my forthcoming "Federalism and the Arab-Israeli Conflict: Prospects and Patterns."

4. These constant variables are discussed in detail in Ben-Dor, "Conflict Reduction Through Negative Peace."

5. Janice Stein, "War Termination and Conflict Reduction or How Wars Should End," *Jerusalem Journal of International Relations*, Fall 1975, p. 16.

6. For instance, Fouad Ajami, "The End of Pan-Arabism," *Foreign Affairs*, January 1979.

### APPENDIX

The multi-state character of the Palestinians is clearly demonstrated in the tables of their geographic distribution. The Palestinian estimate for 1970 is based on Nabil Shaath, "High Level Palestinian Manpower," *Journal of Palestine Studies*, I (1972), p. 81, as slightly amended in Ibrahim Abu Lughod, "Educating a Community in Exile: The Palestinian Experience," *Journal of Palestine Studies*, II (1973), p. 97. The Israeli estimate is based on the official figures of the Israeli Foreign Ministry (1974).

| | Palestinian Estimate (1970) | | Israeli Estimate (1974) |
|---|---|---|---|
| Jordan | | | |
| East Bank | 900,000 | | 600,000 |
| West Bank | 670,000 | | 650,000 |
| Gaza | 364,000 | | 400,000 |
| Israel | 340,000 | | 530,000 |
| Lebanon | 240,000 | | 150,000 |
| Syria | 180,000 | | 130,000 |
| Kuwait | 140,000 | | 150,000 |
| Egypt | 33,000 | | |
| Iraq | 14,000 | Other Arab | |
| Persian Gulf | 15,000 | Countries | 130,000 |
| Libya | 5,000 | | |
| Saudi Arabia | 20,000 | | |
| United States | 1,000 | | |
| Latin America | 5,000 | Western | |
| West Germany | 15,000 | Countries | 150,000 |

# 11

# The Genesis of the
# Carter Doctrine

*R. K. Ramazani*

ON THE EVE of 23 January 1980, President Carter included in
his State of the Union Address to the Congress a plan for the American defense of the Persian Gulf region. The relevant passage of
the President's message, known as the "Carter Doctrine," said:

Let our position be absolutely clear: An attempt by any outside force to
gain control of the Persian Gulf region will be regarded as an assault on
the vital interests of the United States. It will be repelled by use of any
means necessary, including military force.

It is generally believed that the twin crises in Iran and Afghanistan produced the President's commitment, and the address described these crises in the following terms: "The crises in Iran and
Afghanistan have dramatized a very important lesson: our dependence on foreign oil is a clear and present danger to our national security."

At a more general level, however, the President identified three
basic developments that had helped shape "American challenges."
These were: the projection of Soviet military power beyond its own
borders; the overwhelming dependence of the industrial democracies on oil supplies from the Middle East; and the pressure of social, religious, economic, and political change in many nations of
the developing world as exemplified by the revolution in Iran. Nevertheless, the President acknowledged that all three developments
were then focused on "one troubled area of the world." That was
obviously the Persian Gulf region. Hence, the immediate crises
in Iran and Afghanistan must have been uppermost in his mind.

Yet, the question remains: which of these two crises had a greater impact on the President's decision to make such a pledge? The

fact that his statement occurred in the wake of the Soviet invasion of Afghanistan (27 December 1979) rather than the Iranian seizure of the American Embassy in Teheran (4 November 1979) together with the administration's repeated coupling of the Soviet invasion and the security of the Persian Gulf, might leave the impression that of the two crises, it was the Soviet invasion of Afghanistan that probably loomed larger in the decision to commit American forces to the defense of the Gulf region. The President's own message linked the two by stating that the Persian Gulf region was threatened by the presence of Soviet troops in Afghanistan. This essay, however, will argue that the Iranian revolution in general and the hostage crisis in particular contributed more to the President's pledge than the Soviet invasion of Afghanistan. To put it differently, the invasion should be considered as the secondary rather than the primary reason for the American commitment to the defense of the Persian Gulf region.

## Iran's Strategic Significance

Iran had always been accorded a greater strategic significance than Afghanistan in the calculation of American interests in the Middle East before the outbreak of the two crises. The Second World War brought some 40,000 troops (the Persian Gulf Command) into Iran to assist the Soviet Union in the war against Germany. The closure of the Turkish Straits and the relative inadequacy of Murmansk and Vladivostok made Iran the ideal route for furnishing American military supplies to the Soviet Union. President Franklin D. Roosevelt's designation of Iran as "the Bridge to Victory" at the time was a clear acknowledgment of its strategic importance.

Yet, even during the war, the strategic significance of Iran to the United States and other industrial democracies derived from more constant factors than the mere exigencies of the war. As compared with Afghanistan, Iran was a major oil-producing state; was larger in both territory and population; was more advanced socially and economically; was located directly on the Persian Gulf where the increasing American oil interests in Saudi Arabia were at stake and on the strategic Strait of Hormuz through which the bulk of the Gulf oil to the non-Communist world had to flow.

The greater wartime strategic importance of Iran rather than Afghanistan to the industrial democracies has been reflected in peace-time as well. The same constant factors underpinned Iran's basic strategic importance, except that, first, the events of the Cold War and then Detente increased Iran's value to the Western world. With the onset of the Cold War, the United States sought to create a pro-Western alliance system in the Middle East as a means of containing the extension of Soviet power southward. The American concern focused on what Secretary Dulles called the "Northern Tier," which included Iran, Turkey, and Pakistan, and, initially, Iraq, but not Afghanistan, despite its long borders with the Soviet Union. As early as 1931, the Soviet Union had managed to sign a treaty of "Neutrality and Non-aggression" with Afghanistan. This historic commitment of Afghanistan to a policy of non-alignment effectively placed that country outside the purview of an American-sponsored alliance system in the Middle East.

The Soviet Union saw to it that Afghanistan's commitment to a non-alignment policy would continue. In 1955, when the pro-Western Baghdad Pact alliance took final shape with the accession of Iran, the Soviet Union took the initiative to extend its 1931 treaty with Afghanistan. Afghanistan was receptive to the Soviet overtures primarily because of its age-old conflict with Pakistan over "Pushtunistan," and because the most natural access route of Afghanistan to the outside world ran through the Pakistani port of Karachi. In 1955, as in 1950, the interruption of the Afghan trade through that route made Soviet offers of transit rights over its own territory, together with generous offers of economic and technical aid, appear quite attractive. The United States sought throughout the Cold War to bolster the independence and genuine non-alignment of Afghanistan by means of economic and technical aid. However, the overall ties of Washington with Kabul never matched those of Moscow, just as those of Moscow with Teheran never compared with those of Washington.

This was even truer during the Detente era. The overall dependence of the United States on Persian Gulf oil supplies increased considerably and the American oil companies acquired forty percent interest in Iranian oil for the first time. The withdrawal of British forces from the area "east of Suez," including the Persian Gulf region, in 1971, added even more to the strategic significance of Iran. Iran was not only an oil-producing ally of the United States; it was also the only major Gulf nation to enjoy a preeminent position in the Gulf region and especially at the strategic Strait of Hormuz. Furthermore, it was the most populous, the strongest militarily, and the most advanced economic power in the entire region. As such, it was seen in Washington as the most logical country in the region to help maintain Western influence against the Soviet advance and simultaneously insure the uninterrupted flow of oil supplies to world markets. Chafing under the disastrous consequences of involvment in the war in Vietnam, the United States in effect accorded Iran the role of the "policeman" of the Gulf region under the Nixon Doctrine.

## The Security of the Persian Gulf

In the context of the great strategic significance of Iran to the United States in wartime, as in peacetime, and in the Cold War as in Detente, the traumatic effects of the Shah's downfall on Washington must be obvious. But to appreciate the impact of the Iranian Revolution on the evolution of the Carter Doctrine more fully, a distinction must be made between the events before and after the seizure of American hostages in Iran on 4 November 1979. The reason for this distinction is that the evolution of the American conception of security in the Persian Gulf region and the American military buildup surrounding it was quite different. I will take up the security conception first.

Before the seizure of the American Embassy in Teheran, the American conception in the Gulf region had begun to undergo a twofold change. During the Shah's regime, security had a relative degree of concreteness; it was confined to the rather clearly delineated geographic area of the Persian Gulf as a distinct arm of the Indian Ocean. To be sure, the Shah sought to expand the Iranian "security perimeter" into the Gulf of Oman and beyond (1972), but his ambitious pronouncements and even attempted military buildup had no visible effects on United States strategic thinking. The security of the Persian Gulf was perceived in Washington largely in terms of the semi-enclosed sea, oil fields, on and offshore installations, sea lanes, and, particularly, the navigable channels of the Strait of Hormuz.

However, during his visit to the Middle East, Secretary of Defense Harold Brown (9-19 February 1979) seemed to extend the American conception of regional security beyond the Persian Gulf area proper. He envisaged a sharp increase of American military supplies and economic aid to "pro-Western" governments *outside* the Gulf as well as within it, including Saudi Arabia, North Yemen, the Sudan, Egypt, Jordan, and Israel. The Camp David euphoria had not yet spent itself, despite the widespread opposition of the so-called steadfast Arab states, such as Syria and Iraq, and the alienation from this process of Jordan and Saudi Arabia as well.

After the Secretary's visit to the Middle East, national security advisor Zbigniew Brzezinski reportedly proposed to President Carter on 28 February that a "consultative security framework" be established in the region. That framework envisaged a "loosely constructed yet clearly cooperative arrangement among moderate states" of the region, except for Saudi Arabia, which would be marginally involved because of its "sensibilities regarding any association with Israel." Although the President's State of the Union Address subsequently spoke of a "cooperative security framework," it must have had an even wider and more ambiguous meaning than Brzezinski's earlier conception, because of events between February 1979 and January 1980.

What were these events? More important than the apparent expansion of the American concept of security beyond the geographic confines of the Persian Gulf proper after the fall of the Shah's regime, the earliest public indication of the American willingness to commit its own forces to the defense of the Gulf region. When Secretary Brown visited the Gulf (9-19 February 1979), there had been no public talk about any such commitment. Instead, the Secretary emphasized the American willingness to increase military and economic aid. But about a week after his return to the United States, he said in a major interview that the "protection of the oil flow from the Middle East is clearly a part of our vital interest . . . In protection of those interests we will take any action that is appropriate, including military force."

Thus, before the hostage crisis the American conception of security in the Persian Gulf region seemed to be undergoing a basic two-fold change. First, it had lost its previous geographic concreteness under the Nixon Doctrine. Even before the Shah's departure, the Bakhtiar government had committed itself to the reversal of Iran's role in the Persian Gulf; Iran would no longer act as the "policeman" of the region. And after the seizure of power by the revolutionary forces led by the Ayatollah Khomeini (11 February 1979), it was a foregone conclusion that far from acting as an American surrogate in the region, Iran might well play a destabilizing part in the area. In the absence of any other single Gulf state to fill the shoes of Iran, the United States cast about for a number of players under Brzezinski's "consultative security framework," from both within and outside the Gulf.

Second, the single most important tenet of the Nixon Doctrine seemed to be undergoing a dramatic change. The United States had avoided committing itself to the defense of any Third World region. Instead, it had sold vast amounts of military hardware to surrogates, like the Shah's regime, which purchased sophisticated weapons systems in order to protect the security of the Gulf. But after the seizure of power by the Khomeini revolutionary forces, and before the outbreak of the hostage crisis, the United States began to reconsider that position. As seen, Secretary Brown clearly indicated that the United States itself would defend the Gulf region even by military means, if necessary, a notion that was finally incorporated into the Carter Doctrine.

## Force Deployment

Besides the two-fold conceptual change in the American policy in the Persian Gulf, operationally, too, the signs of a changing American position were also visible before the outbreak of the hostage crisis and the Soviet invasion of Afghanistan. The United States began to build up its military forces in the region, upon the departure of the Shah and the emergence of the Khomeini regime.

This actually reflected the first concrete attempt to realize an old idea. Chafing under the impact of the disastrous war in Vietnam, President Nixon had said: "America did not and will not conceive all the plans, design all the programs, execute all the world decisions and undertake all the defense of the free nations of the world. We will help where it makes a real difference and is considered in our interest." Given the general tenet of the Nixon Doctrine that the United States would not commit troops and would instead provide arms to surrogate regional states to defend parallel American security interests in various regions of the world, this statement could leave the impression that outside central Europe, the United States would not commit its own troops.

As a matter of fact, however, as late as the 1960s, the idea of the so-called one-and-a-half wars was current in Pentagon circles. It meant that the United States must have the capability of fighting a small war in the Third World regions of Latin America, Africa, or the Middle East while waging a full scale conflict against the Soviet Union in Central Europe or northeast Asia. Obviously, not everywhere in the Third World could the United States rely on countries like Iran. The Shah's regime had been more than willing to undertake additional security responsibilities in the region, but that was exceptional. In most other settings, the worsening conditions made it seem advisable for the United States to anticipate "brushfire wars."

These conditions were, of course, different from one region of the Third World to another. But what seemed to characterize most of them was the increasing possibility of local wars that might threaten superpower confrontation and impair the prospects of detente. The strategic oil-rich Persian Gulf, for example, was hemmed in by three zones of repeated wars—the Middle East, South Asia, and East Africa. Two factors in particular seemed to induce the increase in regional armed conflict situations. These were the spread of nationalism among an increasing number of new nations and a rise in arms trade across Third World regions, with no major restraints on the part of the major arms suppliers and little restraint on the part of the arms recipients in using them.

Despite the apparent awareness of the trigger-happy conditions of the Third World, no major advance was made on the idea of one-and-a-half wars between the late 1960s and 1977, when the Carter Administration approved a plan for creating a 110,000-member Rapid Deployment Force (RDF). There must have been a variety of reasons for the failure to do so earlier. The American aversion to expansion of military power of any kind in the light of the searing experience in Vietnam must have had something to do with it. Professor Klaus Knorr has argued that the United States' underrating of Third World conflict situations was "culture-bound." Presumably, we unjustifiably projected the relative decline of violence in the Western world and Japan into Third World regions. While this might well be true in general, I believe that the energy crisis, especially in the wake of the Arab-Israeli war of 1973 and the accompanying explosion of oil prices, significantly contributed to the tendency to perceive the Third World challenge more in economic than security and political terms. Not until after the Iranian Revolution and the Soviet invasion of Afghanistan did the United States begin to prepare for "brushfire wars."

Whether for reasons of priority accorded to other military plans or for budgetary reasons, the original nine billion dollar RDF plan did not really get off the ground until after the Iranian Revolution, especially after the hostage crisis. But even before then, the United States began to build up its military forces in the Persian Gulf region. President Carter, for example strengthened United States naval forces in the Indian Ocean-Arabian Sea area in March 1979 by dispatching the 80,000-ton carrier Constellation and several escorting warships to those waters. And on 21-22 June, the Carter Administration decided to add a couple of destroyers to a small flagship and two destroyers, a force known as COMIDEASTFOR; to increase United States task force deployments in the Indian Ocean; to stage more routine "demonstration" visits into Arab countries; and to emphasize high-level contacts with Oman and the smaller shaykdoms of the Persian Gulf. Although these unprecedented moves were perceived with alarm, at least publicly, by American friends as well as others in the region, Washington regarded them as "modest and symbolic." The real point here is that even before the hostage crisis the American position had begun to change. The United States had started to flex its military muscle, whereas it had been reluctant to do so previously. The previous talk of the Carter Administration about the demilitarization of the Indian Ocean now appeared as a naive dream in the context of the turbulent Iranian Revolution.

## Potential Partners

These conceptual and operational changes in American policy in the Persian Gulf region were intensified under the impact of subsequent momentous events, starting with the seizure of the American Embassy in Teheran on 4 November 1979. To take up the conceptual side of changes first, Brzezinski's pre-hostage crisis notion of a "consultative security framework" was for all practical purposes rendered impracticable. As a matter of fact, one might well argue that it had not been such a practical idea to begin with. As mentioned, this notion was to involve American cooperation with an assortment of regional states including Egypt, North Yemen, the

Sudan, Jordan, Israel, and Saudi Arabia. The latter would be only associated with the framework because of its sensibilities regarding any overt tie to Israel. But even this proviso did not make the idea any more pragmatic. This overly optimistic formula hardly had a chance of seeing the light of day because the Camp David Accords had aroused almost universal opposition to American peace-making efforts. How anyone could have believed that such disappointed, if not angry, states as Saudi Arabia and Jordan would then cooperate with the United States in any major way to protect the security of the Persian Gulf region is difficult to say. Perhaps the habitual compartmentalization of the problems of the Middle East into those of the Arab-Israeli and the Persian Gulf zones had something to do with it.

In any event, if there had existed any real chance of cooperation between the United States and such regional countries, it dissipated after the signing of the Egyptian-Israeli peace treaty (26 March 1979). The outcry against the treaty exceeded even the Arab rage caused by the Camp David Accords. The treaty was perceived almost universally as a betrayal of the Arab cause by Egypt. The insistence of Washington and Cairo that the treaty did not constitute a "separate peace" with Israel fell on deaf ears as it, like the Camp David Accords, was seen as foreclosing any real chance for progress toward the fulfillment of Arab aspirations for Palestinian self-determination. The Saudi Arabian concern with the spillover effects of the Palestinian frustrations into the Gulf region was reflected in Oil Minister Zaki Yamani's warning that he would not be surprised if one day the Palestinians, out of a sense of desperation, sank oil supertankers in the Strait of Hormuz.

However slim the realistic prospects of the "consultative security framework" before the outbreak of the hostage crisis might have been, they grew even slimmer afterward because of the conjunction of three separate developments. The White House for the first time in the hostage crisis intimated the possibility of the American use of force against Iran on 20 November. In the afternoon of the same day, the Grand Mosque in Mecca had been seized, and the implied American threat of the use of force, under Article 51 of the United Nations Charter, in "self-defense" against Iran, was prompted by a statement attributed to the Ayatollah Khomeini that the American hostages might be tried as "spies." It is reasonable to speculate that in the rumor-ridden Third World, the news of this threat of American use of force and the crisis in Mecca in combination gave rise to the rumor that the United States and Israel had a hand in the attack on the Holy Mosque in Saudi Arabia. In turn, this rumor triggered the storming and burning of the American Embassy in Islamabad on 21 November.

These events intensified American security concerns in the Persian Gulf. Even before the departure of the Shah and the seizure of power by the Ayatollah Khomeini, the uprisings in Iran (beginning in earnest in January 1978) had increased the American concern with Saudi Arabian security and stability. Quite apart from the American desire to woo Saudi Arabia into a more cooperative posture in the peacemaking process, the unfolding of the Iranian Revolution had made a considerable impact on the unprecedented decision of the United States to commit itself to the sale of F-15 fighter planes to Saudi Arabia as well as Egypt and Israel (May 1978). The eventual fall of the Shah's regime, especially since it was perceived in Riyadh as a reflection of the failure of American policy, had prompted Secretary Brown to assure Saudi Arabia of American support. Whatever positive effects such assurances might or might not have had, the siege of the Grand Mosque intensified American concern with Saudi security and stability.

That concern might not have been as intense if, in fact, the two-week rebellious action in Saudi Arabia could have been merely blamed, as it was initially, on the radicalizing influence of the Ayatollah Khomeini. The pro-Khomeini demonstrations and the presence of some 50,000 Iranian pilgrims in Saudi Arabia at the time had no real connection with the uprising, which was not the work of a group of "fanatics interested only in religious issues." Apparently some "500 disciplined, heavily armed guerrillas intent on destabilizing Saudi Arabia were involved," about eighty percent of whom were Saudi Arabian nationals; the action had been planned for about six months. Secretary of Treasury Miller, who happened to be in Saudi Arabia at the time, denied that Shi'i Muslims had been among the dissidents, apparently reflecting the belief of Prince Nayef, the Saudi interior minister, who had said earlier that no "Iranian Shi'ites" had been involved in the mosque takeover. Whether or not it will prove to be true, as an anonymous Saudi official said to

Steven Rattner of the *New York Times*, that the rebellion was sponsored by "Russians to undermine the stability of Saudi Arabia," the magnitude, the advance planning, the arms, and, above all, the overwhelming involvement of Saudi nationals, all revealed dramatically the fragility of the leading oil-producing ally of the United States.

The Pakistani crisis also intensified American security concern in the region, although its greater impact was on the bilateral relations between the United States and Pakistan. The storming and burning of the United States Embassy, the attack on other American buildings elsewhere in Pakistan, the death of several Americans and Pakistanis, and particularly the slow response of the Pakistani government to the request of the American Ambassador for help to rescue some ninety persons trapped in the Embassy compound in a seven-hour siege appeared to reveal simmering anti-American sentiments that United States officials seemed to deny and forces hostile to American interests in the region seemed to exploit.

The long-standing strained relations between Washington and Islamabad over the reputed Pakistani nuclear weapons program hit a new low in the Pakistani government's failure to carry through its own promise of holding elections in November and returning civilian rule. But aside from these and other elements in the bilateral relations of the two countries, my own observations in Pakistan before the November crisis seemed to indicate a basic difference of views over the developments in neighboring Afghanistan. American officials seemed inclined to take a far more sanguine view of the Soviet designs in Pakistan. Long before the Soviet invasion of Afghanistan, however, Pakistani officials were alarmed. They had in their possession Afghan maps showing the red flag flying over not only disputed Pushtunistan but also Pakistani Baluchistan. In retrospect, it would seem that subsequent events proved the greater accuracy of the Pakistani estimate of the impending Soviet military intervention.

## The Buildup and Access to Installations

Operationally, too, the American military buildup increased by leaps and bounds after the outbreak of the hostage crisis and before the Soviet invasion of Afghanistan. The official American statements repeatedly disassociated the military buildup from the fate of American hostages, claiming only that the Iranian crisis had led the administration to begin "serious contingency planning" for intervening in a Persian Gulf war. We now know that this was only a partial truth, because after the tragic failure of the American rescue mission in Iran (24-25 April 1980), it was revealed that as early as 24 November 1979, the United States had begun to plan for such an adventure. The military buildup was envisaged probably as a means of finally accelerating the plans for a 110,000-member rapid deployment force, mentioned before, and launching the rescue mission when the President deemed it appropriate.

The military buildup was put into high gear after a decision was made on 4 December 1979. A Pentagon team left for Saudi Arabia, Oman, Somalia, and Kenya, led by Robert J. Murray, a Deputy Assistant Secretary for International Security Affairs, on 17 December 1979. Reports at first seemed to indicate that the United States team was to talk to various leaders in the region on access for American naval and air forces to military bases, including those in Saudi Arabia, but it was quickly revealed by State Department officials that the talks would involve "facilities" other than those in Saudi Arabia. With the nightmare of the seige of the Grand Mosque fresh in their memory, the Saudis went out of their way to emphasize that they would reject any request for bases or facilities in their country.

These decisions and moves after the outbreak of the hostage crisis revealed changes in the American strategy beyond the acceleration of the Rapid Deployment Force. Before the crisis, Brzezinski's formula had called for American cooperation with Egypt, North Yemen, the Sudan, Jordan, Israel, and Saudi Arabia, the latter only in the capacity of an associate. But after the crisis, it became clear that the United States had decided against seeking outposts in Egypt and Israel, while no search for Saudi bases or facilities seems to have been envisaged. But the United States had considered joint military procedures, such as joint exercises with Saudi and Egyptian forces. The main concern of the United States was to find air and naval sites to handle the expected increase in port calls by the naval carrier forces that would be on "virtually permanent station" in future in the Arabian Sea and the Indian Ocean.

The principal components of this search for new facilities and improvement of the older ones were five. First, Oman ranked as most important in needed facilities. During the Shah's regime, the two Strait countries had agreed (7 March 1974) to patrol the strategic Strait of Hormuz jointly, but the Iranian Revolution put an end to that arrangement with Oman. The United States was interested in the use of Omani airfields and ports, but the airfield on the island of Masirah, with its close proximity to the Strait of Hormuz and the interior of the Persian Gulf, was of particular interest. Second, the United States had already enjoyed for years access to port and airfield facilities at Mombasa (Kenya) but wished for further access. Third, although the existence of the former Soviet airbase and port in Berbera (Somalia) seemed to make things easier, the installation required extensive repairs. Fourth, the United States had also made use of Djibouti, a former French colony still run by the French, and wished to continue to do so. Fifth, and finally, there were plans to seek funds to enlarge the British-owned base at Diego Garcia in the Indian Ocean, despite its being over 2,000 miles from the Persian Gulf. The relative predictability of its use made it attractive, but the winds of change might well affect it, too.

While the Soviet naval buildup in the Indian Ocean had gone on for about a decade, only the day after the United States decided to plan for a future rescue mission in Iran did the Soviet Union plant a floating listening post in the strategic Strait of Hormuz. On 25 November 1979, a Soviet Navy ship, the 6,450-ton Taman, anchored in the middle of a four-mile slot of international waters, outside the twelve-mile territorial limits of Oman and Iran in the eastern end of the Strait of Hormuz, reportedly to monitor all traffic through the waterway.

## A Hierarchy of Causes

In the light of the foregoing discussions, there is no doubt that the Iranian Revolution was the primary cause in the evolution of the Carter Doctrine. The departure of the Shah from Iran (16 January 1979), the seizure of power by the Khomeini-led revolutionary forces (10-11 February 1979), the seizure of the American Embassy in Teheran (4 November 1979) and the implied American threat of the use of force against Iran, the rebellious seizure of the Grand Mosque in Mecca, and the storming and burning of the American Embassy in Islambad (20-21 November 1979), all contributed to basic changes in American strategy in the Persian Gulf region. These changes underpinned the President's pledge to defend the region by military means if necessary.

However, on balance, the events surrounding the takeover

of the United States Embassy in Teheran produced far greater effects on the Carter Doctrine. The taking of American hostages intensified efforts to build up the Rapid Deployment Force and simultaneously prepare for an eventual rescue mission in Iran. The attacks on the Grand Mosque in Mecca and the United States Embassy in Islamabad intensified the American concern for the security of the Persian Gulf region. The pre-hostage crisis notion of a "consultative security framework" found a different and more concrete expression after the crisis in the rejection of the idea of American outposts in Egypt and Israel, the confinement of cooperation to joint military exercises with Saudi Arabia and Egypt, and determined efforts for gaining access to new air and naval facilities and improving the old ones. All this was, of course, in tandem with the American naval buildup in the Arabian Sea—including two carrier battle groups of twenty-five ships, 150 warplanes, and, after the Carter Doctrine, a new 18,000-man Marine amphibious unit.

While the Iranian Revolution should be considered as the *primary* cause of the Carter Doctrine, the Soviet invasion of Afghanistan also contributed to the eventual pledge of the President. The invasion was more than a rationale for the President to do what he would have done anyway. This is why I suggest that the Soviet invasion of Afghanistan should be regarded as the *secondary cause* of the Doctrine. No matter how serious the impact of the events prior to the invasion, the blatant Soviet aggression against a Third World nation for the first time since the Soviet withdrawal of Red Army forces from Iran in 1946 was clearly an unprecedented challenge. It was condemned by all Muslim states and the overwhelming majority of other nations. While it is impossible to disregard American domestic political considerations in an election year, it would be unfair to attribute merely political motives to the President's pledge on the alleged grounds that he "had to do something." As already noted, the deepening American security concern in the Persian Gulf region prior to the Soviet invasion of Afghanistan had been accompanied by accelerated efforts to realize the old idea of RDF.

Furthermore, the Soviet invasion of Afghanistan was in violation of a tacit postwar understanding between the United States and the Soviet Union. As noted previously, the United States had been satisfied all along with the status of Afghanistan as a non-aligned independent Northern Tier state. Afghanistan had not been included in the American-sponsored alliance in the region, but the postwar American economic and technical aid had been intended to help Afghanistan withstand Soviet pressures and blandishments. Despite the rise of Marxist regimes, the United States had been satisfied with the historical role of Afghanistan as a "buffer" state before the Soviet invasion.

Finally, the Soviet invasion of Afghanistan expanded for the first time the American oil-supply security dilemma definitively beyond the Persian Gulf region proper into South Asia. To be sure, the storming of the United States Embassy in Islamabad had elicited American concern, but its effect, as seen, was limited to the bilateral relations of the two countries. It further aggravated the long-standing strained relations between Washington and Islamabad. But the occupation of Afghanistan by some 80,000 Soviet troops not only brought the potential Soviet menace to the borders of Pakistan and closer than ever to the strategic Strait of Hormuz, but also caused the flow of many hundreds of thousands of refugees from Afghanistan into Pakistan.

## The Ensuing Debate

The implications and evaluations of the Carter Doctrine are beyond the scope of this study. The policy elite and the public seem to be divided between fervent supporters and ardent opponents of the Doctrine, of American military buildup, and of related issues, such as the draft. The division perhaps deepened after the failure of the American rescue mission in Iran. To the opponents of the Doctrine at least, that failure was a concrete indication of the difficulties of undertaking effective military operations in a region some 10,000 miles from the United States, and in an area where the Soviet military enjoys the advantages of geographic proximity.

But before the rescue mission, American public opinion had responded favorably to the President's pledge. A *Washington Post* poll conducted between 23 January 1980, the night of the President's State of the Union Address, through 28 January, suggested that some fifty-two percent of those interviewed agreed that "the United States should take all the steps, including the use of force if necessary, to insure that we have an adequate supply of oil from the Middle East." About thirty-eight percent disagreed, and ten percent expressed no opinion.

My own view of the Carter Doctrine is that the American military buildup is necessary, but not a sufficient instrument of American foreign policy in the region. It is necessary because force must be matched by counterforce. It is insufficient because military force must support rather than replace diplomacy. The Carter Doctrine can be made effective, I believe, if it is in practice transformed from a unilateral statement of American purpose and pledge to a multilateral cooperative plan of action. That is not an easy task. It will require us to persuade our European allies to forge with us a common conception of the nature of the threat and a common strategy to combat it. Above all, the United States will need to convince the regional states that its military buildup in the area is not intended for use against them. Rather, it is to defend their independence and insure the uninterrupted flow of their oil supplies, which, we believe, are goals in keeping with the protection of the vital interests of the United States and other industrial democracies. This is a fundamental challenge to American statescraft for years to come because, as Secretary of Defense Harold Brown in a testimony to the Senate Armed Forces Committee rightly said, the "President's Doctrine" depends upon "support from the people of the area."

# 12
# Comments on Turkey

*Nuri Eren*

IN THIS ESSAY, I have deliberately tried to be freely commentative. I believe that by providing some unexpurgated insight into the thoughts and emotions that underlie Turkish actions and developments, I might be more useful than were I merely to add to the scores of analytical studies on Turkish affairs.

## Cyprus

Over the last two decades, Cyprus has stood above all the other problems that have plagued Turkey, and deserves special attention. It has been the one major national concern that has not caused domestic differences. On the contrary, it has remained the one issue around which the warring political parties have united. The Cyprus problem has at times caused further complications in Turkey's foreign relations, and has drained Turkey's sparse foreign assets. But the island's strategic indispensability made all these troubles worth their while.

Cypriot independence was and has remained synthetic. The island is populated by Muslim Turks who consider themselves Turks affiliated to Turkey, and Christian Greeks affiliated to Greece. None acknowledge any distinct Cypriot identity. Independence came about as a political accommodation between Turkey, Greece, and Great Britain. The struggle started with the Greeks on the island, who comprise eighty percent of the population, and who desired union with Greece.

In the Aegean, Turkey's western coastline is ringed by a chain of islands many of them near her territorial waters. Once owned by the Ottomans, the islands were taken over by Italy during Turkey's debacle in the Balkan Wars. In the Second World War, they kept Turkey bottled off from the Mediterranean, and at the end of the war, both the Germans and the Allies offered to return them to Turkey. But the Italians, in order to forestall Turkish claims, had driven all the Turks away. Turkey accepted the choice of the population and ceded them to Greece, because she viewed her strategic liens with Greece as inalienable.

The Second World War reasserted the local position of Cyprus in the strategy of the eastern Mediterranean and confirmed Turkey's historic feeling about the island's crucial role: Cyprus under the British flag kept Turkey's sea routes open to the West. In the light of this experience, annexation of Cyprus to the chain of Greek islands surrounding the Turkish shores could be strategically disastrous for Turkey's safety. As a result, the Greek call for annexation was countered by the Turkish call for division between the two communities.

Neither solution being acceptable to the parties, independence under Turkish-Greek-British tutelage was seen as the only alternative. The two communities had lived together in ethnic harmony for five hundred years. Turkey and Greece were close allies. Furthermore, extensive public and private help during the war to the ravaged Greeks had promoted friendly sentiments between mainland Greeks and mainland Turks. Under these conditions, the complicated checks and balances in the Cypriot constitution appeared workable. None of the three founders reckoned on the heady wine of independence and on excesses, which could ferment on political ambitions.

The London and Zurich Agreements that created Cyprus were underpinned by the understanding that the Republic of Cyprus would be a condominium between Greece and Turkey, with Britain as an outside partner. It was never meant to create a distinct Cypriot nationality. Neither the Cypriot Greeks nor the Cypriot Turks desired it, and this aspect of the political entity was underwritten by the Constitution. The Turks and the Greeks were accorded their communal chambers with a veto over all vital affairs of state, such as foreign affairs, defense, and security. A Greek president was balanced by a Turkish vice-president. The army would be composed sixty percent of Greeks and forty percent of Turks. Separate communal majorities were required for taxation, education, religion, cultural affairs, personal status; and community taxes were within the jurisdiction of the group. The agreement was satisfactory to Turkey and Greece. Both had achieved their irreducible minimums, and their overriding national interests did not allow for continued strife between the two communities. In fact, the Turkish community's desire for partition and the Greek objective of annexation were forbidden under a Treaty of Guarantee as well as by the Constitution of the Republic. The Constitution declared that "integral or partial union of Cyprus with any other State or a separatist independence is excluded." Those injunctions were reinforced by Article 4 of the Treaty of Guarantee, which endowed the three founders of the Republic—Greece, Turkey, and Great Britain—with the right to take action against infringement of this status.

None of the parties had foreseen how Makarios would run away with independence. Once in the saddle and securely fastened by membership in the United Nations, he undertook to abrogate all the inhibitions placed on independent action. On 30 November 1963, he proposed thirteen changes that he euphemistically called "Suggested Measures to Facilitate the Smooth Functioning of the State and Remove Certain Causes of Inter-Communal Friction." The suggestions aimed to destroy the bi-national structure of the state, enabling the Greek majority to opt for annexation to Greece. On 1 January 1974, he announced his intention to abrogate the founding treaties. Cypriot Greek guerillas moved against Turkish villages, and Turkey intervened by bombing Greek positions. Twenty-five thousand Turks were evicted from their lands or ran away to Turkish enclaves to save their lives.

Makarios could not carry out his plan, but he abolished the Constitution, and the two communities became separated and inimical to one another—as they are to this day. President Johnson, having prevented Turkey's corrective action authorized by the founding Agreements, sought to end the myth of a state without a nation. Acheson and Ball were dispatched with plans for the partition of the island between the two communities. But American diplomacy failed to generate the thrust the plan needed, and Makarios, whose presidency would come to an end, stood as the principal objector to the plan.

The Greek governments were always more unhappy with Makarios than even the Turks. It was well-known that Makarios aimed at delivering Cyprus to Greece with the purpose of becoming its prime minister, in emulation of Archbishop Damaskinos, premier in the late 1940s. The military regime in Greece plotted his assassination. Operation Hermes 1970, Operation Apollo 1971, and

Operation Aphrodite 1974—all failed. But the opposition of the colonels to Makarios turned out to be disruptive of Turkish-Greek cooperation. In 1968, General Papadopoulos squelched the possibility of agreement when he demanded the annexation of the island from the Turkish Premier Demirel. Apparently, the colonels were seeking annexation instead of accommodation to bolster their dwindling support in the country.

An important aspect of the Cyprus dispute is the involvment of the United Nations. It started in March 1964, with the dispatch of a peace-keeping force to contain the civil war between the two communities. It gradually evolved into a forum for negotiation between the sides. Overall, it succeeded in preventing incidents between Greeks and Turks from developing into a civil war. But it has failed to generate and effect an agreement. On the contrary, it solidified differences and encouraged jingoistic inflexibilities. Makarios manipulated the United Nations with great skill. Falsely representing Cyprus as a child of colonialism, he gained the United Nations' sympathy. Masterfully inserting himself into the company of Nasser, Nehru, and Tito, he gained international stature. While condemning Western imperialists, he covertly allowed the Americans to use Cypriot bases whenever the need arose. It was a game that many other Third World leaders played, especially with gullible Americans, in which American confidence and cooperation were gained to enhance their own international status, and then eventually used to the detriment of Western interests.

Ninety-five percent of the members of the United Nations are plagued with problems of minorities demanding new and special rights, and Cyprus was presented as a case where a minority was seeking an equal partnership with the majority. To the membership of the United Nations such an eventuality would create a precedent that would undermine the unity of other states. As in the case of all United Nations disputes the particulars under discussion are of no interest and no consequence if the dispute can provide a precedent reflecting on the national scene elsewhere. On the basis of these facts, year after year, Makarios obtained automatic majorities against the Turkish side. Cleverly, he learned to play according to a third and equally potent United Nations reflex, namely, the negotiating game under the auspices of the United Nations.

The automatic support on which he could rely encouraged

him in his conviction that he would eventually win out. But he erred in believing that the United Nations could effect a solution in the face of Turkey's refusal. All his tactical successes, however, only led him to a strategic failure. His intransigence proved his undoing. It was a mistake that successful disputants in the United Nations make and, in the light of the Arab-Israeli issue and the South African example, is revealing itself more clearly. United Nations incursions into resolutions of disputes end up by fortifying the intransigence of the winners, failing to provide the atmosphere for accommodation that the resolution of any dispute requires.

To Makarios, the United Nations process was a cat and mouse game. With Turkey continually outvoted, he played the negotiating game as an exercise in perpetual procrastination. Blame also rests on Turkey for having allowed herself into the United Nations game. Cyprus was a problem between Greece and Turkey. The basic allegiance of the two communities are to Greece and Turkey. The communities cannot reach a definitive solution without Turkish and Greek acceptance, and Turkey, by ceding the primacy in the discussions to the two communities, gave Makarios the opportunity.

The communities engaged in the negotiating process seriously. By accepting the talks, the Turks evaded negating the United Nations and hoped that persistent airing of their cause would overcome automatic United Nations reflexes against their case. The Greeks on their part, with the United Nations overwhelmingly on their side, expected to nibble at the Turkish position until it would crumble. Both sides were wrong. Experience has proved that in nationalistic international disputes long periods of procrastination in effect become periods of incubation for violent eruption. On 15 July 1974, Makarios was overthrown by his own countryman Nikos Sampson. He seized power with the avowed purpose of effecting union with Greece. On 20 July Turkish troops landed on the island on the basis of the Treaty of Guarantee to prevent annexation.

The Turkish intervention brought about a demographic separation. The Greeks moved to the south and west, the Turks remained in the north and east. In 1963 and 1967, the Turks migrated. In 1974, the Greeks moved. The island became geographically divided, with the Turks holding forty percent of the land. The unitary state that Makarios had so intransigently pursued came permanently to an end.

The cat and mouse game that Makarios so skillfully and skeptically played changed its complexion. With the Turks holding the aces, the Greeks approached the negotiations more seriously. Under the auspices of the United Nations Special Representative, Makarios, leader of the Greek community, met Denktash, head of the Turkish community. In all the years of negotiation no rapprochement had been effected in the opposing purposes of the two communities.

The Turkish community sought a bi-zonal, bi-national federation, with clearly circumscribed authority for the federal government. The Greeks insisted on a unitary state with communal authority clearly limited by a strong federal government.

On 12 February 1977, under the chairmanship of United Nations Secretary General Kurt Waldheim, Makarios and Denktash met. They effected the first break in the deadlock. The agreement subsequently known as the "four point guidelines" provided for an independent, nonaligned, and bi-communal Federal Republic. Territorially, the Republic would be administered by each community in the light of economic viability, productivity, and land ownership. Although the guidelines provided for a federal solution in the ensuing negotiations, the Greek side began, once again, to drag its feet.

The inter-communal talks continued intermittently but no substantial progress was recorded. The Greek side never gave up its reliance on automatic United Nations majorities and the Greek lobby in the United States Congress. In the spring of 1979, the Secretary General of the United Nations pushed for another summit meeting between Kyprianou, who had succeeded Makarios as president, and Denktash, who had become President of the Federated Turkish Cypriot State. The Turkish community, despairing at the intransigence of the Greeks in February 1975, had unilaterally constituted the Turkish entity within the expected Federal State. On 19 May 1979 a ten-point agreement was reached, which incorporated the "four point agreement" effected with Makarios, and called for inter-communal talks to deal with all territorial and constitutional matters. Negotiations were resumed, but the Greeks, once again, could not bring themselves to espouse the bi-zonal, bi-national concept. They could not release themselves from their reliance on the General Assembly. In the talks they continued the verbal mastication, waiting year after year for another General Assembly resolution pressing the Turks. If the present frame continues, the Cyprus issue will be doomed to remain as a permanent item in the United Nations agenda.

As previously stated, the Republic of Cyprus is a state without a nation, and the dispute can only be resolved when the imperatives of this reality are met. Cyprus is a bone of contention between Turkey and Greece. In 1960 the two countries showed that they could compose their interests on the island. Turkey's mainly strategic interests were welded with Greece's mainly demographic requirements. The experience of the last twenty years revealed the weakness in the original agreement, and corrective developments beyond the joint control of the two partners ensued. Today the altered circumstances on the island allow for a much easier composition of the differences between the principal contestants. A geographic division between the two communities has been effected and the constitution of a federal state in which the equality of the partnership between the two communities could be indestructibly established has become much more feasible. But the two communities should not be expected to implement the change. The umbilical cords of the two communities are attached to their respective mainlands. The resolution of the dispute can only be effected by direct Turkish and Greek involvement. In fact, and unfortunately, in the last fifteen years Cyprus has grown into a fulcrum around which Turco-Greek relations evolve. Since both Turkish and Greek governments remain under the continued siege of opposition parties, the prospect of concerted effort to remove this cancerous wart in their relations does not appear promising, even though the strategic situation in Iran and Yugoslavia urgently requires of them a joint front. Hence, the initiative must come from their NATO allies. NATO should provide the umbrella under which they can get together for a final agreement. Camp David yielded an example of the way an outside party can provide the political shield behind which the two contestants can work out their differences.

## Turkey and Greece

Being on the direct line of the Soviet Union's thrust to the Mediterranean, Turkey and Greece require the closest cooperation both politically and militarily. But the Cyprus issue has poisoned them against each other, infecting even their relations with their NATO allies. In fact, not only the two governments' diplomatic stand but the two nations' stance toward the United States, and consequently toward the Western Alliance, has been affected by the ups and downs of the Cyprus controversy. The American embargo convinced the Turks that the United States favored Greece. The lifting of the embargo angered the Greeks, leading them to think that the United States was tilting against them. The net result of this has been the erosion of the wide sense of solidarity with the United States. Worst of all, the geo-political consensus in both countries, an element of strength in their domestic and international relations, was destroyed by yearnings for non-alignment or even a swing toward the Soviet Union.

I would like to repeat what I have previously written for the Atlantic Institute on Turco-Greek relations, which I believe reflects the general tone of opinion among thoughtful Turks and which I also believe is reciprocated by many Greeks.[1]

The Greek and Turkish peninsulae share a strategic unity imposed by the Aegean Sea. Even the Homeric struggles among the ancient Greek states, as well as the Greco-Persian wars, all ended with the inevitable reinforcement of this unity. Observed as it was under the Romans, Byzantines, and Ottomans, this unity procured a measure of peace for the region. Infringed upon, as it was in the nineteenth century by the growing hostility between Greece and Turkey, endless suffering befell both peoples. The two great statesmen of contemporary Turkey and Greece, Mustafa Ataturk and Eleutherios Venizelos, turned back from regional dissension, sealing their claim to greatness by reaching an agreement that reintroduced the concept of the inevitable unity of the Aegean region. Under the umbrella of this accommodation, Turkey and Greece relaxed in their domestic politics and waxed in their international relations.

Such "good neighbor" policies are not new to Aegean politics. The conquest of Istanbul by the Turks in 1453 ended the strangulation of the Greek Orthodox Church by the Byzantine emperors. Mehmet the Conqueror then accepted the coexistence of Islam and Christianity as a fundamental tenet of his state and reinvested the Greek Orthodox Church with authority over its flock. Indeed, in the Ottoman hierarchy, the Greek Orthodox Archbishop ranked next to the Grand Mufti. The Greek Orthodox community became an important component of the Ottoman polity. In practice, the Ottoman state existed as a commonwealth of many nations. Greek and Turk, Arab and Armenian, Bulgar, Serb, and Albanian intermingled without any sense of segregation. Government posts were open to those who could wield a pen. Greeks in active urban centers, and provided with better educational facilities by their Church, retained many posts in the bureaucracy. Romania, for many centuries, was run by Greek pashas.

The estrangement between Turks and Greeks came in the nineteenth century in the wake of the fires of freedom kindled by the French Revolution. The Greek separatist movement started in 1821 with open support by the major imperial powers of Europe. The revolt, in which even romantic nostalgia for the glories of ancient Greece was invoked to gain popular support, culminated in the establishment of Greece as an independent state in 1832.

Independence did not terminate the regional struggle, which continued with increased intensity. With the dismemberment of the Ottoman domain and its partition being a principal European objective, outside powers encouraged the Greeks in their dreams of resurrecting the Byzantine Empire. This "Megali idea" was fed by Greek annexation of the Ionian Islands in 1864, of Thessaly in 1881, of Epirus and Macedonia and many of the Aegean Islands from 1911 to 1913. This continuous extension to the north and into the Aegean developed Panhellenism into the most dynamic feature of Greek foreign policy. Possession of Istanbul appeared its ultimate goal. The mystique of the glories of ancient Greece, inspired by the teachings of history in all grades of the Greek schools, saturated Greek politics with nostalgic irredentism for Constantinople (even though Constantinople as Constantine's city was Roman rather than Greek).

The Megali idea reached its peak in the post-First World War Treaty of Sevres (1920), which accorded to Greece the whole of Thrace as well as western Anatolia. Fighting between Greek army units and Turkish resistance fighters occurred sporadically from 1919 to 1922, simultaneously with the domestic challenge to the Sultanate led by Ataturk. The treaty of Lausanne, negotiated in 1923, left to the Turks the territory obtained with the power of their arms. One of the great accomplishments of the new arrangement was the wholesale exchange of populations, terminating the millenial mixed existence of the two peoples in Anatolia and Greece, which had soured in the nineteenth century and become a major source of trouble. The Treaty of Lausanne established mutually acceptable frontiers in Thrace and a mutually beneficial balance in the Aegean.

In a statement before the Turkish Grand National Assembly in November 1931, Mustafa Kemal Ataturk stated that "the supreme interests of Turkey and Greece no longer oppose each other. It is proper that our two countries should find their security and force in a sincere mutual friendship." Eleutherios Venizelos, one of the great premiers of modern Greece, responded with a similar conviction. His state visit in 1930 was greeted with acclamations of genuine friendship both in Ankara and in Istanbul and resulted in a Treaty of Neutrality, Conciliation, and Arbitration. It contained a protocol that provided for a balance of power in the Aegean, committing the two nations to a partnership in the waters that bathed their shores. On 14 September 1933, the agreement was expanded into a formal pact that confirmed the inviolability of their common borders. Additionally, the agreement pledged them to greater collaboration in their international affairs.

As storms gathered over the horizons of Europe, the Turco-Greek rapprochement encouraged the other Balkan states to make a concerted effort to keep the thunder away from their borders. Turkish initiatives to commit them to joint defense failed, however, in the face of Bulgarian opposition to any large-scale multilateral agreement. Having thus no means for collective security, the Balkan states drifted one by one into war. With the conflict in full action, Turkey brought solace to German-occupied Greece by providing regular food shipments. At the same time, it helped to keep the flame of hope burning by permitting aid to flow to the Greek guerrillas from the Anatolian shores.

In the postwar period, this reservoir of goodwill led to close cooperation between the two countries under the benign umbrella of the Truman Doctrine. Their sense of common destiny was also enhanced by the Communist thrust in Greece and by Soviet demands on Turkey. The extension of the North Atlantic Treaty Organization to the Aegean sealed their bilateral relationship with a multilateral engagement.

Unfortunately, Cyprus has almost destroyed this legacy by bringing the two countries thrice to the brink of war, and juxtaposing them as enemies to the extent that both have come to seek to arm themselves against each other. None of the issues between them, including Cyprus, are insoluble. In fact, they lived with them in peace until aggravation in Cyprus divided them.

First, the question of the rights of the islands in the Aegean is at hand. The chain of islands that begin on the northeastern shores of the Aegean at the entrance of the Dardanelles and dot the whole of the Aegean coastline of Turkey, which never belonged to Greece, were allowed by Turkey to pass from Italian occupation to Greek annexation. Many of them, being within Turkish territorial waters, promoted a lively exchange between Greece and Turkey. In the 1970s, the Greeks sprung two surprises. On the basis of the Geneva Convention of 1958, of which they were a signatory and Turkey was not, they demanded continental shelf rights for each and every one of the islands. Indeed, the Geneva Convention conceded continental shelf rights similar to those of the land states with sea shores. But the convention's ruling applied to such cases as England and Japan, which were huge island states.

Otherwise, the same convention asserted that the continental shelf is the natural extension of the mainland, and islands on the shelf are simply promontories on the continental shelf. Denmark and Holland had run into a similar controversy. The World Court

had decided that the continental shelf rights of the mainland super-
sede the rights of the islands riding on the mainland's shelf. Turkey has indicated her willingness for an equitable arrangement, but
diplomatic talks have not yielded any results.

Simultaneously with the sea-bed issue, Greece sought to extend
the territorial waters of the islands to twelve miles. She has rested
her claim on the preliminary decisions of the Sea Conference, over-
looking the fact that the conference's decision called for exemptions
from the general principle in foreign islands that lie within the waters of mainland states. In 1938, an agreement between Turkey and
Italy, which the Greeks inherited when they were granted the islands, established a six-mile limit. This limit was dictated by the
circumstances of geography to allow Turkey free access to the open
sea. Even under this limit, open access to the Aegean is confined
to five outlets. If the limit is extended to twelve miles, Turkey's Aegean cities will lose free access to each other by sea. At the same time,
the whole western coastline of Turkey will be limited to only two
free outlets.

Air-traffic control in the Aegean has been another important
bone of contention. In 1952, Turkey agreed to allow Greece control of air-traffic over the Aegean. Greece had the tracking facilities, and the two countries were closely knit in the defense of the
area; the Turkish action was a natural consequence of the most
beneficial division of labor between the two.

During the Cyprus crisis, the Greek government, relying on
this agreement, closed the Aegean to international traffic. Air travel
between Greece and Turkey ceased. Flights from Rome and Libya
were forced on alternative routing over Bulgaria. Obviously the
1952 agreement rested on mutual confidence and was not meant
to concede to Greece control of the whole air space over the Aegean
up to the Turkish coastline. The Greek action also gave a forewarn-
ing of what could happen in the sea if the twelve-mile limit prevailed.
Turkey has asked to resume her air traffic control rights, which naturally should extend to midway into the Aegean Sea.

The fortification of the Greek Islands in the Aegean must be
accepted as the worst among these disputes. It disrupts the fundamental agreements on which Turkish-Greek relations have rested in
the last fifty years. In 1923, in Lausanne, Turkey ceded the Aegean
Islands to Greece on the condition that the islands remain demili-

tarized. The Treaty of Paris, which effected the transfer from Italian to Greek rule, confirmed demilitarization. This was an obligation that Greece never contested and honestly fulfilled. But after the Cyprus crisis, covert militarization began. On the basis of evidence offered by Turkey, Greece accepted the contravention. The implications of the infringement of the most solemn agreement on which their mutual confidence rests cannot be minimized. The validity or invalidity of this action can be argued, but its disastrous consequences in causing an erosion of the basic principles of their relationship cannot be disputed. It could easily escalate into a catastrophic race of nibbling at each other's rights, which, in turn, could promote jingoistic rivalries between political parties, destroying the whole edifice of Turco-Greek accommodation.

Fortunately, both governments, in spite of all the pressures from the different parties, have so far succeeded in containing the disputes and in keeping up the dialogue, even though they have not achieved any rapprochement in their divergences. The foregoing reveals that the Greek side has remained more stubbornly extreme in its position both in Cyprus and in the Aegean. From a long-range point of view, the most disturbing aspect of these developments rests on the loss of confidence the Greeks have incurred in Turkey. They have openly taken an inimical stand against Turkey in all international forums. They have threatened Western Germany when she helped Turkey financially. They have aggressively supported the American embargo, whereas the Turks never carried their quarrel with Greece to third parties.

This Greek effort to involve third parties in the dispute appeared to the Turks as evidence of the lack of true affinity in Greece for Turkey. Disputes between two partners cannot always be avoided, but if the partners introduce third parties in the dispute, then the intrinsic worth of the partnership becomes questionable. This conduct is not easily forgivable to President Karamanlis and Defense Minister Averoff, whose statesmanship is beyond question. The grave consequences of this Greek infraction of viable conduct between partners manifested itself in forcing Turkey to retaliation and preventing Greek return to the NATO military fold.

The forthcoming decade promises more strain in superpower relations. After Afghanistan the use of military force is no longer excluded. Yugoslavia without Tito, and Iran in anarchy, could easily prompt military action, exposing both Turkey and Greece to a much easier embrace by the Soviet bear. The game the Turks and the Greeks have been playing with each other could easily turn into tragedy if they persist in torpedoing each other. Unfortunately, the present circumstances of their domestic politics do not allow for a De Gaulle-like approach, which both need. But fortunately, their demands from each other are easily reconcilable. This is a situation in which NATO can act as a shield to bring about an agreement for which both parties are more or less subconsciously ready and which they cannot generate themselves because governments and parties are not strong enough for decisive action.

## Relations with the United States

Like other NATO countries, relations with the United States stand out in the first row of Turkey's international stance. In this essay, Turco-American relations appear as a third item. The reason for our choice is functional. In the last two decades preoccupation with Cyprus and consequently with Greece has dominated Turkey's foreign concerns to the extent of casting shadows of varying intensity on the whole of her international outlook.

The darkest shadow fell on the relations with the United States, ending the love affair between the two peoples, which had begun immediately after the Second World War. At first, they were pulled to each other by strategic necessity. They wedded together against Stalinist expansionism. At the same time, Turkey was caught in a wave of rapid democratization. The multi-party system, which became operative in 1950, worked effectively, providing an example to the rest of the world. To the delight of the American heart, the Turks were the first to volunteer to fight for democracy in Korea, where they displayed exceptional dedication. America found Turkey in every aspect of her national life akin to her own outlook. The Turks found in America the first and only Western ally whose friendship seemed different from the slippery, often deceptive, self-serving embraces of the others. The mutuality of interests that America appeared to recognize and support developed the *marriage de convenance* into a love affair.

In that period the United States responded benignly with military and economic assistance. The ties between the two countries were formalized in various treaties and agreements. Consonant with NATO policy, the Turkish army was modernized with American help. American bases were established as the most important observation posts against the Soviet Union. The quantitative extent of America's military and economic aid is as follows:

UNITED STATES AID TO TURKEY
(in millions of dollars)

|  | 1946-52 | 1953-61 | 1962-74 | 1975 | 1976 | 1977 | 1978 | 1979 | 1980 |
|---|---|---|---|---|---|---|---|---|---|
| Economic aid (total) | 237.3 | 1,093.0 | 1,485.5 | 4.4 | — | 0.2 | 0.8 | 50.3 | 198.0 |
| Military aid (total) | 325.6 | 1,587.6 | 2,554.1 | 109.1 | — | 125.0 | 175.4 | 175.0 | 252.0 |
| Total | 562.9 | 2,680.6 | 4,039.6 | 113.5 | — | 125.2 | 176.2 | 225.0 | 450.0 |

In the 1960s, United States aid policy shifted from grants to loans. At the same time, Turkish economic planning began. Aid became directed to financing projects called for by the development plan. Project orientation required closer cooperation between the donor and the receiver. Inevitably, controversies arose about economic goals—the Turks accusing the Americans of interfering in their domestic affairs; the Americans complaining that the plan was bent to serve partisan political ends overriding general national interests. But the Turkish economy was well under way, recording steadily an annual growth of seven percent of Gross National Product. Adequate flexibility provided channeling aid to balance-of-payments support. These differences between the donor and the receiver did not inhibit the continuation of friendly economic cooperation, which was disrupted by the embargo.

But while working together for economic development, the political atmosphere became increasingly polluted by the developments in Cyprus. In the summer of 1964, when Makarios abrogated the London-Zurich agreements and chased the Turks from the government and their homes, Turkey, in the face of Greek and British indifference, felt coerced to intervene militarily as authorized by the Founding Documents of the Republic. President Johnson intervened to stop Turkish action. The letter delivered to President Inonu in the late hours of 5 June must be quoted here because it is a most important document in Turco-American relations. Its shock on the Turkish national consciousness continues to govern not only Turco-American relations but the totality of Turkish domestic and foreign affairs. It initiated a doubt about the validity of America's friendship, which gradually eroded the national consensus on Turkey's affiliation to the West. The questions raised about Western alignment in international affairs gradually spilled over to Turkey's adherence to Western democracy and economy. Turkish political parties fractured to develop extreme wings, which have plagued Turkey's effective governance since 1973.

President Johnson, in language hardly becoming to an ally of long standing, bluntly stated:

> I am gravely concerned by the information which I have through Ambassador Hare from you and your Foreign Minister that the Turkish government is contemplating a decision to occupy by military force a portion of Cyprus . . . I hope you will understand that your NATO allies have not had a chance to consider whether they have an obligation to protect Turkey against the Soviet Union if Turkey takes a step which results in Soviet intervention.

In reference to the crisis, Premier Inonu wrote:

> With regard to the part of your message expressing doubts as to the obligation of the NATO allies to protect Turkey in case she becomes directly involved with the USSR as a result of an action in Cyprus, it gives me the impression that there exists between us a wide divergence of views as to the nature of the basic principles of the North Atlantic Treaty Alliance . . . Our understanding is that the North Atlantic Treaty imposes upon all member states an obligation to come forthwith to the assistance of any member which becomes the victim of aggression. The only point left to the discretion of the member states is the nature and the scale of their assistance. If NATO members should start discussing the right and wrong of the situation of a fellow member victim of Soviet aggression, whether this aggression was provoked or not and if the decision of whether they had an obligation to assist this member should be made to depend on the issue of such discussion, the very foundations of the Alliance would be shaken and it would lose its meaning.

The damage was done. The Turkish reaction was commensurate with the trust and affection originally placed in America. For the first time "Yankee Go Home" signs made their appearance on university campuses, and numerous anti-American incidents took place.

Into this atmosphere of soiled relations between the two countries, opium broke into the American market. In the high tension of their estranged relationship, Turks became responsible in American newspapers for all the drugs that circulated on the American streetcorners. Although United Nations sources indicated that not more than eight percent of the material on the market could be Turkish, the American government, eager to find a scapegoat, kept its finger pointed at Turkey. The Turkish government responded favorably, cutting production to seven provinces out of the forty-two that produced it. But America was not satisfied. Attorney General Mitchell threatened economic sanctions if Turkey did not end all production. A million and a half farmers would be placed in want but the Nixon Administration did not care. Turkey yielded under the most obvious pressure and prohibited opium production. The public in Turkey again saw this as another manifestation of self-seeking one-sidedness.

The puncture in Turco-American relations led to the embargo, and the embargo led the Turks to limit their relations with the United States. Even though the Turks retained their cool with NATO they began to seek other alternatives. It was like a family relationship in which the partners, though still basically bonded to each other, begin to probe for alternative friendships because of continued aggravations between them. The Turks continued to accept the Alliance as the principal strategic assurance but not with the blind, affectionate dedication with which they had embraced it. The Alliance was a marriage of convenience they could not do without at the moment but they felt free to search for supplementary support. Once the consensus on the West was eroded, naturally, many alternatives emerged.

## Relations with the Soviet Union

Much has been written about the relations between Turkey and the Soviet Union. As a general historical background, I will quote from a study I did for the Atlantic Institute:

In the wake of the First World War, the two revolutions in Turkey and in Russia opened up a completely new phase in the life of their peoples and appeared to end permanently their epic antagonism. Lenin's revolutionary Bolshevik state renounced Russia's traditional messianic compulsions for the south. Ataturk's Turkey turned her back on glories of the Ottomans to become a homogeneous republic dedicated to the status quo.

The Turko-Soviet Treaty of 1921 defined the border between the two countries as permanent. In the 1925 Treaty of Neutrality and Nonaggression, the two states pledged to respect each other's interests against third parties and not to interfere in each other's internal affairs. It thus provided the official frame of their new and close relationship. With no ambitions beyond their borders, the two revolutionary regimes found themselves natural allies in a semi-hostile world. Preoccupied by the preservation of their independence, Moscow and Ankara pursued converging policies in their international diplomacy.

Diplomatic togetherness was reinforced by economic cooperation. In the mid-1930s, the Soviets helped launch Turkey's industrialization with credits and technical expertise. In January 1934, Karl Radek, a celebrated spokesman of Soviet policy, wrote an article entitled "The Bases of Soviet Foreign Policy." He summarized the new relationship as follows: "It used to be an axiom of Tsarist policy that it should strive by every available means to gain possession of the Straits and an ice-free port on the Pacific. Not only have the Soviets refrained from seizing the Straits but from the very beginning they have tried to establish the most friendly relations with Turkey."

In October 1939, the historically unparalleled mutual trust between the two nations came to an abrupt end with Communist Russia's surprising revival of traditional Tsarist demands on the Turkish Straits. Then, in 1940, in exchange for joining an alliance with Germany, Italy, and Japan, the Soviet Union sought "the recognition of the area south of Batum and Baku in the direction of the Persian Gulf as the center of the aspirations of the Soviet Union." It also demanded "the guarantee of a base for light naval forces of the USSR on the Bosporus and the Dardanelles by means of a long-term lease." The same claims were later repeated by Stalin at all the Allied conferences from Teheran and Yalta to Potsdam. Most pointedly, they were made to Turkey on 15 March 1945, when Moscow denounced the Treaty of Neutrality and Nonaggression of 1925 and demanded a new treaty "in accord with the new situation." Moscow declared that the Turko-Soviet border in the east was no longer acceptable and sought to rectify the treaty by acquiring the Turkish provinces of Kars and Ardahan. But Stalin's expansionist ambitions met a determined refusal by Turkey, which was in turn supported by the United States in the context of the Truman Doctrine. The link with the Western defense system was formalized with Turkey's accession to NATO in October 1951.

The disenchantment with the Soviet Union continues to underscore the Turkish national consciousness, even though a normalization of Turco-Soviet relations has been achieved. Nevertheless, the continued attention paid to Turkey by the Soviet Union and the continued offers of economic aid led some Turks to upgrade relations with the Soviet Union as an alternative policy. Naturally, no Turk could rationally conceive of pulling Turkey out of the Western orbit and swinging her to the Soviet orbit. But there could be a middle ground. Non-alignment was in the vogue. Backed by such world figures as Nasser, Tito, and Nehru, it appeared a viable course for middle powers. But Turks soon realized that their particular geo-strategic, geo-political circumstances could not allow a neutral position. Turkey was posited on one of the four most important outlets of the Soviet Union. Of these four she was the most important because she held the gates to the Mediterranean, and to the Middle East where, not only because of oil but because of the unsettled domestic and international affairs of the region, the Soviet Union's greatest opportunity beckoned. Even the man in the street in Turkey realized that international circumstances might arise that would compel the Soviet Union to coerce Turkey to her side irrespective of Turkey's international status. Circumstances over which the Soviets had no control could force Moscow to undertake action against Turkey even if she did not want to.

Nevertheless this restraint did not inhibit Turkey from improving her relations with the Russians. Detente made it politically and psychologically easier. Moscow helped by coming up with large doses of industrial aid. She helped to build the first aluminum works, and she provided the technology and equipment for the second steel mill in the country. Between 1967 and 1979, the aid received from Russia added up to $650 million, which comprised one-third of all aid projects for Turkey for that period.

From the Turkish point of view, the rapprochement with Russia must be accepted as benign. It provides a more balanced position between the two superpowers and fits perfectly with the cardinal principle of Turkey's geo-strategic stance. The principle to which Turkey has adhered through the whole course of the Republic requires Turkey never to lend her geo-strategic position to an offensive against Russia. This was a principle enunciated by Ataturk and followed very strictly during the Second World War, in spite of all the risks it involved with Germany. Turkey adhered to NATO as a defensive alliance.

On several occasions she has proved her strict adherence to the defensive strategy of NATO by refusing any kind of participation in crises that involved the United States in the Middle East. It is a geo-strategic posture that aims to reassure the Soviet Union at the same time, keeping the Soviets from foraging freely in the area. Cyrus Vance appraised it rightly when, in testimony before the House International Relations Committee in 1978, he compared Turkey's relations with the Soviet Union to the Federal Republic of Germany's Ostpolitik. The economic aid obtained also served Turkey well in building up her infrastructure.

From the Russian point of view, it must appear a more than satisfactory development. It has come through disenchantment with the United States. It has shaken the confidence of the Turkish national consciousness in the Western Alliance. At the same time, it has softened Turkish opinion against cooperation with the Communist bloc. The Turkish domestic scene today, in which segments of opinion calling for non-alignment have gained much wider support, forcing governments to ease their ties with the West, indicates the long-range gain to Russia. Russian economic aid helps, also, to reinforce the public sector in Turkey's mixed economy. As the public sector's weight grows, the balance tilts against the private sector. Eventually, the present balanced nature of the economy might fall into jeopardy.

No doubt the rapprochement is a mutually beneficial accommodation, but as in the Ostpolitik of the Federal Republic of Germany, it carries the seeds of geo-political danger. If its pragmatic nature is overlooked and the daily benefits of cooperation are emphasized, it may lead to the loosening of the ties with the Western Alliance, triggering an ideological division of politics. A Russian-oriented faction could easily develop to challenge the diplomatic, as well as the domestic, stance of the country. The nucleus of this faction is now in operation.

## The Third World and the Islamic Group

Disenchantment with the West caused Turkey to look to the Third World as an alternative. But relations with India, Egypt, Algeria—the three leaders of the Third World—were cool if not unfriendly. Turkey could not espouse their militant anti-Westernism, and in the international forums they resented Turkey's pro-Western stance. They responded by raising Makarios's prestige and by following a belligerently anti-Turkish policy in Cyprus. The Turks bent naturally to the Arabs and the Islamic group. The Turkish constitution is rigidly secular, and association with a group of nations pursuing religious policies had to overcome constitutional concerns. In addition, the constitution had to counter the instinct of the Republic against mixing politics with religion. But the disenchantment with the United States was such that even the Republican People's Party, distinguished for its fervent dedication to secularism, espoused it. Since the 1970s, every government that came to power placed closer relations with the Islamic countries as one of the principal objectives in its foreign relations. In all the international forums, Turks began to trail the Muslim group and vote with the Arabs.

Now that the dust is settling on the emotional aspects of Turkey's foreign relations, Turkey's opinion gradually appears to understand how it deceived itself in its search for reliance on the Muslim group.

In wooing the Arabs and the other Muslim countries, Turkey's principal objective was to recruit their support on Cyprus. In the General Assembly vote of 1979 on Cyprus, not one single Muslim vote was recorded in favor of the Turkish stance. In all these years, the Muslim countries have remained adamant about an independent Cyprus under a unitary government, denying obstinately to the Turkish community its request for a federal status for preserving its Turkish-Muslim identity.

The oil moguls, also, have turned a cold shoulder to all of Turkey's pleas for financial help. In the fourteen billion dollars that Turkey has received from the world, there is not a single Arab or Muslim dollar. Recently the Islamic Bank announced a credit of fifteen million dollars for oil purchases. Turkey's annual oil bill is four billion dollars. When her economy almost halted and the OECD rushed to her help, Saudi Arabia had to be coaxed to contribute. Only after insistent solicitation from the Minister of Finance of the Federal Republic did she promise $250 million. The promise has not been realized yet. It is a strange phenomenon that reflects badly on the wisdom and foresight of Turkey's Arab neighbors and Muslim co-religionists.

Since Turkey espoused the Arab cause in the Arab-Israeli conflict, there is no reason for the Arabs to hold back. The Turkish barrier prohibits the Soviet Union from direct pressure and allows the Arabs to enjoy the fruits of Soviet aid as they please. For instance, while arming herself to the teeth with Soviet weapons, Iraq executes its Communist leaders with impunity.

The Gulf states and primarily Saudi Arabia, threatened by the leftist regimes of their Arab neighbors, are sustained by a Turkey with an anti-Communist stance. The precarious position of the Saudi Arabian regime would become instantly untenable if Turkey espoused the cause of Moscow. With Iran under the threat of Soviet influence, Turkey's boosting role has become more crucial. Turkey's affiliation with NATO is, at least, one of the most inhibiting factors that the USSR has to consider in any direct incursion into the Middle East.

Economically, Turkey's agricultural reaches are a geographic boon to her southern neighbors. But none of them have made any effort to avail themselves of this opportunity. Turkey's products might not be as well packaged as the produce from the United States, but Saudi Arabia and the rest must know that the deficiency can easily be rectified if they wish to make the effort. They possess the capital for which they now have difficulty in finding outlets and which Turkey desperately needs to make her produce more acceptable to them.

Turkey has, also, the industrial infrastructure for producing all the different goods and gadgets they require. A conscious effort to expand the Turkish plants to cater to their markets could help not only Turkey to buy her oil but the Arabs themselves in owning joint-ventures to produce for their own markets. All the Arabs can show in economic cooperation with Turkey is a small fertilizer plant involving a few hundred thousand dollars and the Arab-Turkish Bank involving only a couple of million dollars from Libyan and Turkish sources. The United Nations places Turkey among the ten countries in the world seasoned in road construction and maintenance. So far the Arabs have shown little inclination in encouraging Turkey to participate in their construction effort. On the contrary, Turkey has been in effect discriminated against because the Arabs have refused to accept letters of guarantee offered by Turkish banks.

In an article that I wrote recently for *Gunaydin,* I said that in the face of Turkey's efforts to espouse the Arab cause and Turkey's national desire to develop her relations with the Muslim world, the mountain has given birth to a mouse.

Israel is the only country in the area on which Turkey can rely in countering a Soviet thrust into the Middle East. Again Israel and now Egypt are the two countries with which Turkey can cooperate and help the politically primitive polities of the Arab world in effecting the transition to modern statehood. Yet, Turkey, in order to gain Arab support, has jeopardized her relations with Israel and Egypt. She did it at the expense of alienating opinion in the West, and particularly American opinion. In the institution of the embargo this alienation was of considerable impact.

My conclusion in that article was that the Muslim world cannot constitute an alternative to Turkey's affiliation with the West. First, it has not reciprocated Turkey's advances. Secondly, the Muslim world is more divided within itself than any other group. They have evinced their inexperience in statehood by failing to develop a joint world outlook. They have become prisoners to the Arab-Israeli issue and have failed to evolve a realistic attitude and a constructive policy.

Being the most important Muslim state in history and the strongest Muslim state today, Turkey must play a role in the Muslim group. But she will never succeed in gaining that role if she approaches the Muslim states as an alternative to her aggrieved relations with the West.

Turkey must develop a policy of conciliation and cooperation in the Middle Eastern region as a whole. The Palestinian problem has broken its crust, and potential solutions have emerged. Israel has been accepted, though reluctantly, and this is a great advance, but the recognition of Israel is not sufficient. Her survival must be secured. Beneath the euphemism of an independent Palestinian state on the West Bank rests the threat to Israel's existence, as many now expect that the Arab-Israeli conflict will not be resolved by the creation of a Palestinian state. If a Palestinian state becomes inevitable it must be created within a program of conciliation and cooperation for the whole region, a program of development in which Israel, Turkey, and Egypt offer their human resources, their administrative and technical skills for promoting in peace the political, economic, and social progress of the whole area. There are many contradictions between the Arab states that the Arab-Israeli conflict has helped to conceal. These contradictions are in most cases as unsettling as the Palestinian problem. An overall plan for conciliation and cooperation will also help in resolving them. Turkey's approach to the Islamic world can be effective and beneficial only when it is conceived within this concept.

The surface waters are, indeed, choppy and sometimes swell to stormy waves, but the disturbance is on the surface and the deep continues to remain free from serious turbulence. The national consciousness is at times uneasy, but it still retains its basic confidence. People have faith that the fabric will hold. But there are many imponderables affecting Turkey's international posture and economy over which there is no control. The Turks need to remain alert and show a much keener awareness of the uncertainties in their situation. They need to exercise greater self-discipline in politics, and more self-sacrifice in economics.

If, as in the past, crises bring forth the best qualities of the Turks, then we can expect that present hazards will be overcome. The new economic measures have given us a foretaste of the Turks' ability to reassert their best. Let us hope that they will prove themselves as sensible in their politics.

## REFERENCES

1. "Turkey, NATO and Europe: a Deteriorating Relationship?" (The Atlantic Institute for International Affairs, The Atlantic Papers, No. 34).

2. "Turkey's Problems and Prospects: Implications for U.S. Interests" (Report prepared for the Subcommittee on Europe and the Middle East, by the Committee on Foreign Affairs, U.S. House of Representatives, by the Foreign Affairs and National Defense Division, Congressional Research Service, Library of Congress, March 1980).

# 13

# Islam in the Soviet Union

*Alexandre Bennigsen*

THERE ARE between forty-three and forty-four million Muslims in the Soviet Union today; one out of six Soviet citizens is a Muslim. The USSR has the fifth largest Muslim population in the world, after Indonesia, Pakistan, Bangladesh, and India. Muslims are the majority of the population in four main areas: Central Asia and Kazakhstan (28 million); Northern Caucasus (3.5 million); Eastern Transcaucasia (5.5 million); and the Middle-Volga, Southern Urals, and Western Siberia (7 million). Small Muslim groups exist in central Russia in the Riazan *oblast'* (Kasymov Tatars) and in the Lithuania-Belorussia (Lithuanian Tatars). The Crimean peninsula became a Muslim land in the fourteenth century, but since the deportation of its Muslim population (the Crimean Tatars) to Central Asia after the Second World War, it is purely Slavic in population.

Members of Turkic nationalities constitute 75 percent of Soviet Muslims. In 1979, they amounted to just over 37 million. Iranians numbered 3.6 million and the Ibero-Caucasians, 3 million. There also exist smaller ethnic and linguistic groups:

> Muslim Semites, that is, Arabs of Central Asia (20,000?) and "Chalas," Bukharian Jews converted to Islam, who remained, however, crypto-Jewish (1,000?);
>
> Muslim Chinese (Dungans) in Central Asia (54,000 in 1979);
>
> Muslim Gypsies (Luli, Mazang) in Central Asia (about 100,000); and
>
> Muslim Armenians (Hemshins) (1,000 to 2,000?).

There are no Muslims among either the Slavs or the Finnic nationalities. The immense majority of Soviet Muslims are Sunnis of the Hanafi *mazhab,* and only the Daghestanis belong to the Shafei *mazhab.* The Shi'a Twelvers (*Ithna Ashariya*) are a minority. To this branch belong most of the Azeris (4.5 million) and between 50,000 and 100,000 Central Asians, Turks, and Iranians dwelling in cities such as Bukhara and Samarkand.

The other Muslim sects represented in the Soviet Union are: the Ismailis of the Nizarite rite (Aga Khan followers) inhabiting the Pamir (50,000 to 100,000 in 1979); the Ali Illahis ("Those who deify Ali"), an extremist Shi'a sect (10,000 in Azerbaijan); and the Yezidis, adepts of a syncretist sect blending old Manicheism with Islam (30,000 to 50,000 among the Kurds in Armenia).

For sixty years this Islamic culture has been isolated behind a tightly closed iron curtain. Some contacts were cautiously established after the Second World War and once again in 1964, after the downfall of Khruschev, but these were limited mainly to the exchange of religious delegations. Now, with the Afghanistan crisis, the situation has dramatically changed. Contacts between Soviet Central Asia and the rest of the Muslim world have been intensified and broadened. Currently we face a new situation, full of various possiblities, and potentially dangerous for the USSR, the Muslim world abroad, and the West. The object of this short presentation is to briefly analyze Soviet Islam in terms of demographic and political development, and the place of Soviet Islam in the Soviet strategy in the Middle East. More precisely, I shall try to analyze the role of Soviet Islam in the new Soviet policy of expansion in the Muslim world.

## Defining Soviet Islam

In the Soviet Union, the term "Muslim" is commonly used to designate individuals of different nationalities who, before the October Revolution, belonged to the religion of the Prophet. At present, this term has national rather than religious associations. One often hears native Muslims in Central Asia, including members of the Communist Party, declare: "I am a Communist and an atheist," and, "of course, I am also Muslim." The Soviet sources use the expression "non-believing Muslim."

The Muslim community of the USSR is undergoing a veritable demographic explosion. It is a fast-growing young community when compared to the ageing and very slow-growing Slavic nationalities (Russian, Ukrainian, and Belorussians). Between 1959 and 1970, the Muslim population of the USSR increased 45 percent, ranging by nationality from 19 percent to 53 percent while the Russian increase for the same period was only 13 percent, and the total Soviet population increase was 16 percent.

Between 1970 and 1979, the growth rate differential between the Muslims and the Russians increased, and the general growth of the Soviet population was reduced to 8.4 percent, that of the Russians to 6.5 percent. Although during the same period the growth of the Muslim population slowed down, it remained nevertheless high: 23.2 percent. The demographic increase of Central Asian nationalities was particularly spectacular: Uzbeks by 35.5 percent; Kazakhs by 23.7 percent; Tajiks by 35.7 percent; Turkmens by 33.0 percent; and Kirghiz by 31.3 percent.

Although population growth in the Caucasus was slower, it was still impressive. The Azeris increased by 25.0 percent; the Chechens, 23.3 percent; the Daghestanis, 20 to 23 percent. The population increase of the Volga-Ural Muslims was slow in comparison to that of the other Muslim nationalities: Tatars, 6.5 percent and Bashkirs, 10.6 percent.

Demographers, Western as well as Soviet, agree that by the turn of our century, the Muslims of the Soviet Union will represent a community of some 65 to 75 million individuals (compared with a total population of over 300 million). In other words, in the year 2000, one out of every four Soviet citizens will be a Muslim and one out of every five, a Turk. The character of the Soviet Union will be totally different than what it is today.

The contrast between the vitality of the Muslims and the declining birthrate of the Russians and other Slavs (Ukrainians and Belorussians) is due to: 1) the high fertility rate of the Muslims (one of the highest in the world) as compared to the low fertility rate of the Slavs; 2) the unassimilability of the Muslims by the Russians, which is true even of the Volga Tatars, who have been ruled by Russian Slavs since the middle of the sixteenth century; 3) the predominantly rural character of Muslim nationalities (the average ratio of rural to urban population among Muslims is 70 percent to 30 percent, whereas among the Russians it is 30 percent to 70 percent); 4) the persistence of certain family customs favoring large families (early marriage of girls, strict sexual morality, ban on birth control); 5) and the desire to survive as a community (in the case of smaller nationalities) or to outgrow the Russians (in the case of larger ones).

The impact of this demographic growth on the character of the USSR is hard to determine, but it is obvious that the Muslim factor is bound to weigh more heavily on Soviet politics, both foreign and domestic.

One question, however, must be discussed outright: Are those millions of individuals still "Muslims" or are they simply average Soviet citizens of the same Marxist-Leninist background, speaking different languages, but really indistinguishable from their Russian comrades? We must bear in mind that since the Middle Ages the Muslim territories of the Soviet Union—Central Asia, Middle Volga, and the Caucasus—have been an integral part of a brilliant Irano-Turkic culture and not adjuncts, and the prestigious legacy of the past was not—indeed, could not—be wiped out by sixty years of Soviet rule. This means that Soviet Muslims have had, since the Middle Ages, a large and brilliant cultural elite which still exists to-day and which, theoretically at least, can assume intellectual, technical, and economic responsibilities. Uzbekistan, Azerbaijan, or Kirghizia have no need of Russian cadres for their survival as states; and they are, at least, as viable as Southern Yemen or Somalia.

Several Soviet sociological surveys carried out between 1976 and 1980 reveal that the Muslim community of the USSR remains "Muslim" not only in terms of nationality but also in terms of a limited but authentic religious practice. These surveys were conducted in Daghestan, in Checheno-Ingush Autonomous Republic, Uzbekistan, the Karakalpak Autonomous Republic, and in various Tatar areas.[1] They show that 20 percent of the Muslims in these territories are "atheists." The remaining 80 percent are distributed among various categories of believers:

1. "firm" believers, or "believers by conviction," whom Soviet sources call "fanatics." These are members of the older generation, intolerant toward the non-believers, often adepts of various Sufi brotherhoods;

2. believers by tradition who believe in God and observe all religious rites, but do not force their views on their neighbors;

3. those who are "hesitant" and indifferent, who under the pressure of their neighbors and family observe some religious rites and customs.[2] The proportion of atheists to believers is reversed among the Russians who were former Christians: 80 percent for atheists and 20 percent for believers. But generally, even so-called atheists in Muslim territories, high-ranking party members included, are more or less rooted in their religious background and practice

some rites. According to recent Soviet sources, circumcision, religious marriages, and above all, religious funerals are observed by 80 percent to 100 percent of the population.[3] As the saying goes in Central Asia, "a non-circumcised male cannot be a Uzbek" (or a Turkmen, or a Kirghiz . . .), with the corollary that "only a Muslim can be an Uzbek."[4]

This attachment to Islam may help explain the isolation of the Russians from the Muslim community: in Central Asia and in the Caucasus, Islam remains the essential source of reference, more important than Marx or Lenin.

Soviet attitudes toward Islam are ambiguous. Islam is deemed to be a survival of the pre-socialist era and doomed to disappearance. If need be, the "natural" death of Islam may be hurried by propaganda and eventually by administrative and police pressure. Accordingly, anti-Islamic propaganda started around 1928 and continued unabated for more than half a century. Between 1928 and 1941, propaganda was reinforced by a wave of persecutions and forced collectivization. Nearly all the mosques (more than 24,000, in 1913) and all religious schools—*mektep* and *medresseh* (14,500 in 1913)—were closed; Shariyat courts were abolished; and all *waqfs* confiscated. Thousands of Muslim clerics tried as "spies" and "wreckers" were executed or sent to camps. The frontal assault against the Muslim religion was interrupted during the war, but the violent propaganda was resumed around 1953 and still continues. The main themes of this campaign are that Islam is a "foreign" religion, forced on the people of the Caucasus and Central Asia by Arab and Turkish conquerors; Islam is portrayed as a barbaric, primitive, anti-humanist, and generally uncivilized practice, inherently anti-socialist and anti-Leninist because it kindles nationalistic passions and therefore represents an impediment to the creation of the new "Soviet man." But at the same time, Soviet authorities have managed to "domesticate" the higher Muslim hierarchy, namely the muftis and the chairmen of the four Muslim Spiritual Boards of Tashkent, Ufa, Baku, and Makhach-Kala, profiting from the propaganda activity of the muftis in the Muslim world abroad and from their role as moderators within the USSR. However, the official Muslim hierarchy is not a mere "agent" of the Soviet government. It has an independent strategy and its own counterpropaganda, which describes Islam as the "most liberal and the most progressive of all religions, and best fitted to prepare the faithful for the building of true socialism."[5] Soviet authorities are fully aware of the danger represented by this insidious and efficient propaganda.[6]

Recent sociological surveys have disclosed that the level of religiosity has increased during the last five years, if one were to draw a conclusion from the observance of religious rites and respect of traditional customs considered both by the believers and the non-believers as "national" traditions and not only as manifestations of religious belief. Soviet sources specifically mention observance of the fast of Ramadhan, the participation in public prayers at the major Muslim festivals (Aid al-Kabir, Aid al-Fitr, Ashura), and the payment of a voluntary contribution (*sadaqa*) to mosques.

Soviet sources also stress the reappearance in the 1960s of the conservative Sufi brotherhoods, especially the Naqshbandiya and Qadiriya,[7] which are proscribed, semi-clandestine organizations. Nevertheless, in certain areas, such as in Daghestan, the Checheno-Ingush Republic, Turkmenistan, and Kirghizia, they operate almost openly. The Sufi brotherhoods perform services that the official Muslim hierarchy is unable to perform.[8] They maintain a network of Koranic schools and operate hundreds if not thousands of unofficial and illegal houses of prayer.[9] Their adepts perform the same duties as the official clerics (circumcision, burials, prayers) and help maintain among the Muslim masses, rural and urban, a climate of religious intolerance, of xenophobia, and of anti-modernist, anti-secularist, and anti-socialist conservatism.

A specific character of the Soviet Muslim community is its aggressiveness. The Muslims have been neither submissive nor, as too often imagined in the West, totally loyal to the Soviet regime. The sixty-year long relationship between Muslims and Russians since the Revolution has been marked by many dramatic incidents, starting with the Basmachi uprising in Central Asia, which began in 1918 and lasted for more than ten years, until it was crushed by the Soviet army under Marshall Frunze. The rebellion was of the rural guerilla kind and involved the sedentary population of the Ferghana Valley and the nomads of northwestern Turkmenistan and southern Uzbekistan. The war showed the ineffectiveness of the Soviet army against rural guerillas.

The conquest of the Caucasus by the Red Army in 1920 was

followed by another Muslim uprising, this one led by the Sufi brotherhoods in northern Daghestan and in the Chechen country. Guerilla warfare lasted from 1920 to 1922.

In 1941, during the war, when German armies were still thousands of miles away from the Caucasus, a revolt burst out again in
the same area of the northern Caucasus, which lasted until 1943. As
a result, more than a million North Caucasian Mountaineers (Chechens, Ingushes, Balkars, and Karachays) were deported to Siberia
and to Kazakhstan.

There have been several violent incidents since the war in Tashkent such as the so-called *Pakhtakor* revolt, which flared up in 1964
following a soccer match between Russian and Uzbek teams, and
again in Dushambe (Tajikistan) in May 1979.

To complete the picture, one should mention the rural and urban terrorism present in the northern Caucasus, and the general
climate of unrest in Central Asian cities. The phrase "wait until
the Chinese come" is often heard in Tashkent or Samarkand and
often followed by such threatening remarks as "we will paint our
walls with your blood."[10]

Soviet Muslims, however, have the impression that time is on
their side, and that it is useless to endanger their position by an un-
timely confrontation with their Russian "comrades." Theirs is a politically mature community. In 1918, the Russian Communist Party
already contained a number of Muslim leaders, some of whom had
tried to adapt Marxism to the specific conditions of the Muslim world
and had elaborated several bold political programs that were at
once Marxist, nationalistic, and Islamic. Among the most interesting programs were the National Communism of the Tatar Sultan
Galiev, and the pan-Turkic Marxism of the Kazakh Turar Ryskulov.
Not only were these programs fifty years ahead of their time—similar programs are seen today in the Middle East—but they were
also quite realistic in their goals. They had in common with some
contemporary Middle Eastern movements a violent opposition to
"Western imperialism," represented in the USSR not by Europeans
but by the Russians themselves, and a desire to transfer the "revolutionary energies" of the Communist Revolution from Europe
to the Asian and African colonial world.[11]

Stalin was the first among the Bolsheviks to understand the
potential danger of these doctrines to the stability of the Soviet Un-

ion. They were banned as heretical ("bourgeois nationalist"), and their proponents were hunted down during the bloody purges of the 1930s. At present, however, these ideologies survive among the Central Asians and the Caucasians as an intellectual legacy of the past.

Finally, the Muslim community of the USSR remains separated from the Russians. After sixty years of Soviet domination (and for some, such as the Volga Tatars, 400 years of Russian rule) there is no cultural, biological, or linguistic assimilation of Muslim Turks. Mixed marriages between Muslims and non-Muslims are still rare, and, when they do take place, follow the traditional pattern of the Shariyat law. Marriage between a Muslim man and a woman belonging to an *Ahl al-Kitab* community (i.e., a Christian or a Jew) although exceptional, is therefore permitted; but marriage of a Muslim girl outside her community is strictly forbidden. As a rule, children of mixed marriages assume the father's nationality, which means that they remain members of the Muslim community.

The attachment of Muslims to their national languages and their refusal to emigrate to Russian areas of the USSR prove the absence of cultural symbiosis between Muslims and Russians.[12]  In spite of the intense propaganda aimed at promoting the Russian language to the height of universal usage, native language spoken by Muslims persist, as shown by the proportion of Muslims who, in the course of the last Soviet census, declared their national languages as their "first mother tongue."

|  | 1959 | 1970 | 1979 |
|---|---|---|---|
| Uzbeks | 98.4% | 98.6% | 98.5% |
| Kazakhs | 98.4% | 98.0% | 97.5% |
| Tajiks | 98.1% | 98.5% | 98.8% |
| Turkmens | 98.9% | 98.9% | 98.7% |
| Kirghiz | 98.7% | 98.8% | 97.9% |
| Azeris | 97.6% | 98.2% | 97.9% |
| Tatars | 92.1% | 89.2% | 85.9% |
| Daghestanis | ? | 96.5% | 95.9% |

The refusal of the Muslims to migrate outside their territories is illustrated by the number of Central Asians living in the Russian Republic (RSFSR) in 1979:[13]

| | Total population in USSR | in RSFSR | %living in RSFSR |
|---|---|---|---|
| Uzbeks | 12,456,000 | 72,375 | 0.6% |
| Kazakhs | 6,556,000 | 518,060[a] | 7.9% |
| Tajiks | 2,898,000 | 17,863 | 0.6% |
| Turkmens | 2,028,000 | 22,979 | 1.1% |
| Kirghiz | 1,906,000 | 15,011 | 0.8% |

[a] The Kazakhs in the RSFSR are not immigrants, but live in border colonies in the lower Volga, the southern Urals, and western Siberia.

Such then is the general background of Soviet-Muslim relations. We can now examine the present-day position of Soviet Islam in the light of recent developments in the Middle East, and particularly the Afghan crisis.

## Islam in Soviet Strategy

The Soviet Islamic territories have been, since the early Middle Ages, part of the Muslim world and have shared in the fate of other areas of Dar ul-Islam. For the last half of a century, Soviet Islam has been isolated from the rest of the Muslim world and subjected to a systematic and relentless policy of modernization and secularization. In contrast to the rest of the Muslim world, in the USSR, the modernization has been more brutal, more extensive, and imposed by "alien" rulers. As to secularization, its aim was not to adapt religion to the modern world, but more simply to destroy it. It is, therefore, logical that Soviet Muslims reacted to Russian pressure by following a conservative pattern similar to that observed in the Middle East.

Contacts between Soviet Central Asians, Caucasians, and their brethren in Turkey, Iran, and Afghanistan have been limited. Until recently, pilgrimage to Mecca was limited to two chartered flights per year carrying fifty to sixty selected pilgrims. Cultural relations between Soviet Muslim republics and Middle Eastern countries were restricted, and only a small number of Soviet Muslims figured as members of Soviet diplomatic missions, acting mainly as interpreters and drivers. Few ever became ambassadors. But after the downfall of Mohammed Daud, in Afghanistan, in April 1978, a dramatic change occurred. To avoid a complete dislocation of the Afghan government, which had been disorganized by the Communist takeover, a great number of Soviet Central Asian Muslim cadres—Uzbek, Tajik, and Turkmen—were introduced at all levels into the administration of Afghanistan, and late in 1979, several hundred Central Asian non-military cadres were employed in Afghanistan. Thus, for the first time since the Revolution, Soviet Muslims were helping Moscow to build Communism in a foreign Muslim country. It was the dream of the old Muslim National Communists come true. And in December 1979, the Soviet army invaded Afghanistan. The infantry divisions that occupied Kabul had many Central Asian soldiers (probably up to 40 percent); however, most officers and non-commissioned officers were Slavs.

It is certain that during the first two months of the Afghan crisis (January-February 1980), the massive and spectacular presence of Soviet Muslim cadres in the Afghan administration and of Muslim soldiers in the units occupying Kabul helped foster the illusion that all Soviet nationalities, the Central Asian Muslim included, were closely united in a moment of crisis and ready to fight against the imperialists. The USSR displayed in Afghanistan its Muslim face, and it was made to appear that the Afghan operation was basically an "inter-Islamic" affair.

In the spring of 1978, Soviet propaganda directed to the Muslim world began to employ Muslim religious leaders (especially the Mufti of Tashkent, Ziauddin Babakhanov, and the Mufti of Ufa, Abdul-Bari Isaev) as spokesmen, in order to project a positive image of the Soviet treatment of Islam, particularly to conservative states such as Saudi Arabia, Jordan, Morocco, and Tunisia. It seems that Muslim leaders have accepted this role, and during the last two-and-a-half years have acted as Soviet goodwill ambassadors and propagandists abroad. Their main task has been to justify the Afghan adventure, denounce Western and Chinese imperialism, proclaim the vitality of Islam in the Soviet Union, and, finally, counter any anti-Soviet propaganda originating from any Muslim country abroad. There is no doubt that the intervention of Soviet religious leaders has paid off. When the mufti of Tashkent speaks in Mecca or at the University of al-Azhar, his pronouncements carry weight. From this viewpoint, "official" Soviet Islam represents an asset to the government. Without the initial help of Central Asian Muslims, the Afghan enterprise would have been more difficult.

We may safely assume that Muslim religious leaders were willing to help the Soviets expand not just for the sake of propaganda. Their help is being paid for by numerous and important concessions to Islam in the Soviet Union, such as the opening of new mosques, thus promoting a religious revival.[14]

It is also quite likely that the Soviet Muslim non-religious cadres welcomed the invasion of Afghanistan by Soviet troops. This undertaking, as well as others of the same kind in the Muslim Middle East, might represent the transfer of revolutionary energies from Europe to the Middle East and a chance for Muslims to wield greater authority in the administration of their own republics. Furthermore, Soviet Central Asians would probably welcome the transformation of Afghanistan into a Soviet Socialist Republic, for it would add some 15 million new Muslims to the already existing 44 million, hastening the time when they become the dominant ethnic group in the USSR.

In spite of an auspicious beginning to the "Central Asian phase" of operations in Afghanistan, Soviet authorities decided in February 1980, to end it. Soviet Muslim soldiers proved unreliable: their fighting spirit was low, they fraternized with the local population, and some deserted the ranks. All Muslim units were pulled out of Afghanistan and replaced by purely Slavic divisions. At the same time, Central Asian cadres in the Afghan administration were replaced by Russians. Since March 1980, the Soviet Union has been fighting a typical colonial war against Afghan guerillas, who consider the fight against the invaders a *jihad*, a "holy war."

It seems, therefore, that Soviet Islam was an asset for Moscow between April 1978 and March 1980 but turned into a liability afterward. In view of the general climate of hostility that characterizes Russian-Muslim relations in Central Asia and the Caucasus, the Soviets must terminate their Afghan adventure rapidly and victoriously. A failure or even half a success is not permitted. An unfavorable turn of events might have a dramatic impact on Central Asia by showing that the Soviets are not invincible. Continued resistance of the Afghan guerillas might recall the not-quite-forgotten dreams of the Basmachi rebellion of the 1920s.

A failure in Afghanistan might have the same dramatic effect on Russian-Muslim relations that the Russian defeat in Manchuria had in 1905 on various national movements in Poland, Finland, the Ukraine, Georgia, and Azerbaijan. Moreover, a long, Algerian-style guerilla war in Afghanistan would be almost equally dangerous because it might finally supply the groundwork for pan-Islamic solidarity between Soviet Muslims and those abroad. It may have been easy to persuade Soviet Uzbeks or Tajiks to participate in the liberation of Afghan Uzbeks or Tajiks from the domination of the Pashtuns or to protect them from American or Chinese imperialism; but when the Afghan Uzbeks and Tajiks joined in the "holy war" against their liberators, Central Asians could no longer be relied upon.

At present, the Soviets are engaged in guerilla warfare against a Muslim population in a very difficult area of the world. They cannot afford to lose, but it is difficult to imagine how they can win, except, of course, by broadening the conflict. Afghanistan is an ideal place for a generation-long guerilla war.

The Afghan invasion presents an absolute contrast to a sixty-year policy of caution on the part of the Soviets in this area. But, at present, as a result of the Iranian revolution and of the Afghan war, the Middle East has been destabilized, and it is difficult to imagine how it could be restabilized. This is also true of Soviet Central Asia, which, indirectly, has also been destabilized. The long border between Central Asia and Afghanistan has been opened; ideas and information now seem to be circulating more freely in both directions, and, with the war going on, it is difficult to imagine that an Iron Curtain can be drawn once again between the Soviet territories and the world abroad. It is too early to speculate on the final results of this destabilization, but one thing is certain: it would be a mistake to underestimate the historical importance of this development, especially when we remember that the Soviet Union is the last colonial empire.

It seems, therefore, that the Afghan operation is hopeless for all the participants. It is, of course, a major tragedy for the Afghans, who are being subjected to genocide. It has revealed the weakness and division of the Western powers, unable or unwilling to challenge Soviet aggression, and the disunity among the Muslim states abroad, which are unable or unwilling to help the Afghan guerilla *mujahids*. At the same time, it has revealed certain cracks in the Soviet façade,

THE GROWTH OF MUSLIM NATIONALITIES SINCE STALIN'S DEATH

|  | 1959 census | 1970 census | Increase % 1959/1970 | 1979 census | *Increase %* 1970/1979 |
|---|---|---|---|---|---|
| Total Population |  |  |  |  |  |
| USSR | 208,827,000 | 241,720,000 | 16% | 262,085,000 | 8.4% |
| Russians | 114,114,000 | 129,015,000 | 13% | 137,397,000 | 6.5% |
| Total Muslim Population | 24,380,000 | 35,232,000 | 45% | 43,395,000 | 23.2% |
| Uzbeks | 6,015,000 | 9,195,000 | 53% | 12,456,000 | 35.5% |
| Kazakhs | 3,622,000 | 5,299,000 | 46% | 6,556,000 | 23.7% |
| Tatars | 4,968,000 | 5,931,000 | 19% | 6,317,000 | 6.5% |
| Azeris | 2,940,000 | 4,380,000 | 49% | 5,477,000 | 25.0% |
| Tajiks | 1,397,000 | 2,136,000 | 53% | 2,898,000 | 35.7% |
| Turkmens | 1,002,000 | 1,525,000 | 52% | 2,028,000 | 33.0% |
| Kirghiz | 969,000 | 1,452,000 | 50% | 1,906,000 | 31.3% |
| Bashkirs | 989,000 | 1,240,000 | 25% | 1,371,000 | 10.6% |
| Chechens | 419,000 | 613,000 | 46% | 756,000 | 23.3% |
| Ossetians | 413,000 | 488,000 | 18% | 542,000 | 11.0% |
| Avars | 270,000 | 396,000 | 47% | 483,000 | 22.0% |
| Lezghins | 223,000 | 324,000 | 45% | 383,000 | 18.2% |
| Kabards | 204,000 | 280,000 | 37% | 322,000 | 15.0% |
| Karakalpaks | 173,000 | 236,000 | 36% | 303,000 | 28.4% |
| Darghins | 158,000 | 231,000 | 46% | 287,000 | 24.2% |
| Kumyks | 135,000 | 189,000 | 40% | 228,000 | 20.6% |
| Uyghurs | 95,000 | 173,000 | 82% | 211,000 | 22.0% |
| Ingushes | 106,000 | 158,000 | 55% | 186,000 | 17.7% |
| Karachays | 81,000 | 113,000 | 40% | 131,000 | 15.9% |
| Kurds | 59,000 | 89,000 | 51% | 116,000 | 30.3% |
| Laks | 66,000 | 86,000 | 30% | 100,000 | 16.3% |
| Adyghes | 80,000 | 100,000 | 25% | 109,000 | 9.0% |
| Turks | — | 79,000 | — | 93,000 | 17.7% |
| Abkhazians | 65,000 | 83,000 | 28% | 91,000 | 9.6% |
| Tabasarans | 35,000 | 55,000 | 57% | 75,000 | 36.4% |
| Balkars | 42,000 | 59,000 | 40% | 66,000 | 10.0% |
| Nogays | 39,000 | 52,000 | 33% | 60,000 | 15.4% |
| Dungans | 22,000 | 39,000 | 77% | 52,000 | 33.3% |
| Cherkess | 30,000 | 40,000 | 33% | 46,000 | 15.0% |
| Iranians | 21,000 | 28,000 | 33% | 31,000 | 10.7% |
| Abazas | 20,000 | 25,000 | 25% | 29,000 | 16.0% |
| Tates | 11,000 | 17,000 | 55% | 22,000 | 29.4% |
| Rutuls | 7,000 | 12,000 | 71% | 15,000 | 25.0% |
| Tsakhurs | 7,300 | 11,000 | 51% | 14,000 | 27.3% |
| Aguls | 6,700 | 9,000 | 34% | 12,000 | 36.4% |
| Balushis | 8,000 | 13,000 | 62% | — | — |
| Afghans | 2,000 | 4,000 | 100% | — | — |

political and military, and an inability to crush the resistance of poorly armed and politically-divided guerilla forces. One year after their entry into Afghanistan, Soviet troops are still fighting in the same areas—Herat, Logar, Pakhtia, Pandjshir, Ghazni—and have not yet been able to launch an attack on the mountains. At the moment, everyone appears to be a loser except China, which is slowly emerging as a potential friend of Islam. It is protecting Pakistan and helping (or at least pretending to help) the Afghan *mujahids*. And its violent anti-Russian propaganda is certainly enjoying a favorable reception in Soviet Central Asia.

## NOTES

1. Among the most interesting works based on these surveys, we may quote for the Daghestan: I. A. Makatov, *Islam, Veruiushchii, Sovremennost'* (Islam, Believers, Modernity), Makhach-Kala, 1974; for the Checheno-Ingush Republic: *Sotsiologiia, Ateizm, Religiia* (Sociology, Atheism, Religion), Groznyi, 1972; V. G. Pivovarov, "Sotsiologicheskie issledovaniia problem byta, kul'tury,ʲ natsional'nykh traditsii i verovanii v Chacheno-Ingushskoi ASSR" (Sociological research on the problems of customs, culture, national traditions, and beliefs in the Checheno-Ingush Autonomous Republic), in *Voprosy Nauchnogo Ateizma*, Moscow, 1974; and *Kharakter religioznosti i problemy ateisticheskogo vospitaniia* (The character of the religiousness and the problems of atheistic education), Groznyi, 1979; for Uzbekistan: F. S. Saidbaev, *Islam i Obshchestvo* (Islam and Society), Moscow, 1978; Zh. Bazarbaev, *Sekuliarizatsiia Sotsialisticheskoi Karakalpakii* (Secularization of the Socialist Karakalpakiia), Nukhus, 1973; for Islam in general: N. Ashirov, *Islam i Natsii* (Islam and the Nations), Moscow, 1975; *Evoliutsiia Islama v USSR* (Evolution of Islam in the USSR), Moscow, 1975; and *Musul'manskaia Propoved'* (Muslim predication), Moscow, 1978.

2. See Zh. Bazarbaev, op. cit., p. 53; I. A. Makatov, op. cit., pp. 23-31; V. G. Pivovarov, *Na etapakh sotsiologicheskogo issledovaniia*, Groznyi, 1974, p. 158; and A. Kadyrov, *Prichiny sushchestvovaniia i puti preodoleniia perezhitkov Islama*, Leninabad, 1966, pp. 14-15.

3. For instance, for the North Caucasus, see V. Yu. Gadaev, "O kharaktere religioznosti sel'skoi molodezhi" (The character of the religiousness of the rural youth) in *Kharakter religioznosti . . .*, op. cit., pp. 40-57; also, E. G. Filimonov, "Sotsiologicheskoe issledovanie protsessa preodoleniia religii v sel'skoi mestnosti" (Sociological research of the process of overcoming of religion in the rural areas), *Voprosy Nauchnogo Ateizma*, Moscow, XVI, 1974, p. 81.

4. N. Ashirov, *Islam i Natsii*, op. cit., p. 63.

5. The best source for the analysis of Muslim "counterpropaganda" is

the quarterly journal published by the Tashkent Spiritual Board. It appeared in 1946 in Uzbek (in Arabic script) under the title of *Urta Asia ve Kazakhstan Musulmanlarining Dini Nazaria Zhurnali* (Journal of the Spiritual Board of the Muslims of Central Asia and Kazakhstan). In 1969 it was replaced by *Muslims of the Soviet East* in two editions: an Arabic edition (*Al-Muslimun fi al-Sharq al-Sufiyati*) and an Uzbek edition in Arabic script (*Sovet Sharkining Musulmanlari*). In 1974 English and French editions, and in 1980 a Persian edition, were added. An excellent analysis of the journal is given by N. Ashirov in his *Musul'manskaiia Propoved'*, op. cit.

6. T. Izimbetov, *Islam i Sovremennost'* (Islam and Modernity), Nukhus, 1963, p. 78, writes: "Muslim modernist leaders are as dangerous as the conservatives." Sharaf Rashidov, first secretary of the Central Committee of the Communist Party of Uzbekistan, declared at the VIIIth plenum of the Central Committee of his Party: "Muslim clerics are cleverly adapting themselves to the new conditions of the Soviet life . . . . It would be a great mistake to imagine that they are fighting a losing battle . . . ," in *Pravda Vostoka* (Tashkent), July 13, 1963.

7. Sufi brotherhoods or *tariqat* ("path" leading to God) are secret but mass societies, especially strong in North Caucasus, where they have several thousands of adepts (cf. V. G. Pivovarov, "Sotsiologicheskie isledovaniia," op. cit., p. 316, where it is noted that in the Checheno-Ingush ASSR, "more than half of the Muslim believers are adepts of a Sufi *tariqat*"). The Naqshbandiya is a Bukharian order founded in the fourteenth century; the Qadiriya, a Baghdadi order founded in the twelfth century.

8. The official Muslim hierarchy controls probably not more than 300 "working" mosques.

9. Soviet literature on the Sufi brotherhoods is very important. Among recent works one may mention: S. M. Demidov, *Sufism v Turkmenii*, Ashabad, 1978, and by the same author *Turkmenskie Ovliady* (The holy tribes of Turkmenia), Ashabad, 1976; I. A. Makatov, "Kul't Sviatykh v Islame" (The Cult of the saints in Islam), *Voprosy Nauchnogo Ateizma*, III, 1967, pp. 164-185; S. Mambetaliev, *Qyrqyzystandagy Musulman Sektlary* (Muslim sects in Kirghiza), Frunze, 1966 (in Kirghiz); by the same author, *Sufizm zhana anyng Qyrqyzstandagy agmdary* (Sufism and its trends in Kirghizia), Frunze, 1966 (in Kirghiz): A. Safarov, *Paidoish va mohiati ichtimoyi Darvishi* (The origin and the social character of the Dervishism), Dushambe, 1975 (in Tajik); N. Basilov, *Kul't Sviatykh v Islame* (Cult of the Saints in Islam), Moscow, 1970.

10. On this subject, see Rasma Karklins, "Islam: how strong is it in Soviet Union? Inquiry based on oral interviews with Soviet Germans repatriated from Central Asia in 1979," *Cahiers du Monde Russe et Sovietique* (Paris), Vol. XXI-I, January-March 1980.

11. On this subject, see A. Bennigsen and E. Wimbush, *Muslim National Communism in the Soviet Union–A Revolutionary Strategy for the Colonial World*, Chicago, University of Chicago Press, 1979.

12. One may object that Soviet Muslims are numerous in the Adminitration, in the CPSU, and in the Komsomol, but for the majority of Muslims, Communism is a technique of power (to be used eventually against their Russian comrades), not an ideology.

13. *Vestnik Statistiki,* Moscow, 7, 1980, pp. 43-44.

14. According to *Muslims of the Soviet East,* an average of five new mosques have been opened every year during the last three years.

# 14

# The Islamic Community of China

*June Dreyer*

## Ethno-Demographic Data

THE GOVERNMENT of the People's Republic of China (PRC) has been very reticent about providing demographic data for its population as a whole. There has been only one official census, in 1953, and the media typically use the same well-rounded figure for several years without change—for example, 600 million during the entire period of the Cultural Revolution and 960 million at present. In addition, the PRC maintains that, in keeping with its policy of freedom of worship, no registrations are made by religion and no such records are kept.[1] Despite this claim, a *Beijing Review* article of December 1979 stated that China has 10 million Muslims.[2] However, this is almost certainly inaccurate, and was probably derived by adding population statistics for the eight largest ethnic groups known to be consistently Muslim in faith. Although a recent *Congressional Record* puts the number of Muslims in China at 50 million,[3] this writer would estimate the figure at no more than 12 million.

Muslims are found all over China, reflecting the variety of paths by which their forebears reached the celestial kingdom: via trade routes to the south and east and via invasion routes from the north and west. There are Muslim colonies in most of the major cities, including the large eastern metropoles of Beijing, Shanghai, and Tianjin. Rural Hainan Island, far to the southeast, has a sizeable Muslim community, as does Tibet's Lhasa, the holy city of Lamaist Buddhism. There are so-called Panthay Muslims in Yunnan province in the southeast. The largest concentration of Muslims is, however, in China's northwest, where their influence, and even their numbers, were predominant for many centuries. This is particularly true of the four northwestern "Muslim belt" provinces of Xinjiang, Qinghai, Gansu, and Ningxia.

Eight ethnic groups of some size are virtually wholly Muslim in faith: the Turkic Muslims (Uygurs, Kazakhs, Uzbeks, Tatars, Salars, and Sibos), Persian Muslim Tajiks of Xinjiang, and the Hui, who are concentrated in Qinghai, Gansu, and Ningxia. So-called "scattered" Hui are also found in most Chinese cities. The Hui consider themselves ethnically distinct, and both the Chinese Communist Party (CCP) and its Guomindang (GMD) predecessor government have conceded to this claim. Finally, the Miao of South China, the same group known in Indochina as Meo, have had a substantial number of converts to Islam.

Save for the Shi'ite Tajiks, the overwhelming majority of China's Muslims are Sunni. Furthermore, Sunni and Shi'ite differences have been muted. A nineteenth century explorer noted that although a certain mountain pass served as a dividing line between Shi'ite Tajiks and Sunni Jagatai Turks, the two groups were in constant communication across the line, and intermarriage was not infrequent.[4] Differences among ethnic groups were similarly submerged.

The term "Hui" is often used interchangeably with "Chinese Muslims," as distinct from Turkic or other Islamic groups in China. However, since this chapter deals with all Muslim believers in China, it would be misleading to refer to the Hui alone as Chinese Muslims. By Chinese Muslims, we will designate all citizens of China who follow the Muslim faith, regardless of ethnic group.

Muslims are found in a variety of professions; Ekvall noted "a tendency to follow the more adventurous of the subsidiary callings, or those which require more hardihood or daring. Such occupations as innkeeper, trader, muleteer, carter, soldier and the like attract many more Muslims, proportionately, than Chinese."[5] Many Muslims, including the Uygurs, Hui, and Miao, are engaged in sedentary agriculture, while the Kazakhs and Kirghiz are nomadic herders. Popular professions for urban Hui are, in addition to trade, the butchering of cattle and ownership of "pure and true" restaurants, which conform to Islamic dietary strictures. Such establishments enjoy a reputation (among non-Muslim Chinese) for high sanitary standards and are well-patronized by them. All of China's Muslims are reputed to be excellent soldiers. Each Islamic group, save the Chinese-speaking Hui, speaks its own language. Before 1949 those who were literate—an estimated 20 percent of the population, though most males had had some training in the Koran—read Arabic.

Birth rates, particularly for the Turkic Muslim groups, were high, although Ekvall, speaking of the Gansu-Qinghai-Ningxia Muslim belt, notes that the Hui birthrate was lower than that of the Han.[6]

The socio-political organization of Islamic communities in the Muslim belt was cohesive, with whole villages tending to be either Muslim or Han and their inhabitants having little to do with one another. In the urban coastal areas where Muslims were a minority, they tended to cluster together on certain streets, forming Muslim enclaves within the city. The largely Turkic Muslim groups of Xinjiang were more decentralized around local clan and lineage groups, but overlapping ancestral connections provided links among the groups, as did their common Muslim faith.

Muslim leaders were powerful individuals, able to mobilize large numbers in battle on very short notice. When organized around such a strong leader, different clans and ethnic groups were welded into a formidable fighting force. This was particularly true when the cause was a holy war, into which many Muslim grievances quickly escalated.

## Historical Background

Traditionally, China's Muslims were a problem for the state. Seeking to remain independent, they refused to accept certain important tenets of the Confucian ideology that formed the basis of the Chinese state. Instead, they adhered to a value system that sharply contrasted with Confucianism in several fundamental areas.[7]

One area of disagreement concerned the matter of loyalty. Confucianism conceptualized the emperor as the link between heaven, earth, and the beings that dwelt thereon. He was considered the ruler of *tianxia*, all under heaven, and as such was owed the loyalty of all under heaven. Muslims, by contrast, gave their loyalty to Allah.

Another area of divergence concerned the locus of values. Confucianism fostered the belief that China was the fount of civilization—indeed, the very word China means "middle kingdom," with connotations of centrality. Those who refused to acknowledge this superiority were *ipso facto* barbarians, to be looked down upon. China's Muslims, in turn, looked down upon their non-Muslim countrymen because they were infidels. Muslims regarded Islamic, not Chinese, civilization as the repository of ultimate values, and looked beyond China's borders to Mecca as the symbol thereof. Their schools sought to impart the wisdom of the Koran and other Islamic classics and not, as in Chinese schools, the works of Confucius.

Muslim rebellions or the threat thereof allowed the northwest to remain largely autonomous of central government rule in the 1920s and 1930s, a period that saw Muslim warlords in three provinces and a Muslim governor briefly in a fourth. However, this pattern of confrontation also had its exceptions. In areas where Muslims were not numerous, accommodations were made to local norms. It was possible for a Muslim to be a conformist in the outward manifestions of speech, dress, and the exterior design of his dwelling. Yet, when he stepped into the walled courtyard of a mosque, he could reaffirm his Muslim heritage. While outwardly Chinese in style, the inside of his home would contain Arabic calligraphy and ritual bathing facilities. Such acculturated Muslims might attain positions of respect within the local community, and several became nationally prominent. One of the great Ming dynasty explorers was a Muslim, as were two of Chiang Kai-shek's leading generals.[8] However, the overall relationship between Muslim and non-Muslim communities in China was characterized by distrust and wariness.

The infant Chinese Communist Party, on its celebrated Long March to escape decimation by Chiang Kai-shek's GMD government, was nearly wiped out by Muslim cavalry just before reaching its destination at Yenan.[9] The CCP, at that time weak and desperately in need of allies, worked hard to win the favor of the local Muslim population. It downplayed, and frequently actually ignored, the anti-religious component of Marxist ideology, made significant concessions to Islamic customs, and even promised Muslims a vaguely defined independence.

Although the party did win over a number of people who later proved useful as both symbols and administrators, the CCP's pre-1949 efforts to convert Muslims to Communism were relatively unsuccessful. Most Muslim areas were either conquered after bitter fighting, or went over to the Communist side only when CCP victory was a foregone conclusion.[10] In sum, with a few exceptions, Communist ideas and organizations had little impact on Chinese Muslim communities before the CCP came to power in 1949.[11]

## Treatment of Islam by the Communist Authorities

In general, the treatment of Islam in post-1949 China has close-ly followed the party line at any given time, swinging from relative tolerance when moderate pragmatists were in power to repression when radical ideologues held sway. Initially, despite the outspoken atheism of its Marxist ideology, the CCP government approached China's Muslims with caution. Party rule was tenuous in many other parts of the country besides those inhabited by Muslims, and the new government's international position was not yet well estab-lished. The party was mindful of the economic and political con-sequences of a Muslim rebellion when its authority in the country as a whole was still to be consolidated, and was wary of the inter-national ramifications of cooperation between Chinese Muslim dis-sidents and foreign governments hostile to the CCP.

Tactically, a policy of toleration of religion was called for, and such a promise was indeed contained in the Common Program of 1949.[12] China was declared to be in a transition period in which the form of government would be the People's Democratic Dictator-ship—a united front of all patriotic elements in Chinese society led by the CCP in its role as vanguard of the proletariat. As long as they did not oppose socialism, religious leaders as well as upper class per-sons and representatives of various other groups were encouraged to participate in the building of a new China.

The Common Program's promise of religious freedom was repeated verbatim when a formal constitution was ratified in 1954. According to Article 88 thereof,

Every citizen of the People's Republic of China shall have freedom of re-ligious belief.[13]

The new constitution, which went into effect in 1975, changed the focus only slightly, by guaranteeing the freedom not to believe, as well as the freedom to believe. As enunciated in Article 28,

Citizens . . . enjoy freedom to believe in religion and freedom not to believe in religion and to propagate atheism.[14]

This same wording was used in Article 46 of the 1978 constitution.[15]

The consistency of these statements obscures both differences in the party's attitude toward different religions and shifts in the party's attitude toward religion in general. CCP leaders tended to look most distrustingly on faiths that were highly centralized and had their centers of direction outside the country. Thus, Daoism, Confucianism, and certain Buddhist sects were felt to have the least potential for serious harm, while Catholicism was regarded as most dangerous. Chinese Muslims did, of course, look to Mecca, far beyond their country's borders, as the center of their faith, but the degree of political control exercised from the holy city in Islam could in no degree be compared to that emanating from Rome. Moreover, the Middle East was an area in which Communism itself had aspirations. These factors, combined with the party's genuine fear of provoking a Muslim uprising, meant that Islam fared considerably better than Catholicism under CCP rule.

Initially, it was announced that religious observances might go on as before, with customs to continue as long as they did not interfere with production. Which practices were actually inimical to production would later be the subject of differing interpretations, but apparently it was not a serious issue in the early years of the PRC. A government decree of September 1952 ordered that Muslim customs must be respected by schools, the army, work places, and government institutions. Ridicule was forbidden. Special cook stoves were to be set up where there were sizeable numbers of Muslims. Subsequently, a joint decree by the ministries of finance and labor and the Nationalities Affairs Commission allocated funds for this purpose.[16]

Following the Soviet example, so-called autonomous areas were established in areas where ethnic minorities lived in concentrated groups. Muslim ethnic groups were included in this allocation: the Xinjiang Uygur Autonomous Region was founded in 1955 and the Ningxia Hui Autonomous Region in 1958, each equal in status to a province. Other autonomous areas existed at prefectural (*zhou*), county (*xian*), and township (*xiang*) levels. The practice of giving political recognition to one's ethnic group rather than to religion would later also become an issue between the party and Muslim groups. Muslim schools, like all schools, came under the jurisdiction of the ministry of education, but continued to operate. Muslim "pure and true" restaurants and other trades also continued to function. In accordance with the 1952 decree mentioned above, Muslim factory workers who worked with Han, and Muslim children who attended Han schools, were given separate stoves to conform to their dietary strictures. Muslims in the People's Liberation Army (PLA) were granted special facilities for ritual bathing. All Han who might come in contact with Muslims were warned to respect Muslim customs. Muslims were permitted to slaughter cattle for major festivals without payment of the customary tax, and received special food allocations at these times. Other customs, including circumcision, polygamy, and early marriage, were also permitted.

Mass organizations oriented toward religion were founded by the party, allegedly to show its solicitude for Chinese believers. The best-publicized of these was the Chinese Islamic Association, founded in 1953. Among other activities, the Association issued two separate editions of the Koran and several additional works of Islamic theology. It also organized pilgrimages to Mecca. In 1955 the Chinese Institute of Islamic Theology was established to train imams and Islamic scholars. Moreover, "to foster intellectuals highly learned in Islamic theology, the institute gave special research classes where students from all parts of the country took courses in the Koran, the *Hadith* (the doings and sayings of Mohammed), the *Fiqh* (Islamic law), Chinese Islamic history, world Islamic history, and the Arabic language."[17] The Chinese Institute of Religious Studies was also sponsored by the party; scholars were permitted to use its modest 100,000 volume library to study Islam as well as other religions.[18]

Party propaganda tended to stress the benefits of its policies to believers. However, substantial numbers of Muslims were less than pleased by this vaunted special treatment. Numerous uprisings occurred in the 1950s, all of them, insofar as can be ascertained, localized in area and without a coordinating center.

Muslim grievances against the new government abounded. Food shortages and tight rationing were frequent in the early 1950s. For many Muslims who had previously been economically better off than their Han neighbors, the leveling effect of rationing meant that their living standard declined not only absolutely but relatively as well. At the same time Chinese cadres (bureaucrats) received preferential treatment in food and clothing allocations.[19] Some mosques had their property confiscated, and in other places, Muslims who complied in good faith with a registration order were subject to interrogation, torture, and prison sentences because of real or fictive ties with the KMT.[20]

Another point of contention was the Korean War, which Muslims resisted on grounds that, as this was not a holy war, they did not wish to participate.[21]

The Muslim-oriented mass organizations also had disadvantages from the point of view of their constituencies. "Youth Study" clubs, which the government ordered mosques to set up in order to provide political, Islamic, and general education to educated Muslim youth of the area, proved insufficiently Islamic and overly political for the *mullas,* and were unpopular with the students. Several infiltrators were found to be among the study club members: they were tasked with Communist propaganda work, disruption of mosque administration, and with reporting back to the party on the attitudes of the religious leaders.[22] And the Chinese Islamic Association seemed more determined to give the government control over China's Muslims than to foster the growth and development of the faith. For example, one may surmise that only those who cooperated with the party were chosen to go abroad on the pilgrimages organized by the Association.

The socialist education classes that religious leaders, teachers in Muslim schools, and others had to attend contained heavy doses of Marxism and materialism, which were offensive to the beliefs of many in their audiences. Muslims were also annoyed by didactic speeches on atheism and similar subjects delivered by Chinese cadres in railway cars or other public places to their captive audiences.[23]

Economic policies, which infringed on both Muslim customs and incomes, were also annoyances. The relatively mild degree of collectivization introduced in the early 1950s had unwelcome repercussions for Muslim farmers and shopkeepers. The government's increasing control over their lives and livelihoods was worrisome, as was the increasing presence of Han Chinese and the threat of having to change their lifestyles still more as larger, more advanced forms of collectivization were introduced.

In short, party policy during the 1949-56 period could be regarded as overtly tolerant, while covertly there was harassment and a progressive narrowing of Islamic autonomy. Muslim leaders were not unaware of the steady diminution of their powers, and some resisted. Those who did so openly were generally removed on grounds that they were "counterrevolutionaries operating under the cloak of religion." Those who cooperated with, or at least acquiesced in, this narrowed scope of activities were deemed progressive and could hope to stay on or even to be promoted into positions vacated by persons who had been declared counterrevolutionaries. In one such step, Burhan, the Tatar governor of Xinjiang, was named president of the Chinese Islamic Association in 1955. At the same time, he was removed from the position of governor of Xinjiang, which he had held since Guomindang days, and replaced by Seypidin, an Uygur and party member. These moves coincided with a change in Xinjiang's status from province to autonomous region, the new status also being portrayed as an example of the party's largesse.

## Dissent Based on Islam

When in 1956 and 1957 the party asked the masses to criticize it, in the so-called Hundred Flowers Campaign, the pent-up grievances of Muslims and others poured forth. The long list of complaints included protests that:

"All Muslims everywhere are one family [and not separate nationalities]"
"Muslims fight for religion and not for country"
"The *ahron* and not the cadres are the leaders of Muslims"
"Religion and the CCP cannot stand together any more than fire and water can mix"
"Muslim cadres are anti-religious and traitors to their people"
"The policy of nationality autonomy is meaningless"
"Muslims should have a separate state without Han"
"Muslim stoves are too few and dirty"
"Muslim women rolling up their trousers [to work in the fields] is anti-religious"
"Participation in cooperatives is forbidden by religion"
"As the cooperatives become larger, the Muslim way becomes narrower"
"Before, the few were poor and the rich many. Now, the rich are few and the poor many"[24]

The party appears to have been genuinely shocked by this outpouring of grievances from its Muslim population, as indeed it was shocked by unexpectedly harsh criticisms from other groups in the PRC. Retribution was swift, beginning with the launching of an anti-rightist campaign in mid-1957.

As it concerned Islam, the campaign allegedly aimed at separating progressive from right-wing Muslims—as previous campaigns had actually done. However, the effects of the anti-rightist movement were more far-reaching, amounting in fact to an attempt to destroy the institutional basis of the faith, and to discredit religious leaders personally as well.

Mass meetings were held to denounce various Muslim counter-revolutionaries, and accusations included graphic details of the sordid practices religious leaders were said to have indulged in. Some were said to have suppressed culture among their people by forbidding them to sing certain songs, and attend theatrical performances or dance the *Yangge* [a traditional north Chinese Han Folk dance]. Other imams were said to have treated their family members cruelly and beaten those who sang party songs. Many imams and *ahron* had also emphasized the differences between believers and non-believers, and had indulged in black-marketeering, the illegal slaughter of animals, and other violations of law. Exploitation was found to be widespread, and unreasonable fines and taxes were levied for religious or quasi-religious purposes. Those Muslims who resisted their corrupt leaders allegedly were brutally beaten or killed.

Struggle meetings and denunciation sessions generally took place under the supervision of the party's United Front Work Department, which had responsibility for nationalities work, or of the Nationalities Affairs Commission, which was the governmental counterpart of the UFWD. This was in line with the party's attitude that nationality, not religion, was the primary category for classification and differentiation. Where the persons attacked were officers of the Chinese Islamic Association, that organization was used to attack them.

The sense of conflict created by the revelation of crimes was doubtless the focal point of such meetings. Yet the party also took pains to refute the criticisms the accused rightists had made against it. The party was particularly anxious to convince people of the absurdity of the statement "All Muslims under heaven are one family" ( *tianxia huihui shi yijia*). The party-controlled media responded that more than ten of China's nationalities were Muslim. Some had mutually unintelligible languages and most had varying customs. Moreover, there were also ten different sects of Islam in the country. Obviously, then, it was ridiculous to speak of Islam as one big family. For similar reasons, it was erroneous to equate nationality interests with religious interests. While some persons made these mistakes simply because they were not thinking clearly, this could hardly excuse the conduct of such a well-informed and prominent person as Ma Songting. His intent was believed to be the deliberaste muddling of distinctions between religion and nationality to "throw a foreign religious cloak over this political greed."

Despite the barrage of propaganda designed to prove that Muslim complaints were the work of a small number of counterrevolutionary malcontents, the party appeared to make efforts to improve some of the conditions the "malcontents" had complained about, at least in the early stages of the anti-rightist movement. A July 1957 speech to the National People's Congress confirmed the allegation that Muslim cook stoves had not been set up in some places, and stated that because Muslim workers were forced to eat cold food, their attitudes toward work and study had been adversely affected. In other places, Muslim kitchens were found to be "cold, cramped, and dirty."[25]

The same National People's Congress voted to create the Ningxia Hui Autonomous Region (NHAR), thereby giving a significant proportion of China's Muslims political recognition through the creation of an administrative division equal to a province. This decision was implemented in 1958, in the face of significant opposition from Han Chinese. No less a person that Premier Chou En Lai explained to Han critics that creation of the NHAR would undercut the slanders of reactionary instigators using religion as a cloak to stir up anti-Han feelings, and would help to reduce the strained relations between the Hui and Han.[26]

The unity of the nation was a major theme of party propaganda on religion during 1958. A forum held in Henan province at this time was told that,

. . . rightists are isolating the minorities by creating dissension under the guise of protecting the interests of minorities and their religion. Such actions not only endanger the solidarity of the nation, but also the peaceful development of the minority nationalities.

As a solution,

. . . the conference decided that the solidarity of the nationalities must be strengthened by giving every minority nationality family a thorough socialist education and by organizing them to learn advanced experiences from the Han so that the great unity of all nationalities will be consolidated around the Han.[27]

The theme of unity based on or consolidated around the Han Chinese took on increasing momentum, and had escalating con-

sequences as the party geared up for the massive social and economic transformation known as the Great Leap Forward.

With those persons who might be in opposition either purged
or cowed into silence by the anti-rightist campaign, radical changes
were introduced in August 1958. Muslims were included with Han
in the same communal mess halls—where pork dishes were prepared. Special accommodations for Muslims, such as ritual bathing
facilities and pure food restaurants, were also abolished. There
was increased encouragement of intermarriage, which Muslims
had long opposed. A letter to the editor of the official organ of the
Young Communist League, *Zhongguo qingnian* (Chinese Youth)
posed the question: "Is intermarriage between Han and Hui young
people permissible?" The editor naturally said that it was, explaining that opposition was due to "outdated views." Such persons "must
be helped to understand that a happy marriage should rest on common political aims and true love."[28] Progressive Muslims were also
said to be demanding that their exemptions from the provisions
of the marriage law of 1953 be ended; they now wished monoga-
mous marriage and legal sanction of divorce. They had also come
to know the dangers of early marriage, and now wished to have the
same minimum age qualifications applied to them.[29]

The Chinese Islamic Association was formally abolished in
October 1958, at almost the same time as imams "spontaneously"
began to work in the fields. Women, too, were reportedly willing
to throw off the fetters of feudal superstition and were abandoning their restrictive clothing and houshold chores to join men in
the fields. There was a large-scale confiscation of lands owned by
the mosques, with the masses again allegedly demanding an end
to this feudal exploitative custom.

The economic disasters and social disruptions wrought by the
Great Leap Forward are too well known to bear repetition here.
Party and government leaders strove to revitalize their badly shaken
country, and many of the policies introduced during the Great Leap
Forward were either rescinded or lapsed. The Chinese Islamic
Association quietly reappeared, with Burhan again its chairperson.
A reorganization of the communes allowed smaller mess halls with
special separate provisions for Muslims.[30] There is no evidence,
however, that confiscated property was returned to the mosques
or that those mosques that were closed during the Great Leap

Forward were allowed to reopen. Given the acute shortages of food and other commodities that followed the Leap, it is unlikely that many religious leaders would have been allowed to leave full-time production. And the regulations against polygamy were not rescinded, although it is possible that cadres ignored its existence. Despite the reappearance of official statements on freedom of religion, it is obvious that Muslims were not being encouraged to practice the basic elements of Islam, and were clearly being discouraged from contributing any significant portion of their incomes to the faith.

Still, there is no doubt that party and government were far more tolerant of the Islamic faith after 1959 than they had been in 1957 and 1958. Official media again announced the observance of major Muslim festivals, and at least some mosques were being maintained by the government.

The new tolerance was motivated partly by a desire to avoid rebellion and a deepening of the economic crisis, and partly by foreign policy considerations. The Sino-Soviet dispute, smoldering quietly for years, had been exacerbated. Anti-Chinese Muslim minorities in Xinjiang province were believed to be colluding with Soviet authorities, and indeed there had been an unpleasant incident in Ili prefecture in 1962. The Chinese authorities attempted to halt a mass exodus of tens of thousands of Muslim minority peoples from the PRC to the Soviet Union, which called forth a demonstration of protest by many of those who had hoped to cross the border into the USSR. Han Chinese soldiers fired on the group, killing and wounding several dozen members. This touched off sympathy demonstrations and rioting in other areas of Xinjiang. Soviet propaganda made much of the incident, and radio broadcasts were beamed from stations in Soviet Central Asia to China, emphasizing how much better Muslim minorities were treated in the Soviet Union than in the PRC.[31] China's tolerance, therefore, was partially a result of its desire to refute these accusations.

Another foreign policy consideration, which attended the PRC's decision for tolerance, was a desire to win friends among the Islamic countries of the Middle East and Africa. The Chinese Islamic Association sponsored touring groups from these countries in China and groups of Chinese Muslims made return visits abroad. Visiting dignitaries from Muslim countries were met on arrival in the PRC by delegations that included members of the Chinese Islamic Association, and the Association generally hosted a banquet for them as well. Those few mosques still open were made available to the visitors for prayer.

This greater leniency toward the practice of the Islamic faith, together with other decisions that were pragmatic in nature, were associated with a particular group in the Chinese elite that assumed leadership when the Great Leap Forward's deficiencies became evident. Their policies were not satisfactory to those who held more radical views.

In 1966, Chinese students were organized into so-called Red Guard groups and told by Mao to "bombard the headquarters" [of established conservative authority] and "destroy the four olds" [old ideas, culture, customs, and habits]. Wall newspapers, often crudely printed or handlettered in large characters, expressed the Guards' attitudes and frequently echoed the views of radical leaders. One which was seen in Beijing during the fall of 1966 dealt with religion, demanding that the authorities close all mosques, abolish religious associations, abolish the study of the Koran, abolish marriage within the faith, and prohibit circumcision.[32] A second poster outlined a ten-point program for the eradication of Islam, including immediate abolition of all Islamic associations in China. Muslim priests were to work in labor camps, Muslim burial practices were to be replaced by cremation, and Muslim festivals and holidays[33] were no longer to be observed. Some mosques were apparently vandalized by Red Guard groups early in the Cultural Revolution, but this seems to have been a result of youthful overreaction. Still, it was clear that the mood of those who guided the Cultural Revolution was emphatically anti-religious. The Chinese Islamic Association again disappeared, and the official NCNA excoriated "Soviet revisionist renegades" for "zealously fostering the forces of the Church and encouraging religious and superstitious activities in the country."[34]

Muslim resistance apparently was encountered, although we have no first-hand confirmation. The PLA's 21st army was moved from Lanzhou, the capital of Gansu into the Ningxia Hui Autonomous Region, and the two leading Muslims in the NHAR party apparatus, first secretary Yang Qingren and his leading deputy, Ma Yuhuai, were both purged. They were accused, among other crimes, of having tolerated counterrevolutionary Muslims such as Ma Zhenwu, who had been one of the principal targets of the anti-rightist campaign of 1957-58.[35]

In neighboring Gansu province, first party secretary Wang Feng was charged, *inter alia*, with consorting with "reactionary religious leaders of the nationalities and spreading the theory that religion is eternal."[36] Pre-Cultural Revolution policy was castigated as a "policy of surrender to the enemy, because it did not exterminate religious and feudal leaders."[37]

Despite the generally hostile climate of the Cultural Revolution, some manifestations of Islam continued. In February 1969, NCNA indirectly confirmed the continued existence of Hui middle schools by noting that the students of one in Shanghai had organized more than one hundred Mao-thought study groups.[38] However, the report gave no details on the status of religious instruction in the schools, or on whether special dietary provisions were being observed. Bairam and Corban festivals were also observed in 1968 and 1969, with NCNA noting that Muslims from Asian and African countries, including ambassadors and diplomatic officials, attended Corban services at Beijing's Dongsi Mosque and sent greetings to fellow Muslims in China.[39] These diplomats may have been the main reason that the mosque continued to function at all. One index of the importance the PRC attached to good relations with the Muslim countries of the Middle East may be seen in the PRC's recall of all its ambassadors save one during the Cultural Revolution. That individual was posted to Cairo, and was one of the few diplomatic representatives Beijing had in the area at that time. During 1970, the Chinese Islamic Association reappeared.[40] Although Burhan, its previous director, had been purged, the new head was also a Muslim.

Attitudes toward religion were further moderated with the fall of radical leader Lin Biao and China's decision to seek new international allies. However, there was violent protest from Yunnan Muslims in 1975 against a government call to give up the observance of Friday as a religious holiday.[41] And a *People's Daily* article of approximately the same time warned against "counterrevolutionaries operating under the cloak of religion" in the Xinjiang Uygur Autonomous Region,[42] indicating that a similar policy may have been tried there.

## The Current Status of Islam

Official attitudes toward Islam became still more tolerant after the death of Mao and subsequent overthrow of the chief remaining radical leaders, the so-called Gang of Four, in late 1976. For the moment, at least, dissent based on Islam seems to have abated.

Two major factors seem to have influenced the new leadership's tolerant policy. First, they perceived the country's economy to be on the brink of ruin as a result of their predecessors' misguided policies. Liberalization of attitudes toward those who had been discriminated against by the previous regime because of their religion, class background, or political views would, the leadership hoped, encourage the former outcasts to work harder—to "arouse their socialist enthusiasm." This would in turn encourage the growth of the economy.

Second, a combination of oil diplomacy and a resurgence of militant Islamic sentiments gave the Middle East increased weight in the world balance of power. The Chinese conviction that the PRC's arch-enemy, the Soviet Union, had designs on the Middle East made it imperative that China seek to counter growing Soviet influence there. Clearly, a country that treated its Muslim population well could more easily win friends in the Middle East than one which did not.

Numerous policy changes followed from this change in attitude. Leaders who had been purged because of their religious beliefs, or because of alleged capitulation to believers, reappeared. Burhan, then eighty-four, attended the opening session of the Fifth National People's Congress in 1978,[43] his first public appearance since the Cultural Revolution. Hui leader and former NHAR First Party Secretary Yang Qingren reemerged as head of the Nationalities Affairs Commission;[44] his former deputy, Ma Yuhuai, was elected a secretary of the NHAR party committee.[45] Ma Songting, originally removed from his position in the China Islamic Association during the anti-rightist campaign of 1957-58, regained his status.[46]

In September 1979, those Hui of Yunnan province who had been implicated in the July 1975 uprising there were rehabilitated. It was explained that the Gang of Four's policies had "abominably insulted" the Hui, who had developed "profound resentment," leading to the 1975 unrest.[47] Muslims in Lhasa were also rehabilitated, and given government aid to build schools, run restaurants, and facilitate normal religious activities.

Institutions concerned with religion in general and Islam in particular were revived as well. In April 1980, the China Islamic

Association held its first meeting in seventeen years, electing, among others, the venerable Burhan to the position of honorary chairperson and Ma Songting to the office of vice-chairperson.[48] Local Islamic Associations resumed their activities as well, including those in the major cities of Tianjin, Shanghai, and Beijing.

In turn, the Association denounced the discredited Lin Biao-Gang of Four leadership and protested Soviet actions in Afghanistan in accordance with the party line. More importantly, the National Association organized groups of Chinese Muslims to visit other countries with powerful Muslim communities. During the closing months of 1979 and in early 1980, delegations toured Pakistan, Iran, Bahrein, Oman, Kuwait, and the Yemen Arab Republic.[49] Typical schedules included visits to holy places, prayers with local Muslims, and participation in Islamic conferences. The delegations served to create goodwill for the PRC, and to show foreign countries that China treated its Muslims well. Clearly, then, they functioned as adjuncts to Chinese foreign policy.

The existence of mosques and their activities were publicized by official media. A foreign visitor to Beijing in May 1978 was told that the Dongsi mosque was open only on Fridays—with her itinerary having been arranged such that she was not in the capital on that day.[50] Just a few months later, however, groups of tourists were being guided through its premises, and holiday services, which included foreign guests, received television coverage.[51] Qinghai province's renowned Dongguan mosque was reopened,[52] and the Niujie mosque in Beijing received government help in carrying out needed repairs.[53]

As further evidence of the government's increasingly benign view of Islam, the twentieth anniversary of the founding of the NHAR in October 1978 was celebrated with great fanfare. A large delegation of high-ranking party and government officials attended the festivities, which received sustained attention from the media. As a spinoff of the celebrations, numerous articles appeared in the press intending to show the party's great solicitude for Chinese Muslims, their customs, and the economic progress they had achieved since 1949.

Other concessions were made by the government. Muslims are allowed to marry at the age of eighteen, whereas the minimum age for Han Chinese is twenty-five for women and twenty-eight for men.[54] Muslims, as well as all Chinese minority ethnic groups, are also exempt from birth-control measures designed to limit families to two children. Traditional burial practices are retained. Although the government encourages cremation since it is "more economical, hygenic, and saves valuable land," Muslims are buried according to tradition in white shrouds and in graveyards. Circumcision is still widely practiced.[55] Arabic signs in Muslim homes and traditional motifs in art, music, and dance continue to survive,[56] although the latter are tailored to suit current propaganda themes.

In the early 1970s a push to get Uygurs and Kazakhs to write their languages in the roman-letter *pinyin* alphabet used by most of the rest of China now seems to have lost momentum; visitors have noted that many residents continue to use Arabic script. The government is sponsoring research that will lead to the publication of a history of Chinese Islam.

While Muslims indisputably enjoy a greater amount of religious freedom now than in the recent past, one must not conclude either that the government's special provisions for religion are motivated by altruism, or that it espouses true freedom of religion in the Western humanist sense of that term.

The government's definition of freedom of religion is bound to differ from that of true believers. The director of China's Institute for Religious Studies has said explicitly that "religion cannot be separated from politics." Its deputy director asserted that "God arises from fear," adding that the Chinese no longer need religion, but that it is valued for its historical and educational role.[57] These attitudes are certain to be reflected in the curriculum of the religious schools, and in the research work the government has proudly announced its willingness to sponsor. Official media emphasize that the observance of religion must not be allowed to interfere with productive labor, and that "counterrevolutionaries operating under the cloak of religion" will not be tolerated.

Given the restrictions on religious practice and the discrepancy between officially sanctioned Islam and orthodox Islam, it is entirely likely that some sort of unofficial Islam exists. Hard evidence is lacking. However, a foreigner who spent several years studying at Chinese universities recounts that while visiting the capital of Shanxi with fellow students in 1975, the year in which government policies caused Muslim uprisings in at least two other provinces, he asked his guides to take him to see the mosque. One of them, a local resident, said he thought it had been converted into office space. The students, incredulous, decided to investigate. With the aid of a guidebook, they located a Muslim neighborhood, but were bewildered by the maze of alleys running between innumerable mud-plastered walls. A local Muslim, mistaking the group for fellow believers, led them to an unprepossessing door in one of the walls. Stepping through, they found themselves in a large, impressive mosque dating from the early eighth century. In one courtyard, repair work, done by the members with their own time and money, was in progress. In another, over a hundred men ranging from twelve to eighty in age, knelt on prayer mats. The elders, however, perhaps feared official sanctions if too many outsiders learned of their presence. When the young man returned two years later, a "no visitors allowed" sign had been hung outside the door.[58]

## Islam and National Cultural Identity

Unlike Catholicism in Poland or the Orthodox Church in Russia, the Muslim faith in China is in a minority position, and cannot serve to bolster a Chinese national identity. As the center of the Muslim faith is located in Mecca, far beyond China's borders, Islam might even be considered inimical to the strengthening of a Chinese national identity. Although Islam's 12 million adherents certainly constitute a sizeable group, they are dwarfed by the billion person total population of the PRC. Therefore it is unlikely that any future evolution of Chinese national culture will include any significant Islamic component.

To bring Islam as closely as posible in line with a unified Han Chinese national identity and with the country's economic development model, the PRC has attempted to isolate hard-core Muslim dissidents from their followings and to strengthen the hands of those of Muslim origin who are amenable to reform measures. In the process of co-optation of the amenable, the independent institutional basis of the faith was destroyed. Party policy has also encouraged attachment to ethnic group rather than religious faith. In that these separate ethnic groups are smaller than the community of believers in Islam as a whole, the emphasis on ethnic rather than religious identification would further reduce the possibility of unified Muslim resistance to PRC policies.

It is highly unlikely that a change in regime would result in greater freedom of religion. Any move away from tolerance of Islam would be tempered by China's need to maintain friendly relations with the Middle East. A Muslim rebellion could also play into the hands of the Soviet Union, as happened in Xinjiang in 1962. Still, as the PRC's behavior during the Great Leap Forward and Cultural Revolution shows, pragmatic policies may be abandoned under certain circumstances in favor of more ideologically pure policies.

The changes that the Communist government has made in the ambience of Chinese Islam are substantial. Yet, more than thirty years after the founding of the PRC, it is evident that even the urban Muslims of the northeast, who are surrounded by Han and greatly outnumbered by them, continue to regard themselves as separate. This remained true even during the periods when mosques were officially closed and Muslims were left without an organized, independent priesthood to guide them. Where the concentration of Muslims is greater, Muslim communities are still cohesive.

In conclusion, Islam in China seems to be healthy despite its loss of an independent institutional base. Although perhaps not as decentralized as some Muslims claim, Islam is not as dependent on hierarchy and organization as many other faiths. The loss of structures that permitted free interaction of Muslim leaders to discuss topics chosen by themselves and to convene at times and in places of their own choosing was undoubtedly a blow. But it has not been a fatal one.

Chinese official sources stress that it is mostly the elderly who still believe in Islam. While confirming the basic truth of this, foreign visitors to mosques in 1975[59] and 1978[60] also observed worshipers ranging from twelve years through middle age. Moreover, it is not unlikely that, as often happens in the West, those who do not now attend services will feel drawn to do so in their later years.

The present government's relative tolerance of Islam facilitates the practice of the faith. Yet even if a new radical leadership were to come to power, and in the unlikely event that good relations between China and the Muslim states of the Third World were no longer valued, Islam might well survive. Chinese Islam, due to its newly expanded contacts with the outside world, may develop an attraction to militant Islamic nationalism, or may try to establish links with fellow Muslims that are not sanctioned by the Chinese government. This is likely to pose real problems for the PRC leadership. Despite its desire to maintain good relations with Middle Eastern countries and to present an image of toleration to the world in general, the leadership is likely to restrict the practice of Islam in China in an effort to reduce outside influence on its Muslim population.

It is difficult to tell how effective the government's policy of giving priority to recognition of ethnic over religious identification has been in eroding the sense of Islam as a community. It is possible that, contrary to the hopes of the party, increased ethnic identification may ultimately reinforce Islamic loyalties. Given the examples of the USSR and Yugoslavia, it is conceivable that ethnic identifications will be strengthened over the course of time, and that the common Muslim faith of various minorities, newly trained in technical and administrative techniques, will facilitate their banding together to rid their areas of the Han presence. At this point Islam would assume an integrative role, reinforcing a common interest in opposing the Han. Thus, the government's encouragement of ethnic over religious ties will not necessarily diminish the importance of the latter.

As for the faith itself, if present trends are any indication, it appears that it will be the folk aspects of Islam that survive—a shared sense of separateness based on the mutual observance of certain rituals, and possession of a common culture different from that of the Han Chinese—rather than religious faith in the orthodox sense of the term.

## NOTES

1. "Peking Reopens Institute for Studies on Religions," *Washington Post* (WP), 22 September 1978, p. B6.

2. *Beijing Review* (BR), 22.51 (21 December 1979): 16.

3. *Congressional Record*, S 16191, 20 September 1976.

4. Sved Hedin, *Through Asia*, New York, 1899, Harper & Brothers, Vol. II, p. 696.

5. Robert B. Ekvall, *Cultural Relations in the Kansu-Tibetan Border*, Chicago, 1939, University of Chicago Press, p. 17.

6. *Ibid.*, p. 20.

7. The standard work on Chinese Islam is Marshall Broomhall, *Islam in China: A Neglected Problem*, London, 1910, Morgan and Scott. See also

Raphael Israeli, *Chinese Versus Muslims: A Study of Cultural Confrontation,* Ph.D. dissertation, University of California, Berkeley, 1974.

8. For a fascinating account of Chinese Muslim views of the Guomindang, see Yang Ching-chih, "Japan—Protector of Islam," *Pacific Affairs,* 15.4 (December 1942): 478. Translation of an article in Dagongbao, Chongqing.

9. Nym Wales, *Red Dust,* Stanford, 1952, Stanford University Press, pp. 75, 146; Ekvall, p. 25.

10. For a summary of this process, see June Teufel Dreyer, *China's Forty Millions,* Cambridge, Mass., 1976, Harvard University Press, Chapter 4.

11. John M. H. Lindbeck, "Communism, Islam, and Nationalism in China," *The Review of Politics,* 12.4 (October 1950): 473-488.

12. The Common Program was passed in the fall of 1949 by a conference said to represent all strata of Chinese society, but in actuality carefully orchestrated to present the views of the Chinese Communist Party. It served the country in place of a constitution until formal elections could be held, at which time (1954) the delegates ratified a formal constitution.

13. *Constitution of the People's Republic of China,* Beijing, 1954, People's Publishing House.

14. BR 18.4 (24 January 1975), p. 17.

15. BR 21.11 (17 March 1978), p. 13.

16. Ma Jian, "The Hui People Will Always Walk With the Communist Party," (speech to 4th Session of First National People's Congress), *Xinhua banyuekan* (New China Bimonthly), No. 17, 1957, pp. 91-95.

17. Burhan Shahidi, speech to Third National Conference of the China Islamic Association, New China News Agency (NCNA), Peking, 8 November 1963, in United States Consulate General, Hong Kong, *Survey of the China Mainland Press* (SCMP), 14 November 1963.

18. WP, 22 September 1978, p. B6.

19. Kao Hao-jan, *The Imam's Story,* Hong Kong, 1953, Dragonfly Books, pp. 68-74.

20. *Ibid.,* pp. 31-34, 37, 78.

21. MZTJ, No. 6, 1958, p. 4

22. Kao, pp. 20-21.

23. See Kao, pp. 38-47 and 48-57 for accounts of two such conversations.

24. See the collection of complaints enumerated in MZTJ, No. 6, 1958, pp. 1-15.

25. Ma, p. 91.

26. See SCMP, No. 1588, p. 1; SCMP, No. 1549, p. 1.

27. *Henan Ribao* (Henan Daily), 29 March 1958.

28. *Zhongguo qingnian* (Chinese Youth), 16 October 1958, trans. in United States Consulate General, Hong Kong, *Excerpts from China Mainland Magazine,* No. 151, pp.28-29.

30. SCMP, No. 1770, p. 17.

31. Zunin Taipov, "Eyewitness Account: On the Other Side of the Barricade," *Kazakhstanskaya Pravda*, 29 September 1963, p. 4 in *Current Digest.*

32. MacInnis, p. 292.

33. *Ibid.*

34. *New China News Agency* (NCNA), Peking, 27 February 1969.

35. Beijing Radio, 27 May 1966 in *Foreign Broadcast Information Service* (FBIS), Asia No. 105, 1966 (66-105), p. CCC 5.

36. Lanzhou Radio, 18 September 1967.

37. Lanzhou Radio, 14 January 1968.

38. NCNA Beijing, 28 July 1969.

39. NCNA Beijing, 28 February 1969.

40. *China Notes*, 9.4 (Autumn 1971), p. 45.

41. *South China Morning Post* (Hong Kong), 11 July 1975.

42. *Renmin Ribao* (People's Daily), 30 September 1975.

43. NCNA Beijing, 23 February 1978 in FBIS-CHI-78-28, p. E4.

44. Beijing Radio, 5 March 1978 in FBIS-CHI-78-52, supplement 1, p. 72.

45. Beijing Radio, 25 April 1980 in FBIS-CHI-78-80, p. M1.

46. NCNA Beijing, 7 April 1980 in FBIS-CHI-80-68, p. L14.

47. NCNA Kunming, 10 September 1978 in FBIS-CHI-79-240, p. Q4.

48. NCNA Beijing, 11 April 1980 in FBIS-CHI-70-73, p. L4.

49. See, for example, NCNA Beijing, 3 December 1979 in FBIS-CHI-79-234, p. I1.

50. Barbara L. K. Pillsbury, " 'Horseback Observations' About Hui in the People's Republic of China," unpublished manuscript, May 1978, p. 2

51. Agence France Presse (AFP), Hong Kong, 11 November 1978 in FBIS-CHI-78-220, p. E10.

52. Xining Radio, 3 August 1979 in FBIS-CHI-79-152, p. T1.

53. NCNA Beijing, 6 April 1980 in FBIS-CHI-80-68, p. L14.

54. WSJ, 26 October 1977, p. 1

55. WP, 22 September 1978, p. B6; AFP Hong Kong, 13 October 1978 in FBIS-CHI-78-199, p. M9.

56. Pillsbury 1978, p. 3; WSJ, 26 October 1977, p. 1

57. WP, 22 September 78, p. A-1.

58. Tim Brook, "Dying Gods in China," *Commonweal*, 55.15 (4 August 1978): 493.

59. Brook, p. 493.

60. WSJ, 22 September 1978, p. 6

# Index

Afghanistan, 10, 23, 29, 36, 37, 45, 49, 51, 52, 65, 66, 69, 73, 76, 107, 136, 143, 165, 166, 170, 172, 175, 178, 179, 192, 206, 213, 214, 215, 216, 218, 237.

Algeria, 49, 90, 91, 93, 94, 97, 103, 199.

Ansar, 117, 118, 120, 121, 122, 123, 126.

Asad (Hafiz), 43, 44, 47, 56, 129, 130, 131, 132, 133, 134, 135, 136, 137, 138, 139, 140.

Ataturk, Kemal, 188, 189, 196, 198.

Ayatollah Khomeini. See Khomeini, Ayatollah.

Baath, 43, 44, 46, 69, 84, 97, 106, 129, 130, 131, 132, 134, 135, 137, 138, 139.

Bahrein, 94, 237.

Begin, Menachem, 41, 48, 65, 148.

Carter, Jimmy, 66, 78, 165, 168, 169, 171, 172, 177, 178, 179, 180.

China, 29, 218, 221, 222, 223, 224, 225, 229, 231, 233, 234, 235, 236, 237, 238, 239, 240, 241, 242, 243.

Cyprus, 181, 182, 183, 184, 185, 187, 188, 190, 192, 193, 194, 195, 200.

Egypt, 9, 10, 11, 16, 17, 18, 27, 28, 29, 30, 32, 35, 36, 37, 38, 39, 40, 41, 42, 43, 45, 47, 48, 49, 50, 51, 53, 56, 58, 59, 61, 63, 64, 67, 68, 69, 72, 84, 86, 90, 91, 92, 93, 94, 95, 98, 100, 101, 103, 105, 106, 107, 108, 109, 110, 111, 112, 113, 114, 115, 116, 117, 119, 120, 121, 127, 133, 135, 137, 138, 143, 149, 150, 151, 152, 154, 155, 156, 169, 173, 174, 176, 178, 199, 202.

England, 11, 181, 182, 183, 190.

Faysal, King, 142, 143, 144.

France, 11, 45, 90, 91, 93, 99.

Greece, 45, 181, 182, 183, 185, 187, 188, 189, 190, 191, 192, 193.

Gulf States (Shaykhdoms), 50, 52, 101, 169, 170, 173, 178, 201, see United Arab Emirates, Kuwait, Bahrein, Qatar, Oman.

Husayn, Saddam, 29, 31, 32, 48, 56.

Iran, 9, 10, 11, 16, 22, 23, 27, 29, 30, 31, 32, 37, 41, 45, 48, 49, 50, 64, 67, 68, 71, 72, 73, 74, 76, 77, 81, 83, 84, 90, 91, 92, 93, 95, 96, 97, 101, 103, 135, 143, 148, 165, 166, 167, 168, 169, 170, 171, 173, 174, 176, 177, 178, 179, 187, 192, 201, 213, 237.

Iraq, 9, 10, 17, 18, 28, 29, 31, 35, 36, 42, 43, 45, 46, 49, 56, 58, 68, 76, 90, 91, 92, 93, 96, 97, 98, 101, 103, 109, 125, 126, 134, 135, 137, 138, 139, 167, 169, 201.

Israel, 9, 10, 11, 28, 36, 37, 41, 42, 45, 48, 49, 52, 53, 59, 62, 64, 67, 73, 76, 84, 85, 86, 89, 91, 92, 93, 94, 95, 100, 105, 106, 107, 113, 114, 115, 130, 133, 135, 138, 139, 143, 147, 148, 150, 151, 152, 153, 154, 155, 156, 157, 158, 159, 161, 169, 173, 174, 176, 178, 202.

Japan, 9, 10, 75, 77, 78, 99, 171, 190, 197.

Jordan, 9, 45, 47, 48, 49, 58, 64, 69, 90, 91, 93, 94, 98, 133, 147, 151, 152, 153, 155, 156, 157, 158, 159, 162, 169, 173, 176, 214.

Khomeini, Ayatollah, 9, 10, 30, 31, 45, 48, 68, 69, 82, 96, 170, 173,

THE LIBRARY
ST. MARY'S COLLEGE OF MARYLAND
ST. MARY'S CITY, MARYLAND  20686